Charl

PLAY

Charlotte Jones' first play, *Airswimming*, was premiered at the Battersea Arts Centre, London, and later broadcast on Radio 4. *In Flame* was premiered in 1999 at the Bush Theatre, London, and revived at the New Ambassadors, London, in 2000. *Martha, Josie and the Chinese Elvis* premiered at the Bolton Octagon in 1999 and transferred to the Liverpool Everyman. It won the *Manchester Evening News* Best Play Award of 1999, and was recently revived at the Watford Palace Theatre. Charlotte Jones won the Critics' Circle Award for Most Promising Playwright in 2000 for *In Flame* and *Martha, Josie and the Chinese Elvis*. *Humble Boy* was awarded the Susan Smith Blackburn Award 2001, the Critics' Circle Best New Play Award, 2002, and the People's Choice Best New Play Award, 2002. *The Dark* premiered at the Donmar Warehouse in 2004.

CHARLOTTE JONES

Plays One

Airswimming

In Flame

Matha, Josie and the Chinese Elvis

Humble Boy

Introduced
by the author

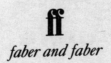

faber and faber

This collection first published in 2004
by Faber and Faber Limited
3 Queen Square London WC1N 3AU
Published in the United States by Faber and Faber Inc.
an affiliate of Farrar, Straus and Giroux LLC, New York

Typeset by Country Setting, Kingsdown, Kent CT14 8ES
Printed in England by Mackays of Chatham plc, Chatham, Kent

A CIP record for this book is available from the British Library

0-571-22596-9

2 4 6 8 10 9 7 5 3 1

Contents

Introduction

It has taken me a long time to call myself a playwright. When I wrote *Airswimming*, my first play, I was an out-of-work actress, working part-time in a shop ironing clothes. *In Flame* was written on my order pad at a pie-and-cider restaurant in Pimlico, where I worked as a waitress for one pound an hour. *Martha, Josie and the Chinese Elvis* was the first play of mine which was properly commissioned by a theatre, but I continued to waitress and I also sold clothes at Columbia Road flower market at the weekend. By the time I wrote *Humble Boy* I had given up waitressing and I worked at home in my front room on a computer which I had managed to buy from the royalties that I received from the Octagon Theatre, Bolton. About this time if people asked me what I did I would mumble that I wrote scripts. 'Scripts' sounded less pretentious, more accessible than 'plays'. 'What sort of scripts?' they would ask. 'Mostly theatre,' I would say, as I watched their faces fall. 'But I've written an episode of a TV series too,' I would add, to brook what I felt to be their inevitable disappointment. I come from a resolutely untheatrical family. My father has earned a deeply honest living selling used cars. To say I was a playwright seemed to me akin to saying I had chosen the path of the shepherd. A solitary, lonely, old-fashioned (and poverty-stricken) path that no one in their right mind would willingly choose.

I always start with an image. With *Airswimming* I saw a woman trying to trepan herself with a hand whisk. I happened to read in a book about the injustices

committed against the mentally ill: 'A Miss Kitson and a
Miss Baker were placed in a Hospital for the Criminally
Insane in the 1920s for bearing illegitimate children and
not released until the 1970s.' That was the line that
started me writing. There was something terribly moving
to me in hearing their names – genteel English names,
the names of posh girls who should be coming out into
society, not being incarcerated for being out of wedlock.
Those names with the dismissive and distancing 'a'
before them – 'a Miss Kitson and a Miss Baker' –
reading those names was the trigger to wanting to write
their story. A story about bad girls trying to be good –
a world where it seemed inevitable to me that Doris Day
should become the patron saint of all that is wholesome
and perfect and feminine.

I like to have a title to each new play before I start it.
I like writing the title at the beginning – it grounds me.
It has become almost a matter of superstition. The child
must be named before it is born, baptised immediately, in
the traditional Catholic way. And I think *Airswimming*
is the title I am most pleased with; it came very easily
to me, very naturally, before I had committed one line
of dialogue to paper. It expressed perfectly to me the
emancipation that the two women find in each other in a
world where they are denied the simple act of coming up
for air – and yet still they swim! Finding that first title so
easily has made my search for the right title in
subsequent plays much, much harder.

With *In Flame* it was the vision of an old woman
nearing her death who tap-dances that sparked the play
off in my mind. *In Flame* is perhaps the most personal of
my plays. I was in my early thirties when I wrote it and
troubled by the map of my own life. It also seemed to
me that my generation of women had been brought up
to have infinitely more choice in our lives than our

mothers ever had; we had been raised to want it all but somehow we still managed to make fatally bad choices. Each successive generation learns from the mistakes of the past but finds cunning ways of making their own unique errors. My paternal grandmother was diagnosed as senile when I was writing it and she suffered a slow, undignified, painful and often funny slide into a random but often joyous language all of her own. As much as I love spectacle and the moments that transcend language in theatre, I think my overriding obsession is with words – like Felix Humble in *Humble Boy* – the need to find the right word, the right title, the right name for a character. So having a character who is losing her grip on language was in some ways the perfect dramatic challenge for me. And perfect that her last expression should be a wordless epiphany – tap-dancing her way into oblivion.

Martha, Josie and the Chinese Elvis began with the picture in my mind of a girl with learning difficulties ice skating in her front room. Lawrence Till, who commissioned and directed the play, gave me a very firm brief: the play should speak to the Bolton audience and it should be a comedy. In fact, he said to me every third line should be funny. I'm not sure I succeeded in that exactly, but I think it is my sunniest play in many ways. It was a happy time for me personally: I got married the year it was produced and hung up my waitressing apron for the last time. It has been said that I write about dysfunction and this play perhaps has the most dysfunctional cast of characters of all my plays. But I never think of my characters as dysfunctional; malfunctioning perhaps describes it better. I think I write about the place and the moment where function and dysfunction meet; the 'I don't know what came over me' moments that we all have. The play takes place on the Feast of Epiphany and it is a play about revelation. All the characters transform into better versions of themselves. I treasured one comment that an audience member said to me after seeing the show: 'I started off thinking I wouldn't sit next to any of these weirdos on a train and ended up by thinking I wanted to invite them all round my house for Christmas.' The first night in Bolton was very magical and the play received a ten-minute standing ovation – my proudest theatrical moment. The play had spoken to the audience.

Humble Boy started with the image of an overweight, unhappy bumble bee of a man buzzing around his child-hood garden. It had the longest gestation period of any of my plays. I thought about it for about a year before I wrote anything. If I analyse it, which I try not to, I can see my plays are often quite heady concoctions. *Airswimming* combines witchcraft, Doris Day, trepanning and cross-dressing. *In Flame* has tap-dancing, cartography and Alzheimer's. Cross-dressing crops up again in *Martha, Josie and the Chinese Elvis* along with sex, domination, ice-skating and Elvis impersonation, but perhaps the play with the strangest fruit is *Humble Boy* – with its wild mix of bees, *Hamlet* and astrophysics. It is difficult, after the fact, to know exactly how I made all these connections in the act of writing. All I can say is the bees came first, and I would not like to stand up in court and trace chronologically the timing of the rest. I know I wanted to a do a big mother/son play and the more I thought about Felix and Flora the more I realised they owed something to Hamlet and Gertrude. So what would happen if Polonius became an earnest little charity shop worker called Mercy? And Claudius a boorish coach driver? And Ophelia a single mum? It seemed like a good joke to me. And I like good jokes, quite as much as I like the big visual moments. I like it when I can turn on a dime – when you're laughing one minute and wondering why you were laughing the next. But still part of me resists the term 'comedy' for any of my plays. I'm old-fashioned – I want to make 'em laugh and make 'em cry in equal measure. *Humble Boy* has turned into my biggest hit so far, with a West End and a New York run and productions all over the world. I think it is the saddest comedy I have written.

Just as I struggled to come to terms with myself as a playwright I think all my characters are in search of and simultaneously in denial of their own identities – whether it be Dora imagining herself as a great female soldier, the Chinese Elvis trying to find his voice as Timothy Wong or Felix Humble searching for the Eureka moment that will define him as a great scientist. I think, thank God, that my search for identity is over. *Humble Boy* has bought me a study – a room of my own at last. A room in which I hope to write more plays. I am also a mum now – my young son listens to me type and points sadly up the stairs to my study and says, 'Mummy working.' I will have to continue to write plays in order to pay for the therapy he will need when he is older to deal with the emotional scarring that hearing me type behind a closed door has caused him . . . Still, you never know, he might not be that bothered. As long as he doesn't want to become an actor we'll be all right. It has taken me six years and five plays and it does depend how I feel but most of the time now when someone asks me what I do I smile and say, 'Playwright.' I am a playwright.

Charlotte Jones
Brighton, May 2004

AIRSWIMMING

For Anna Mackmin

Airswimming was first presented by Sweet Desserts Theatre Company at the Battersea Arts Centre, London, on 31 January 1997. The cast was as follows:

Persephone/Porph Rosie Cavaliero
Dora/Dorph Charlotte Jones

Director Anna Mackmin
Designer Kirsty Twaddle
Lighting Sue Baynton
Choreography Scarlett Mackmin

Characters

Persephone / Porph
Dora / Dorph

SCENE ONE

Lights up.

An institutionalised interior. Drab and hostile. Possibly tiled like a bathroom or swimming pool.

A tin bath. And a staircase or possibly a stepladder. A box. A picture of a saint (Saint Dymphna) on the back wall.

Dora is polishing vigorously, whistling. Persephone enters with cloth in hand, looking bewildered.

Dora It's like the trenches.

Persephone Trenches?

Dora Yes, it's like being in the trenches.

Persephone What?

Dora *Here.* It's like being in the trenches here.

Persephone Oh.

Dora You're the new girl.

Persephone What? I don't know, yes.

Dora How's your elbow?

Persephone I beg your pardon.

Dora Elbow?

Persephone Fine, thank you.

Dora Good, here we need strong elbows. We have no need of a nicely turned ankle, an elegant wrist, a swan-like neck. No, here you need damn good elbows.

7

Persephone I see.

Dora Lots of elbow grease.

Persephone Yes.

Dora Bath. You're supposed to clean the bath. Get to it, then. At the double.

Persephone Sorry.

Dora Come on, long bold strokes. We've got to do the floor, the stairs and the bath before four. Trouble is, there's never any proper training here. Wouldn't let it happen in my regiment. Don't like sloppy work.

Persephone I can't, I mean I never have. I don't know how to.

Dora That's neither here nor there.

Persephone (*on the verge of breakdown*) I'm very tired.

    Pause.

Dora Ever heard of Catalina de Frangipani.?

Persephone No, no, I haven't.

Dora Didn't think so. In 1657 Catalina was training to be a nun, First Order of the Weeping Magdalenas. On the night before she was due to take her vows, she escaped the convent, scaling a twenty-foot-high wall. Incidentally she was only four-foot-seven. Yes, she scaled that mountainous wall and ran away and joined the army. Fought for the Spanish all over South America. She made a lousy Weeping Magdalena you see, but a formidable soldier.

Persephone I'm sorry?

Dora Apparently she survived on twenty-seven minutes' sleep every night. Lived till she was ninety.

Persephone Oh.

Dora Being tired did not enter into it.

Persephone No. (*Persephone starts to clean. Stops.*) It's just that I'm not quite sure where I am. Or why I'm here.

Dora They didn't brief you?

Persephone What? No. Nobody's told me a thing.

Dora Negative. Well, the duty falls to me. You are now an honorary Dymphonian.

Persephone What?

Dora The new girl. A freshman. A private, of course. But you must prepare yourself for a long haul.

Persephone I'm sorry I don't . . .

Dora St Dymphna's Hospital for the Criminally Insane.

Persephone I'm in hospital?

Dora For the Criminally Insane, yes. St Dymphna's – there she is. (*She gestures towards picture.*) I am Dora Kitson and we are now on polishing duty. The year is, correct me if I'm wrong, which incidentally I never am, 1924. All present and correct. I've been here since 1922. Yes, stationed here July 4th – American Independence Day – funny that. The irony is not lost on me, believe you me. I shall be your superior officer for a while, but don't worry, I'm not one to pull rank. We do this polishing duty for one hour each day. The rest of the time we shuffle and look crazed. They prefer it that way. This is probably the only time we get to talk as they need two of us to do it. They generally leave us alone. The last one was too feeble to do it any longer. To tell you the truth she wasn't up to much. Deaf mute, you see. Nice enough soul but talk about blood out of a stone. I'd have given her compassionate leave straight off. No, I need someone with their wits about them. Beleaguered lot here, you see. They prefer them with at least one of their faculties missing. Have you got all your faculties, Miss – sorry what did you say your name was? Mmm? . . . You look all right. But then you never can tell. Although usually they've lost it in the eye department. But you can begin to lose it, you see, when there's no one to talk to – you know, discuss tactics, that sort of thing. I've been there, oh yes I have. Which is why I'm rather pinning my hopes on you, Miss . . . what did you say your name was? . . . Hoping you're a bit of a wit and raconteur. Liven up the barracks. Well, all this waiting, you see. Never know when the battle might commence. But you look all right. Good soldier material . . . Well, at least you can speak, not like the last one . . . You can speak can't you?

Persephone There's been a mistake.

Dora Ah yes, a fine soprano lurking in there.

Persephone There's been a terrible mistake.

Dora Very probably. There are always mistakes. But they are seldom rectified.

Persephone I must contact my father.

Dora No contact with outside world, I'm afraid. But I'm thrilled you're here. I've waited two years for you.

Persephone You don't understand. I must get a message through to my father. I absolutely must. I have to speak to someone in authority. Can you call them for me?

Dora It won't do you any good. It's better not to make a fuss. I've tried it and I know. Damn nearly court-marshalled I was.

Persephone Please, you're not listening to me. Please, please, I need to speak to my father. Please help me.

Dora All right, there there. Deep breaths and all that. Who brought you here?

Persephone Well, Daddy, but . . .

Dora Your father brought you here?

Persephone Well, Daddy called the Doctor, you see. I was just at home. In the nursery. Minding my own business. And this doctor came. A nasty, nasty man. He asked me all sorts of impossible questions. I couldn't answer them. I'm rotten with questions, you see. I'm not very bright, Daddy says. And I just couldn't answer them, try as I might. And then they restrained me, you see. I was jolly upset. All the questions you see. Mind you, I put up a fight. Oh yes I did. And Daddy called me a witch. He called me a witch. Then he brought me here. To convalesce, he said. It all happened so quickly you see.

Dora Yes we must learn to be on our guard at all times.

Persephone Well, I suppose it's only for a short time. I have been unwell. To convalesce, he said.

Dora That's it. That's the spirit. We might as well finish this now.

Persephone Sorry.

Dora Yes. It's all right. You find ways of getting through it. You won't think so at first. But you will.

Persephone I'm only here for a short time. I just didn't realise . . . till I'm better. Just till I'm better.

Dora Absolutely. Would you mind getting some water? Round the corner to the right.

Persephone Yes, very well. Sorry.

Persephone exits.

SCENE TWO

We are suddenly in a new reality. Lights change. It is brighter, less hostile.

Persephone re-enters, but she is now Porph, wearing a bad Doris Day wig.

Porph Dorph, Dorph. Oh my God. You've got to help me. Please, Dorph.

Dorph Porph, calm down, what is it? Slowly. Take deep breaths.

Porph Oh Dorph. I've never been so scared. This big dastardely man came up. You know, with a big black moustache. And a very false smile. And unnaturally white teeth.

Dorph Do we have to go through this again, Porph?

Porph Yes, yes. I was very scared. He asked me lots of questions. And I couldn't answer them. So he chased me. He chased me here and there and over there and under there . . .

Dorph Yes, all right. What questions? Let's go through this. Tell me. What questions did he ask you?

Porph I don't know. I'm not sure.

Dorph Of course you know, come on Porph.

Porph I don't remember – impossible questions.

Dorph Like what?

Porph I don't know.

Dorph I'm not listening any more, Porph.

Porph No, no, Dorph. Very hard questions. The hardest type of questions, sport and leisure questions.

Dorph Sport and leisure questions?

Porph Yes.

Dorph That's new. Like what?

Porph Like, 'In which sport did Betty Wilson make head-lines during the 1950s?' Very hard questions. Especially for a girl, Dorph.

Dorph Yes.

Porph And then he chased me.

Dorph Cricket.

Porph What?

Dorph Betty Wilson was a cricketer. Fast bowler. Famous for her bouncers.

Porph Yes, all right.

Dorph Am I right?

Porph I don't know.

Dorph I think I am.

Porph Anyway, the point is he chased me all over the place and I was screaming and screaming and here's the really weird thing, Dorph: no sound would come out of my mouth. And then he tied me to a tree. And I couldn't breathe. And nobody could hear me. You couldn't hear me, could you, Dorph?

Dorph No, Porph.

Porph And I thought I was going to die. And I was frantic and I was crying, and I was tearing my hair out.

Dorph I thought you were tied up.

Porph I was . . . I was but I could just reach my hair. It was slightly longer then.

13

Dorph And then what happened?

Porph I managed to get free.

Dorph That was lucky.

Porph Yes, but I'm completely exhausted.

Pause.

Dorph There was no man was there, Porph?

Porph No, Dorph.

Dorph And he – that man that didn't exist, he didn't ask you any questions did he? And if he had asked you questions you might have been able to answer them, mightn't you? They might have been easy questions, mightn't they? And then he didn't chase you and tie you to a tree because, besides that he didn't exist, there are no trees around here, and he didn't have any rope and you didn't need to scream for help and if you had I would have heard you, wouldn't I, because, besides that there is nothing wrong with your voice-box, I have exceptionally good hearing and anyway there was no man, with or without a moustache and you have been safe here with me all morning, so you're not in any danger are you, Porph?

Porph No, Dorph . . . well I'm glad we cleared that one up.

Dorph Good.

Porph But Dorph, what if I was in critical danger?

Dorph I'm losing my patience with you.

Porph What if I accidentally fell into a persistent vegetative state?

Dorph I might find it difficult to tell, Porph.

Porph Dorph! What if I was struck by a herd of marauding beasts and I didn't have clean knickers on and then I got sucked into a swamp against my will and then I became a Christian against my better nature and I was forced to wear Lycra and then I lost my vitals and in the meantime my cortex was crumbling and I didn't know the way home?

Dorph You really are a terrible worrier, Porph. The worst case scenario doesn't always happen. You mustn't torment yourself. You're here with me and nothing and nobody else matters.

Porph Thank you Dorph. You help me get through things. I didn't think you could but you do.

Dorph Good.

Porph Have you noticed? I'm wearing it.

Dorph What?

Porph My new Doris Day wig.

Dorph Ah, so I see.

Porph Do you know what?

Dorph What?

Porph I think it's time for a song in my new Doris Day wig.

Dorph I've got to do some reading, Porph.

Porph Only a quiet one. A lullaby. Doris' million-dollar hit from *The Man Who Knew Too Much*, co-starring James Stewart. Are you ready, Dorph?

When I was just a little girl
I asked my mother what will I be
Will I be pretty, will I be rich

Here's what she said to me
Que sera sera –

Sing along if you want to, Dorph.

Whatever will be will be
The future's not ours to see
Que sera sera.

Porph sighs.

Porph What a truly beautiful song Dorph.

Dorph I think it is unrivalled in the beauty stakes, Porph.

Porph And very deep, don't you think? I find it oddly comforting, you know. When I'm a little bit down in the dumps. Or under the weather, I just think to myself, '*Que sera sera*,' and I really genuinely feel a whole lot better.

Dorph Doris Day never skimps on the truth does she Porph? She tells it like it is.

Porph Thank you for that, Dorph . . . what are you reading?

Dorph A book of spells.

Porph What's it like being a sister of Wicca, Dorph?

Dorph What?

Porph You know the 'w' word . . . (*She whispers.*) Witch.

Dorph Oh, you know, Porph. It has it's ups and downs. You're your own boss. You're not cooped up in an office. But there's not much security. No long-term pension plan; and there's always the risk that your neighbours will duck you in the village pond or burn you to death.

Porph Yes, there is that. Why do people do such terrible things to other people?

Dorph Witches are evil, Porph. They're destructive. They cut off male members and eat them for breakfast. They're sexually crazed.

Porph Well, you're not that, are you, Dorph. You never get it at all.

Dorph I'm not a witch, Porph.

Porph But you said –

Dorph I said sometimes I felt like a witch. It's very different, Porph. I just don't trust people any more. It's better if we keep ourselves to ourselves.

Porph You know Doris has lost complete faith in people now. That's why she founded the Doris Day Pet Foundation. She's dedicated her life to animals now.

Dorph That woman really is a saint, isn't she, Porph? Let's hope she gets recognised very soon for what she's done for mankind.

Porph That day is coming very soon, Dorph.

Dorph Good. Time for bed. Don't forget to say your prayers.

Porph Dear Lord, God bless Doris Day and the Doris Day Pet Foundation and let Doris get the Nobel Prize for . . . Literature or something soon and God bless Porph and Dorph and keep us safe and together forever. Amen.

Dorph Good girl. Go to sleep. I've got some tidying to do.

Lights change.

SCENE THREE

Dora and Persephone are cleaning, but Persephone in a very half-hearted way.

Dora Good morning. It could be worse, we could be on laundry duty.

Persephone ignores her.

Yes, they've got quite a system going there.

Pause.

The delirious wash, the imbeciles carry the linen to dry, the melancholy iron it and the monomaniacs fold it and put it away. And we have to sleep on those sheets. No wonder we all have nightmares. Yes, it's a shame. After all, even nutters need their beauty sleep, what do you think?

Persephone What are you?

Dora I'm sorry?

Persephone What's wrong with you?

Dora Nothing.

Persephone Why are you here, then?

Dora Why are you here?

Silence.

It's hard at first, I know. But you have to keep focused. Like Joan of Arc. Incarceration didn't get her down. She took it like a man. Refused to wear frocks. Had a short crop. They thought it was deviancy. I try to be deviant whenever I can. *Vive la deviance.*

Persephone Are you mad?

Dora I beg your pardon?

Persephone Criminally insane. Well, I assume you are. You seem to be.

Dora Certainly not. I resent the suggestion. Criminally Insane. The idea of it! Unless a predilection for Spanish cigars counts.

Persephone What?

Dora That's what first got them alerted to me. To my deviancy. I enjoyed the odd smoke. Shouldn't have done it. It's not *de rigueur*. But whether it's criminally insane, that's a different matter. What do you think, Miss – umm?

Persephone About what?

Dora Smoking cigars.

Persephone I think it's perfectly foul. I can't believe any one in their right mind would want to.

Dora Ah, typical woman. There are pleasures in this world that you know nothing of.

Persephone Well, I'm rather glad. Life isn't supposed to be all pleasure.

Dora Ah, indeed you are so right, Miss – umm. In fact you have inadvertantly hit upon our little motto here. What is the Latin now? *Vitam sine pleasurae*, or some such. Life without joy. We Dymphonians live by that. Not that we feel sorry for ourselves, oh no. They also serve who only sit and polish. I can see you're going to fit in here, Miss Umm –

Persephone I'm not here for long.

Dora Oh.

Persephone No. I'll be leaving any day now. They're coming back to get me, you see. So there's no point getting your hopes up about me. I'll be leaving you very soon.

Dora Ah, what a shame.

Persephone Yes, isn't it? But it can't be helped, I'm afraid. I'm coming out very soon you see. Before the King. My parents are arranging a huge party at the Dorchester. I'll be dressed in white satin from head to toe. So I can't possibly miss it. It will be the most important day of my life. Apart from my wedding day. So I have to be there. In the meantime I just have to sit tight. Get strong. This is just my convalescence home – I'd have preferred Geneva or somewhere Swiss. I can't understand why they chose here. But ours is not to reason why. What will be, will be, Mummy always says.

Dora Does she now?

Persephone Yes, like one time I wanted this hat. It was huge and pink with big squashy flowers all over it and I thought it was the most beautiful hat in the world but looking back on it it was rather vulgar but at the time it would have made me very happy but Daddy said I couldn't and I was so vexed I cried and cried and all Mummy said was, 'Ours is not to reason why, Persephone Baker, what will be, will be.' Which I found oddly comforting at the time although it would have been better to have the hat I think, in fact, looking back on it, it wasn't comforting at all and I should have had the hat even if I never wore it. I said to Reggie – (*Looks at Dora.*) – well it doesn't matter. I didn't get the hat and now I'm here we're not allowed to have pretty hats so maybe it's just as well. Although I shall need one for my coming out. So I'll just sit tight. But don't get it into your head that I'm staying. Because I'm not. I expect they're

coming any day now. At the end of the week probably.
A fortnight at the most . . . (*She trails off.*)

   Pause.

Dora Persephone Baker.

Persephone What?

Dora Your name.

Persephone What about it?

Dora Nothing. I just didn't know it. You hadn't told me.
I'm very pleased to make your acquaintance, Miss Baker.

Persephone Yes. Well. It won't be for long.

Dora No, clearly. We'd better get down to this, then.
Sharpish. Before you get whisked away.

Persephone Yes, we'd better.

Dora Yes, like Persephone to the Underworld, Hades
will return and take you thither.

Persephone I beg your pardon?

Dora The Greek myth, you know . . . Well, we'd better
get on with this.

Persephone Oh. Yes.

Dora And by the way, Miss Baker, you have a lovely
voice. Music to my ears.

Persephone Oh, right. Thank you.

Dora Yes. Feel free to break into song at any time.

SCENE FOUR

Porph goes to the box and gets out her wig and puts it on. Dora gets a book out and starts to read.

Morph sings from 'Everybody Loves a Lover' by Richard Adler and Robert Allan

Dorph Guess I might be trying to read, Pollyanna.

Porph You're always reading.

Dorph Yes, so be quiet.

Porph What are you reading?

Dorph You won't be interested.

Porph Yes I will. I like books and I have a wide range of hobbies and interests.

Dorph Trepanning.

Porph What?

Dorph It's about trepanning.

Porph That's nice.

Dorph Yes.

Porph What is it?

Dorph Trepanning?

Porph Yes.

Dorph It's drilling two small holes in your skull, about here and here.

Porph Why?

Dorph To make you feel happier.

Porph Happier?

Dorph Yes.

Porph Are you sure?

Dorph Yes.

Porph It doesn't sound much fun to me.

Dorph Well, you don't need to do it.

Porph Oh Dorph, are you unhappy again?

Dorph What could I possibly be unhappy about?

Porph I wish I could help you.

Dorph You don't have to stay with me. You can go at any time.

Porph Shush now, Dorph. You know Bob Hope once said about Doris, that she had the rare quality of making people feel good just by walking on stage.

Dorph If only she were here now, Porph.

Porph Yes, but I think that in this wig there is a striking similarity between myself and Doris. Let's see if I can do it. Hold on Dorph. (*Porph walks off stage and walks back on à la Doris.*) Feel any better, Dorph?

Dorph That was uncanny, Porph.

Porph Did I have that rare quality of making you feel good just by walking on stage?

Dorph You do have a rare quality, Porph.

Porph Shall I do it again?

Dorph I think I've had my fill.

Porph So you feel better?

Dorph It has affected me greatly.

Porph I was imbued, just for that second, with the spirit of Doris, I think. I can feel her presence even now, Dorph. Can you?

Dorph Porph, when I'm with you I can truthfully say that I can't get Doris Day out of my head. I shut my eyes and she is there, I close my ears and I still hear her, even in sleep I cannot quite rid myself of the image of this woman who, after all, only made a handful of films almost four decades ago.

Porph You are very lucky Dorph. It's like she's your spiritual guide. You're very. very lucky.

Dorph *Que sera sera*.

Porph Now put away that book. Neither I nor Doris will hear any more of you bedpanning yourself.

Dorph Trepanning.

Porph Yes, all right. Drilling holes in your head. I've never heard the like. Now I've got a surprise for you. (*She collects a present from the box.*) Here.

Dorph What is it?

Porph Well open it.

Dorph Is this what I think it is? Because really it's not a problem, Porph.

Porph Open it!

  Dorph opens it.

Dorph What is it?

Porph Its a Moulinex hand-whisk.

Dorph What do I want with this?

Porph It's battery-operated.

Dorph Yes?

Porph It's a brilliant labour-saving device.

Dorph It's an instrument of evil.

Porph Oh, Dorph. You can do all sorts with it.

Dorph Like what?

Porph Stir and whisk and whoosh things up in a bowl. Ingredients. Whirr. In a bowl.

Dorph I don't need this. I never bake. You know I never bake. I've made a point of never baking. Take it back, Porph.

Porph But it's my present to you. I like it. It's made by Moulinex. Please can we keep it?

Dorph Oh, all right.

Porph Can I have a cat as well?

Dorph Porph, I've told you, no. You can keep the whisk but a cat is out of the question.

Porph Oh all right.

Dorph Don't sulk. It's time for bed.

Porph Do you feel any better, Dorph?

Dorph Yes thank you. I'm fine.

Porph You worry about what other people say about you, don't you?

Dorph No, no, come on, I'm tired.

Porph Can I sing to you?

Dorph If you like.

Porph Can it be Doris?

Dorph Of course. It's always Doris, Porph.

Porph What shall it be. I know –

'Make someone happy
Make just one someone happy
Make just one heart
The heart you sing to
One smile that cheers you
One face that lights when it nears you
One man you're everything to.

Dorph That's nice, Porph.

Porph You sleep, Dorphy. (*Porph collects whisk quietly, still singing, then looks troubled.*) Dorph, are you asleep?

Dorph Yes.

Porph I need to ask you something very urgently.

Dorph What?

Porph Was Doris Day a virgin?

Dorph What?

Porph It's all right, you can tell me.

Dorph She wasn't to begin with, but then she became one.

Porph Like me.

Dorph Yes Porph, like you.

Porph That's good. Goodnight, Dorph.

She settles down to sleep immediately. Dorph looks troubled.

Dorph Goodnight.

SCENE FIVE

Dora Do you want to do the bath or the stairs?

Persephone I think you've mistaken me for someone who gives a damn.

Dora I'll do the stairs then.

Silence.

The folks didn't show?

Silence.

So how are you settling in then, Miss Baker? Perfectly comfortable are we? It's not the Dorchester, is it? Although most of our guests stay for much longer. It's the camaraderie I think. Have you met some of the others? Oh, it's just like a barracks here, we all muck in, help each other. Although insolence to our superior officers does not go unnoticed. But we have fun, oh yes we do. There's even talk of a ball, you know. Our own big coming-out party. Except none of us will be. Coming out, that is. More of a staying-in ball. But we know how to have a good time. Agnes is always good value. Have you met her? Mad as a snake and horny as a ram – one tooth and no hair to speak of. She'd make rather a good gun dog, come to think of it. Little terrier, you see. Yes, some of them are really wild. Some of them are just children. Lots of cripples . . . Drawn from all walks of life. No we don't stand on ceremony here. I wonder where you'll fit in, Miss Baker.

Persephone I'm a moral imbecile.

Dora What?

Persephone It says so in my notes. I had to see the doctor. He left me alone and I read them. I'm a moral imbecile.

Do you know what that is? Reggie would know, I'm sure of it. Anyway, they're not coming to get me, are they? That's clear enough even to a moral imbecile.

Dora I'm sorry.

Persephone No, you're not. Anyway I'd better get down to it. I'd like to finish the stairs since I always get the bath.

Dora Feel free.

Persephone Yes, and I'd like to point out here and now that I'm afraid I don't like you. You don't have any manners, you talk too much and you seem to think you're a man when clearly you're a girl. In fact you remind me of my Great Aunt Martha. I hated going to see her when I was little because she barked like a dog and stank like one too. She was jilted, not unsurprisingly. Nobody liked her. I'm sure she would have fitted in very well here. Anyway, Miss Kitson, fate has dealt us a cruel blow in putting us together, but Reggie would have told me to be brave and put up with it. So put up with it I shall.

Dora Who's Reggie?

Persephone It's none of your business.

Silence.

Dora People don't warm to me, it's a funny thing. Even the last one. The deaf mute. She didn't actually say anything but the way she would occasionally spit at me gave her away you see . . . Yes. So. Your Great Aunt Martha. Reminds me of Hannah Snell, you know. She was jilted in 1745. I'm remarkable with dates, had you noticed? Anyway, yes, she was jilted but she didn't go to seed, oh no. She joined the navy. Another top-drawer soldier. She received twelve wounds at the British Naval assault on Pondicherry in 1748. Even extracted a ball from her own groin to prevent discovery of her sex. Just think of it! Perhaps that's what old Martha should have done. The naval bit, not the groin bit.

Persephone I'm really not interested.

Pause.

Dora It's certainly not necessary that we like each other.

Persephone Good.

Dora Although it might be nice. And I have a plan that might involve you.

Persephone (*reluctantly*) What?

Dora Keep it under your hat.

Persephone I haven't got a hat.

Dora No, of course. Well, would you like to hear it?

Persephone If you really must.

Dora (*confidentially*) Code name of operation: GOD.

Persephone GOD?

Dora Get out of Dymphna. Date of operation, any day now.

Persephone Great.

Dora Time of operation: sixteen hundred hours.

Persephone Couldn't you wait till after tea?

Dora Short-term and long-term aim of operation: to get out of Dymphna.

Persephone God help us, you're talking about escaping. And how exactly are you going to escape?

Dora Well, I'm still working that one through. Still a bit tied up on the logistics. But I thought two heads would be better than one.

Persephone Miss Kitson, look around you. People die before they get out of here. And if we did get out, who would have us? We have no family. We have no money. We have no hope.

Silence.

Dora At times like these I think of Judith, of her courage. Flirted with the attacking General, drank him under the table and then whacked off his head and stuck it in a picnic basket.

Persephone Please. Please. You're not helping me.

Dora I'd like to be able to help you.

Persephone Well, you can't. Nobody can. I just have to put up with it. What will be, will be. I think it would be very much better if we spent this hour in silence, don't you?

Pause.

Dora I'm sorry if I'm annoying you.

Pause.

Persephone It's not your fault. (*Persephone goes to clean the picture of St Dymphna.*) She's got a lot to answer for.

Dora What? Ah, the Venerable Dymphna.

Persephone Who was she, anyway?

Dora Born 1034. Woman of extraordinary beauty. Unfortunately her father thought so too. He repeatedly forced himself on her until she bore his child, which he murdered, and she starved herself to death. Now she's our patron saint. Patron saint of moral imbeciles.

Persephone Why do people do such terrible things to other people?

Dora There are those who would say she was on a losing wicket to begin with. With a name like Dymphna.

Persephone It is a peculiar name.

Dora Terrible name. Dymphna. With a name like that what else could she be but patron saint of the mentally unbalanced?

Persephone Well, she'd better start pulling her finger out because I'm a moral imbecile. And I'm in bloody trouble.

SCENE SIX

Porph Good morning Doris.

Dorph reads. Porph sings.

> Teacher's pet, I wanna be teacher's pet
> I wanna be huddled and cuddled
> As close to you as you can get.

Dorph Are you going to give me trouble today?

Porph (*sings*)
> I wanna be dated and rated
> The one most likely
> At your side.

Dorph I know you.

Porph I thought maybe we might go swimming later.

Dorph (*sings*)
> I wanna take home a diploma
> And show Ma
> That you love me too.

Dorph No.

Porph Oh, Dorph!

Dorph No.

Porph But I love swimming.

Dorph I told you it's better if we stay here. Anyway, the baths are filthy. You'll get verrucas.

Porph I like verrucas.

Dorph Porph!

Porph Can I have a cat, then?

Dorph Look, we'll go swimming later.

Porph Really?

Dorph Yes. But a different kind of swimming. Much less hazardous.

Porph Sometimes I am weighed down by the boredom of my life.

Dorph How about a story?

Porph Yes!

Dorph Good girl. Now. Let's see. Our story today is of Persephone.

Porph Persephone.

Dorph Yes. Persephone lived with her mother, Demeter.

Porph Demeter.

Dorph And her two sisters, Artemis –

Porph Artemis.

Dorph – and Athene –

Porph Athene.

Dorph Yes, thank you, Porph, you don't have to repeat all the names.

Porph Sorry.

Dorph And Persephone was very beautiful with hair like spun gold. And she lived happily with her mother and sisters.

Porph Like us?

Dorph Yes like us Porph. Until one day –

Porph Oh no!

Dorph What?

Porph Something bad, I know.

Dorph A man came. His name was Hades.

Porph A big ugly dark hairy Turk of a man.

Dorph Yes all right, Porph. Who's telling this story?

Porph Sorry, Dorph.

Dorph And he saw Persephone with her hair like spun gold and he wanted her. Like he'd never wanted anything else before.

Porph Like I want a cat?

Dorph Porph!

Porph Sorry, Dorph.

Dorph So he stole her away. And took her to the Underworld. Now Demeter loved her daughter so much that she lost her marbles.

Porph I lost my marbles once.

Dorph Yes, well, she wanted her daughter back so much that she decided to use the only power she had to bring her back.

Porph She cut off his member.

Dorph No, she withered the crops. She turned summer into winter.

Porph I bet you could do that, Dorph. And what did the hairy bloke do?

Dorph Well, the two of them struck a bargain. They decided to share her. Demeter had Persephone for the summer months and Hades had her for the winter.

Porph (*appalled*) And what did Persephone say?

Dorph The story doesn't tell us what she said, Porph.

Porph Couldn't she speak?

Dorph Oh yes, I think she had a lovely voice.

Porph Then why didn't she stop them?

Dorph Perhaps they didn't listen to her.

Porph Frankly, I am appalled at the outcome for poor Persephone. I feel very sorry for her, Dorph.

Dorph Yes, well.

Porph Someone ought to help the poor girl out.

Dorph It's all right, Porph.

Porph No, but I mean –

Dorph No, it's all right, Porph. Because, you see, in the film version, Persephone is played by Doris Day.

Porph (*relieved*) Oh I see, and she manages to win them all over with her sweet girl-next-door image, natural good looks and extraordinary singing voice.

Dorph Exactly.

Porph Well, that's a relief. We love Doris, don't we, Dorph?

Dorph She made happy pictures about happy people, Porph.

Porph And when she cried, she cried funny . . . How do you do that, Dorph?

Dorph Only Doris knows.

Porph I don't think I'd like it if everybody laughed at me when I cried.

Dorph No, well, that's why Doris Day is a major motion picture star and you're just Porph.

Porph Yes, I see, Dorph.

Dorph Now come on for your swimming lesson.

Porph Where are we swimming, Dorph?

Dorph We're going to swim through the air, Porph.

Porph Do you know, Dorph, I feel like Calamity Jane when I'm with you.

Dorph Is that good?

Porph (*impersonates Doris Day*) Why of course it is, yes, siree, you give me the finest time in Chicagee. Better even than Wild Bill Hickock.

Dorph Come on then, Calam, get the goggles.

They get goggles, swimming caps and nose-clips out of the box. They put them on.

Dorph I think you might have to lose the wig, Porph.

Porph No, no, Dorph. See I've got my swimcap on.

Dorph Are you ready, Porph?

Porph Let's get cracking.

Dorph Right.

Music. Doris Day: 'Fly Me to the Moon'.

Let's go.

They hold hands and do a synchronised airswimming routine. At the end of the routine they put their things away and revert to St Dymphna's.

SCENE SEVEN

Persephone Stairs.

Dora Bath.

Pause.

Persephone Sometimes, Miss Kitson, I imagine I'm in a film. I'm the heroine, naturally.

Dora Naturally.

Persephone And one of those dastardly men comes up. You know the sort – with mad eyes and fierce black moustaches. And anyway, he's tied me to the lampost or even better the railway tracks. And the train is coming. Well, of course I'm quite frantic. I'm screaming for all I'm worth.

Dora I expect you're a dab-hand at screaming.

Persephone Yes, well, I look extremely beautiful even though I'm dishevelled. I'm very worried, but then part of me knows that I'll be saved in the end.

Dora Your hero.

Persephone Exactly. My hero. But of course he doesn't come until the very last moment. It would ruin it all if he arrived too early. All hope must be lost. I must be on the absolute brink of disaster.

Dora Of course.

Persephone He snatches me from the jaws of death. Do you ever have fantasies like that?

Dora Not exactly like that, no.

Persephone (*persisting*) But say you did. If someone was going to snatch you from the jaws of death, who would it be?

Dora Well, I suppose it would have to be Mariya Bochkereva.

Persephone I don't think I want to know.

Dora Yes, remarkable woman. Russian Bolshevik soldier. Founded an all-woman crack corps of two thousand high-grade volunteers. Called them the Women's Battalion of Death.

Persephone Really.

Dora Yes I quite fancy being snatched from the jaws of death by two thousand Bolshevik women with rifles.

Persephone looks at her incredulously. Pause.

Persephone Anyway, the point is I suppose that I want someone to snatch me from the jaws of all this. I know I shouldn't but I can't help myself.

Dora Who would it be?

Persephone Reggie. You know, I can see him striding down those stairs to sweep me off my feet.

Dora I'd have to have them widened.

37

Persephone What?

Dora The stairs . . . If Mariya Bochkereva and her Women's Battalion of Death were going to save me.

Persephone Yes, well, there's no point thinking about it, is there?

Dora returns to her cleaning but notices that Persephone is lost in thought.

Dora Where did you meet him?

Persephone You're not really interested.

Dora Why not? It might make you feel better. Get it off your chest and all that.

Persephone I doubt it.

Dora Suit yourself.

Persephone At a friend's twenty-first birthday party. I met him at a friend's twenty-first. I fell in love with him at first sight.

Pause.

He was thirty years older than me. He had a wife. He had two chidren. He was an acquaintance of my father's. Madness, I know. There was never any question of ever breaking anything up. Although his relationship with his wife was very, very patchy.

Dora I see.

Persephone He asked me to dance. I turned bright beetroot. I was quivering all over. We got up. On the dance floor I was electrified from head to foot. Afterwards he crumpled and I crumpled. I'd never known a man cry and he blubbed like a schoolboy. He was crying for me, which was most gratifying. He was bonkers about me. And I absolutely adored this man.

Pause.

Haven't you ever felt anything like that for a man, Miss Kitson?

Dora Well, I suppose I admire a man in a uniform. But then again it's more the uniform than the man, I think.

Persephone Oh, how could I have expected you to understand, you of all people?

Dora Sorry.

Persephone No, you're bloody not. Oh, what have I ever done to deserve you? I don't think I can bear this much longer. (*Pause.*) Never say never, Mummy always said. But don't you see that here you can always say never. I'll never see Reggie again, never kiss him and hold him. I'll never see my family, never come out, never get married, never wear fine dresses, never buy hats. The weight of it all is killing me. I'll never dance again, for God's sake. I'll never dance. And I'm such a fine dancer. The best, Reggie said. I can't bear it. Never to get up and dance. Simply dance. The only certainty in my life is you. An unhinged cigar-smoking monomaniac transsexual. I must have done something really terrible. Beyond terrible.

Pause.

Dora I'll dance with you.

Persephone (*horrified*) What?

Dora I'll dance with you.

Persephone YOU!

Dora Why not? I don't see Reggie anywhere. And I want to help in some small way. It's worse for you because you're a lady. And there's nothing to say we can't dance. Well, actually I can't dance. But I'm willing to give it a

39

go. You could teach me something simple. Then I could be the man. And lead. It might make us feel better. A bit of exercise. A bit of fun.

Persephone NO! I mean no, thank you, Miss Kitson, it's very kind of you. But I don't think it's a very good idea. I mean you're not trying to . . . I mean, you don't find me –

Dora Good God, no. Nothing like that. I'm sorry. Stupid idea. Forget I spoke. Stupid, stupid idea. You wouldn't catch Joan of Arc doing the Charleston. Forgive me, I don't know what came over me.

Persephone Yes, well, you're not a man. No, well, I mean you're not Reggie. And we've no music. Someone might see us. We'd mess up the floor. I mean, I haven't got the right shoes. I don't need to dance that desperately.

Dora Yes, all right, all right. It was stupid. (*Dora starts cleaning vigorously.*)

Persephone I'm sorry about what I said earlier. You're not that bad.

Dora It doesn't matter.

Pause.

Persephone Oh damn it to hell. No, come on. You're perfectly right. Dancing always makes me feel better. What's the worst that could happen? Someone will find us and think we're moral imbeciles. Which we are anyway. I'd love to dance, Miss Kitson. Thank you for asking me. Let's dance. We were born to dance.

Dora Well I wouldn't go quite that far.

Persephone I'll teach you the steps. No, wait, wait, we must do this in style. Throw away our cleaning rags. Now picture this: I am wearing a full length shimmering silver halter-necked dress. My bosoms are just showing. I'm holding a long diamante cigarette holder. My hair is piled up and divine. I'm an actress. Adored by thousands. What about you?

Dora Well . . .

Persephone Come on, what regiment.

Dora Oh I see. Well maybe the Twenty-First Lancers. Or I've always quite fancied the Green Jackets. At a push the Blues and Royals and if I could swing it, the Scots Dragoon Guards.

Persephone Who has the nicest uniform, Dora?

Dora Well the Twenty-First's have splendid crushed velvet vermillion epaulettes.

Persephone Perfect. Perfect. Now I need an entrance. Hold on.

Dora I think you just set yourself alight with your diamante held cigarette.

Persephone Thank you for bringing that to my attention, Sergeant.

Dora Colonel. At the least.

Persephone Colonel then. Now you wait there. (*She is at the top of the steps.*) Look the other way. Then spot me from afar.

Dora How can I do that if I'm facing the other way?

Persephone You sense me. Everyone has turned to look at me. Even the orchestra has stopped momentarily. Now, Dora, try it again. Remember I am the most ravishing creature you've ever seen. Everyone is hopelessly in love with me.

Dora I'm a soldier. I'm trained to keep my reactions in check.

Persephone Well, just this once your guard has dropped. Now try it.

Dora does.

Fine, fine. Now I'm making my entrance. Everyone is applauding. (*She comes down the steps.*) Now you approach me. Slowly and purposefully. Don't look down. You can't keep your eyes off me.

Dora Can I go back and try that bit again?

Persephone Very well. Now take my hand. Kiss it.

Dora does so reluctantly.

Now ask me to dance.

Dora Excuse me, Miss Baker, would you care to dance?

Persephone Thank you kindly. Now put your arms around me. Not so stiff.

Dora It will be something slow and stately, won't it? Nothing too frantic.

Persephone Listen for the music, Dora. Oh yes. It's romantic. Now follow me.

Dora I should lead.

Persephone You don't know the steps. Look, you'll pick it up and I'll pretend to follow . . . That's it. Not bad, Dora. That's it. Splendid. For a couple of imbeciles we really can trip the light fantastic. Oh yes, Dora. I'm there now. I'm almost there.

They dance. Music: Doris Day, 'Move Over Darling'.

SCENE EIGHT

Porph You're such a good dancer, Dorph.

Dorph Thank you, so are you.

Porph No, I'm not.

Dorph Yes, you are. You're very good at lots of things.

Porph Like what?

Dorph I don't know. Well, airswimming for one. You and me are the number one Great British synchronised airswimming team.

Porph I'm no good at anything. I'm stupid.

Dorph Don't say that, Porph.

Porph Can I have a cat?

Dorph does not answer.

Sometimes I feel like nothing good will ever happen. It'll always be the same or worse.

Dorph Nothing is either good or bad but thinking makes it so.

Porph Don't be clever.

Dorph Come on, smile.

Porph I have never been one for artifice. It is a characteristic I despise. I am always exactly what I am. I always show exactly how I feel.

Dorph What are you talking about?

Porph Doris said that.

Dorph I might have known.

43

Porph Yes. If I am happy, I bloom with it, she said. And I'm exactly the same. And today I'm bloody miserable. I've got nothing to look forward to.

Dorph You never know what's round the corner. Your life is full of golden opportunity. Anything could happen.

Porph Like what?

Dorph I don't know. Anything. You could meet the Queen. Eat oysters and champagne.

Porph I prefer tea and crumpets.

Dorph All right, tea and crumpets, and you'll wear white, you'll be a dream in white when you meet the Queen – satin and lace and voile and chiffon and gossamer and creamy calico.

Porph I always look very drawn in white

Dorph Porph, you have to make things happen. You can't wait for them to come to you. What would you most like to happen?

Porph I don't know. It's like I lost something really good along the way and I can't remember now what it was.

Dorph We'll get it back, Porph. We're the only ones who can make it happen.

Porph Okay.

Dorph What's that, Porph? What's that? (*Dorph goes to the box and gets out the hand-whisk which she treats as a telephone.*)

Porph What?

Dorph I'm sure it's, yes I thought so, it's the phone.

Porph But –

Dorph Hold on, Porph. Yes, yes, she is – it's for you.

Porph I'm not in.

Dorph I'm sorry, Porph can't get to the phone right now, can I take a message? Yes, yes, right, great. Yes, I'll tell her. Okay, thanks. Porph – you're going to have a baby.

Porph What?

Dorph Yes, any day now. A little girl. A natural birth at home. The labour will be quite painful, but over quickly.

Porph Who was it?

Dorph Oh Porph, I'm sorry. I didn't take their number. I could ring 1471.

Porph No. I suppose it doesn't matter who it was, does it?

Dorph No, Porph.

Porph A baby girl, you say? A sister for . . . I'm glad the birth won't be too traumatic. You can be present if you wish. I'll keep the placenta. Yes I shall lightly grill the afterbirth and serve it with wild mushrooms and prosciutto ham.

Dorph I don't think that's strictly necessary, Porph.

Porph It's very nutritious. What shall we call her?

Dorph Something noble. Like Artemis the Hunter.

Porph Do you know, I think I prefer Doris? My God, she's going to be pretty and sexy too, but only in moderation. Yes, she must be pure. Pure as peaches. Oh, and I shall love her, Dorph, with such a big piece of my heart.

Dorph I know, Porph. I know you will.

Porph I shall teach her to speak and walk and love and sing and dance and swim –

Dorph In the air, Porph.

Porph In the air, Dorph, and I shall feed her on satsumas and crispbreads.

Dorph That's a bit harsh, Porph.

Porph She must be thin, Dorph. And she'll be mine. All mine and no one will take her away from me.

Dorph No, Porph.

Porph Are you sure?

Dorph Yes.

Porph is by now cradling her imaginary baby.

Porph But no Dorph, you see sometimes they come in the middle of the night, when you least expect them. You don't know who they are and they ask all sorts of questions. And everything depends on you getting the questions right. And sometimes you just can't get them right. And they say terrible things to you. Things to send you mad. And then you lose it, you see, Dorph. You lose the thing that was the most precious thing to you. And there's nothing you can do. Nothing.

Dorph It's all right, Porph. That won't happen any more. I promise.

Porph There's nothing you can do. There's nothing anyone can do. I've lost her, Porph. I've lost another one. I can't hug her into life. I just can't.

Dorph Yes you can. You're stronger now, Porph. You can hug her into life. This time it'll be all right. She'll be happy and healthy and American as apple pie.

Porph Like Doris?

Dorph Just like Doris. Sing to her, Porph. Sing to your baby.

Porph Yes. Oh she's crying, isn't she? She's so tired. She needs to sleep.

Dorph That's it, Porph. Sing her to sleep.

Porph (*sings*)
Once I had a secret love
Who lived within the heart of me
All too soon my secret love
Became impatient to be free
So I told the friendly stars
The way that dreamers often do
Just how wonderful you are
And how I'm still in love with you.

During this:

Dorph Let's put her to bed now, Porph.

She takes the imaginary baby as Porph sings and puts her in the bath. We are back in the hospital.

SCENE NINE

Persephone I know I've been bad. But you can bring him back to me now. Please, please. I'll be good now. Just give him back to me now. Give him back. I demand that you give him back to me.

Dora What is it, Persephone?

Persephone They've done the most dreadful thing to me.

Dora What? Who? Who's done this?

Persephone I don't know. I don't know where he is. I put him down somewhere. (*She searches frantically*). Where's the water? You need plenty of hot water. He's here somewhere. Help me find him, Dora.

Dora Who is it? Who have you lost? Is it Reggie? Reggie's not here, Persephone. But it's all right. I'm here.

Persephone No, no. Stupid. Not Reggie. The little fish. My little toad. Where is he?

Dora I don't know.

Persephone Well, somebody must know. I'm going to the authorities.

Dora All right now, calmly, from the beginning. Where did you get the fish? Did you win him at the fair?

Persephone I don't know.

Dora Did Reggie give him to you?

Persephone He definitely had something to do with it. But perhaps it was Nana.

Dora Nana?

Persephone Only Nana would speak to me. She brought me my meals. I was in that nursery for months. Dirty, dirty girl. He was swimming around in my tummy. The little guppy. And then the pain. Phew, Dora. I said, 'Nana, my tummy button hasn't opened yet.' 'Lots of hot water,' she said. He was such a naughty little fish. But he was there all of a sudden. (*She laughs*). He jumped out like a salmon. Plop. The little slippery blue and red fish. Big brown eyes. He was the best thing I've ever had. Much nicer than that big hat. But then they took him away from me. They took him away.

Dora I'm sorry. I'm so sorry.

Persephone (*dawning realisation*) They brought me here because of the fish, didn't they? I shouldn't have had the fish at all. Only witches have fishes in their tummies. What a mess.

Dora Yes.

Persephone He was the only thing I ever had and they took him away from me. He didn't even have a name. I couldn't even give the bloody fish a name.

Pause.

Dora Come on, we'll name him now. Hold him, Persephone, come on, hold him. (*She hands an imaginary baby to Persephone.*)

Persephone But –

Dora That's right. Mind his head. We need some water. Wait there. Don't drop him. That's it. Right. By the power invested in me by . . . by . . . by St Dymphna, I baptise you . . . what? What do you want to call him?

Persephone What about Bastard?

Dora Persephone!

Persephone Well, he was a bastard fish, wasn't he?

Dora We can't call him Bastard.

Persephone Why not?

Dora Well, it would ruin his chances with the army for one thing. No hope of Sandhurst with a name like that. Come on think, Persephone, what's he called?

Persephone I don't know. (*She looks hard into her arms*). Finlay. Yes, Finn. Finn, my little amphibian boy.

Dora (*with water*) I baptise you Finn in the name of the Father and of the Son and of the Holy Ghost . . . There,

Persephone. He's got a name. He's yours now. They can't take that away.

Persephone What can I do for him?

Dora Just love him. That's all any mother can do.

Persephone Oh yes, I shall certainly do that. I would have liked to dress him in sailor suits. But never mind. What will be, will be. I'm tired now. Phew, the pain of it, Dora.

Dora You sleep now. You deserve some rest. I can do the polishing today.

Persephone I want a big breakfast, I think. Eggs and crumpets.

Dora I'll see what I can do.

Persephone What year is it now, Dora?

Dora 1926.

Persephone Oh God. I've been here long enough now haven't I? How much longer will it be, Dora?

Dora I don't know.

Persephone Please tell me how much longer.

Dora The Great War lasted for four years.

Persephone Four years! What's great about that? But what about the Thirty Years War, how long was that?

Dora It was longer.

Persephone Yes! And what about the Hundred Years War? What about that? That went on for ever, didn't it?

Dora Yes, yes it did. There's no telling when it will stop. We have to put it out of our minds. We have to keep fighting. We're in this campaign together now. And we have to keep fighting.

Persephone Oh, Dora, let's not think about it any more.

Dora No, we'll start again tomorrow. Each day is a new day.

Persephone Thank you, Dora. You're so strong. I was wrong about you. And about Reginald. I'd rather be in your regiment. I don't know what I'd do without this hour every day. Polishing. Ah well. Chin up. Good night, Dora.

Dora Good night.

SCENE TEN

Dorph Porph, come here, we need to practise some questions.

Porph Why?

Dorph I've thought it over and we need to be prepared. In case someone comes.

Porph But you promised me. You promised me I was safe. You said the dastardly man would never come. You said you'd protect me.

Dorph It's better to be prepared, Porph. That's all. I'm trying my best, but I might not always be around.

Porph But you promised!

Dorph I'm not as strong as you think. Sometimes you can't stop bad things happening. I'm just saying we should be prepared. Now come on. They'll be easy questions. You'll enjoy it.

Porph Okay.

Dorph Right, let's see. What was Doris Day's real name?

Porph She was born Doris Mary Anne von Kappelhof to German Catholic parents in Ohio on the third of April 1924.

Dorph Correct. What life-threatening event happened to Doris at the age of fifteen?

Porph She suffered a double compound fracture of her right leg when the car she was travelling in crashed into a train.

Dorph Correct.

Porph I hope he doesn't ask me that. You know I get upset when I think about it.

Dorph We have to be prepared, Porph. Right. In which film did Doris star with Jimmy Cagney?

Porph *Love Me or Leave Me.*

Dorph Correct. What was Doris's favourite film of the films she made?

Porph *Calamity Jane.*

Dorph Correct. What was Doris's favourite pie?

Porph Ah, a trick question! Well, most people assume it's apple when in fact. of course, it's peach.

Dorph Is the right answer! You see, you're very good at questions, Porph.

Porph Well, I'm sorry, Dorph, but a five-year-old could get these questions right.

Dorph That's right, Porph, there's no need to be scared. Now how long have you known me?

Porph For ever!

Dorph And have I ever upset you in that time?

Porph You're my best friend, Dorph. What do you mean?

Dorph We're just practising questions, Porph. I've never hurt you, have I?

Porph You won't let me have a cat.

Dorph No. I mean wicked hurt.

Porph Of course not. I don't like these questions, Dorph.

Dorph No all right Porph. You must be strong. People say bad things about me. We have to tell the truth.

Porph What things?

Dorph That I hurt people. I make people mad. That I made you mad. That I made your baby die.

Porph No, no, no, no. I won't hear any more. You're getting confused. It was all such a long time ago. They don't know you. They don't know you like I know you.

Dorph We just have to tell the truth. That's all.

Porph Yes, yes, all right, Dorph. Now I've got a question for you. It's very hard.

Dorph Try me.

Porph Why was Doris Day such a good actress?

Dorph Ah, I know this one.

Porph Come on then.

Dorph Because she was always confident, upbeat and absolutely sure of her destiny.

Porph Like us?

Dorph No, Porph, I don't really think so, do you?

Porph No, I didn't think so either. (*Pause.*) What do we do now?

Dorph Sit tight, Porph. We could be in for a long haul. So sit tight.

> *Time passes. Perhaps some music (Doris Day, 'Sentimental Journey') and stylised movement to show Persephone and Dora ageing in the hospital.*

SCENE ELEVEN

Dora I think these stairs are clean, don't you?

Persephone I can see my face in this bath.

Dora We've done a bloody good job, haven't we?

Persephone Well, we've been doing it for a very long time, haven't we?

Dora And all this polishing has made me strong, you know. Arms like iron. I could swim the Channel, the Indian Ocean. When I get out they won't catch me for toffee. I'll join the Royal Irish Hussars. Fight the Huns. Do my bit . . . What is it?

Persephone My hair. My hair's grey. How terrible. When did this happen?

Dora Don't look.

Persephone I thought I looked better than this.

Dora You do.

Persephone My hair. My hair is –

Dora It's *brown*. Your hair is lovely and brown.

Persephone (*equally appalled*) Brown?

Dora Blonde, then. Yes, it's like spun gold.

Persephone Is it?

Dora Of course.

Persephone (*she decides to look away from bath*).
Thank you, Dora. (*Pause.*) What year is it?

Dora Let's see. The date. Damn it. This isn't like me.
1930-something? 1940? It couldn't be, could it?

Persephone How long have we been here?

Dora Well I came in '22 and you came in '24. How old
am I? How old are you?

Persephone I forget. I was just about to come out then.
So I must have been twenty-one.

Dora Ten years? Twenty years? I don't know. It's not
like me. I just don't know.

Persephone I wonder what we've missed? At any rate,
it's got easier, hasn't it?

Dora In a way.

Persephone We must have missed things, though.

Dora Don't look back. Don't look forward. Sit squarely
in the centre of each moment.

Persephone You're much stronger than I am, Dora.

Dora No, I'm not.

Persephone Oh yes you are.

Dora No, the difference is I deserve this and you don't.

Persephone What rot. Never say that, Dora. Nobody
deserves this.

Silence.

Dora My brothers all died.

Persephone I didn't know you had brothers.

Dora Three of them. In the war. All felled. Bang, bang, bang. So young.

Persephone I'm sorry, Dora.

Dora George was the eldest. Quiet chap. Very serious, academic, you know. Should never have been a soldier. Then Harry. The joker. Bit of a cad. You'd have liked him. But it's Alfred I think of most. Beautiful, angelic boy, with a mop of curls. Eighteen when he was killed. Eighteen. I should have done it. Fought the good fight.

Persephone You're a girl. A woman, Dora. You couldn't have done it.

Pause.

Dora Flora Sandes did it. In the Great War. She was a vicar's daughter. Captained a Serbian infantry unit against the Bulgarians. Brave as a bulldog. She was a vicar's daughter.

Persephone Well, I'm very glad you weren't a soldier. Or a vicar's daughter, for that matter.

Dora I should have done it though, don't you see? Died for King and Country.

Persephone No, Dora. No

Dora Instead of which this has been my National Service. The Royal Dymphonians. First Regiment. I've been a Dymphonian man and boy. Dymphonians are known for their stoicism. We're the backroom boys, really – we're not the heroes, but we put in bloody years of service.

Persephone I think you're very brave. The bravest of the brave.

Dora Ha. An unsung hero. Perhaps I should award myself some medals. Decorations of valour. Polish them up. For another year's service. And another.

Persephone So you should.

Dora (*looks at Persephone*) A bit of you thinks I'm mad. You do, don't you?

Persephone Dora!

Dora It's all right. I don't mind. But I mean, the whole soldier thing. Come on, I am a bit unhinged, aren't I? What was it? You hit the nail on the head once. 'A cigar-smoking monomaniac transsexual?'

Persephone That was years ago. I did think so at first. But not any more.

Dora I don't know how long I can keep it all up.

Persephone What?

Dora Active service, you know.

Persephone Dora, we've come this far. What do you mean?

Dora I want to retire. With a good pension.

Persephone Perhaps we will.

Dora No we won't . . . I'm not as sharp as I was. My fingers are all thumbs. I won't be able to change the fusillage. Won't be able to change it quick enough.

Persephone A minute ago you were going to swim the Indian Ocean.

Dora (*laughs*) Bravado, Persephone. Truth is I'm a coward. Always have been. That's why I fit in here. With all the other lost souls.

Persephone We're just tired. There's only so much polishing a person can do. It has got easier, Dora.

Dora Not for me.

Persephone I'll help you. You've always helped me in the past. It's my turn now.

Dora It's all right. I am fine really. Perhaps I will rest, though. I wish I could remember what year it was. Yes just get my head down for a while. Lay low. I should know what year it is, though.

Persephone That's the beauty of it. It can be any year we want.

Dora Not military doctrine, but perhaps you're right. And I am exhausted, you know. Always on my guard, you see. In case they shave off my hair and find the Devil's mark.

Persephone Shh. Shush now, you rest. It's your turn to rest.

SCENE TWELVE

Dorph Where is it? Where is that bloody thing? She loses everything. Where the hell has she put it?

Porph Dorph?

Dorph Ah you, yes. You. Where have you put it? Where is it? Come on, where have you hidden it? Quickly. I haven't got all day.

Porph What, Dorph? What? You're frightening me.

Dorph That bloody thing. Your bloody thingummy-gadget. You know. Your fantastic labour-saving device. I need to save my labour. So where the hell is it?

Porph It's in the box.

Dorph Well come on then, get it. Come on, I need it. You keep telling me how good it is. I need to try it.

Porph Dorph, what is it?

Dorph Just get it. Give it to me. Quickly. Come on.

Porph gets hand whisk and gives it to Dorph, who presses it to her head.

Dorph That's no bloody good. Plug it in. Come on, I need some power. It doesn't bloody work. Bloody typical. Bloody Moulinex.

Porph No, please stop, Dorph. You're scaring me. I don't understand. What are you trying to do?

Dorph What does it bloody look like? I'm trepanning myself with a hand whisk. I'm trying to bloody well trepan myself with a sodding bloody hand-whisk.

Porph Please stop. Please, please, Dorph.

Dorph I can't even do this. God, give me strength. What are you doing? Are you completely thick? Turn on the power.

Porph It's battery-operated but I forgot to get any batteries.

Dorph I don't believe it,

Porph You'll hurt yourself.

Dorph That's the idea.

Porph No, please, Dorph.

Dorph Don't you dare take it from me. Go away. I'm telling you for your own good. Go away. Leave me alone. Do you need me to spell it out for you? I don't

59

want you here any more. Do you hear me? Where's the book? Where's the bloody book?

Porph What book?

Dorph The trepanning book, you idiot. Jesus Christ, where have you put it?

Porph I didn't touch it.

Dorph You must have done. You touch everything. You can't keep your thieving hands off anything. Get out of my life, Porph. Go back to your family.

Porph No, no, please, please stop.

Dorph I can't understand this. It won't work. It won't bloody work. I got the wrong bloody book. I should have got the bloody beginner's book.

Porph What?

Dorph Trepanning for bloody beginners. For people who only want a small bit of happiness. That's all I want. A small bit of happiness. Nothing major. Just a bit of peace and quiet. On my own. What part of my head do I drill the holes in? I can't remember. Are you still here? BUGGER OFF! Go on, just sod off. I don't want you here any more.

Porph is beside herself.

Stop snivelling. You're a grown woman. You're not a child. God knows I've let you be a child for too long. You've got to grow up. Take some responsibility. Get a life! Leave me in peace.

Porph I don't want to leave you.

Dorph Well, I'll be leaving you soon enough whether you like it or not.

Porph I won't let you go.

Dorph And how exactly are you going to stop me, Porph?

Porph I'll take care of you. You won't be unhappy any more.

Dorph You can't.

Porph I can. I'll be like Doris Day in *The Thrill of It All* – you know, when she plays Beverley Boyer and forsakes her own thriving career in soap commercials to look after her husband and children.

Dorph (*deadly*) Shut up about Doris Day.

Porph But we love Doris.

Dorph No, Porph. YOU love Doris. I haven't even a passing interest in her. Do you know why? Because she's bland. She's completely fucking bland. I don't believe a word she says in her films. Her world doesn't exist. I can't bear her synthetic singing voice. And I hate blondes. I hate her, in fact. In fact, I would go as far as to say Doris Day has sodded my life up. She's completely sodded my life up.

Porph But Doris wouldn't hurt anyone.

Dorph Oh no! You know what, Porph? Doris Day is a sham. A complete fabrication. A PR exercise.

Porph No she's not.

Dorph And another thing you didn't know about Miss Perfect American Pie. She's a dyke, Porph. She didn't like Cary Grant. Oh no! She preferred Debbie Reynolds.

Porph How can you say such things? I don't believe you. It's not true. That's disgusting.

Dorph Porph, it's staring you in the face.

Porph No.

Dorph She was a plain, good old-fashioned carpet-muncher, Porph. Take it or leave it.

Porph Dorph, say you're sorry. Say you're sorry to Doris.

Dorph What?

Porph You heard me. Say sorry to Doris.

Dorph She's not here.

Porph She's always here.

Dorph No, Porph, Doris Day is at this moment running a home for bewildered dogs on the other side of the Atlantic.

Porph Yes, yes, and as she loves animals so she loves us. So say sorry to her.

Dorph Grow up.

Porph Since she isn't actually here, you can say sorry to me. In fact I have often been told there is an uncanny resemblance between myself and Doris Day.

Dorph No there isn't.

Porph Yes there is, I think you'll find.

Dorph No, Porph. Let me tell you as your friend, that you are living a lie. You're not a bit like Doris Day. You're too short, you're too dumpy, you have no style and you look bloody ridiculous in that wig.

Porph (*slowly takes off wig*) I hate you.

Dorph Good. That's a start. Pack your bags. Take your bloody whisk and go.

Porph I won't. I won't leave you. You can say what you like. I'm not going anywhere.

Dorph Can't you see what you're doing to me? You're driving me mad. I can't cope with it any more.

Porph I'll help you.

Dorph Nobody can help me. I'm a lost cause. I'm not a very nice person, Porph. I'm not Doris Day. I'm wayward. I'm a witch. All my children are bastards. I have to be punished. I hurt people. I destroy things. They should lock me up and throw away the key. Just leave me to prepare myself. Find your family. Go back to them. You could still be happy. You've still got a chance.

Pause.

Porph I think that was a little bit melodramatic, don't you? That's quite enough of that sort of behaviour. You just be quiet now, Dorph. It's my turn to do something for you. Come on, Dorphy. You've always done everything for me.

Dorph You can't do anything for me.

Porph I can wash your feet, for a start. Have you seen the state of them? Cleanliness after Godliness, Dorph. There, sit there, give me your feet. Holy Dymphna, Dorph, they stink! There now, just relax. You're very, very tense, Dorph. Let me wash them. That feels better, doesn't it?

Porph washes Dorph's feet.

When I had my baby, I washed his feet. Tiny feet. So perfect. Like your feet.

Dorph Are you sure I haven't got six toes?

Porph That's enough now. Just put it all out of your mind. There, do you feel better?

63

Dorph Thank you, Porph, I do. I just need to get some fresh air. I won't be long. But you must be on your guard. We have to be vigilant from now on.

Porph I won't let you down, Dorphy.

Dorph Thank you, Porph. I won't be long.

Dorph exits. Porph sits on the steps. Possibly some music plays (Doris Day, 'When I Fall in Love'). She tries to stay awake but gradually falls asleep.

SCENE THIRTEEN

Dora enters and talks to the sleeping form

Dora Persephone. I know you're asleep. I don't want to wake you. I think it's time. Lay down my arms and all that. It's time to lie down and take it like a man. I don't know what year it is, you see, Persephone. I just don't know.

Pause.

I thought I was inviolable to attack. As stiff an upper lip as my pater. I only wanted to wear men's clothes. Smoke a few cigars. A few shiny medals and a cricket box, you know the sort of thing. I thought we'd get out one day. Reward for years of service. We'd be handed it all on a silver platter. But the current's too strong, isn't it, old girl? My God, we've been treading water for years, haven't we? When we should have been swimming. Hades took us to the underworld, didn't he, Persephone? But Demeter and the family just forgot about us. Forgot about us for years and years. How could they have done that? That's not how it was supposed to be. We were supposed to see the Spring again, weren't we?

Oh, listen to me rambling on. You're right, I do talk too much.

It's over now for me. You're still in with a chance. I did think you were a bit giddy at first, but you're full of gristle, aren't you, Persephone? I've enjoyed our little chats. We've had a rum deal but we've made the most of it. I'll just go quietly. Don't want to make a song and dance of it. No need for the Last Post. Although the Victoria Cross might be nice. Awarded posthumously. Fix it for me, Persephone, would you? That would be nice.

She looks at her and leaves. Persephone shifts in her sleep.

Persephone Dora? (*She goes back to sleep.*)

SCENE FOURTEEN

Dorph enters

Dorph Porph? Porph? Weren't you able to stay awake for even one hour? (*Dorph sits and looks at the sleeping Porph.*) It's time, Porph. Be strong. Tell the truth.

Suddenly a light picks out Porph. She wakes up abruptly. During the next, Dorph fills the bath with water.

Porph Who is it? Whoever it is, go away.

Dorph You know who I am, Porph.

Porph No I don't. Go away.

Dorph Come on, Porph. Don't be stupid.

Porph I'm not stupid.

Dorph You know why I'm here, don't you?

Porph (*unsure*) Yes.

Dorph How long has she been a witch, Porph?

Porph I don't know who you're talking about.

Dorph Come on, Porph, don't mess me about.

Porph I'm not.

Dorph I thought you were good at questions.

Porph I am. I am.

Dorph You know what happens to bad girls. You don't want that to happen to you, do you now?

Porph No. No, I don't.

Dorph Why did she become a witch?

Porph I don't, I don't know.

Dorph Porph, I'm losing my patience with you.

Porph I know. I know.

Dorph Why did she become a witch?

Porph Because she was always confident, upbeat and absolutely sure of her destiny.

Dorph Good girl. That's more like it. Who did she choose for her incubus, Porph?

Porph Cary Grant. No. No. Debbie Reynolds.

Dorph Where did the Black Sabbat take place, Porph?

Porph The Dorchester.

Dorph What music was played there and what dances did she dance?

Porph Doris Day.

Dorph What dances, Porph. Come on.

Porph We tripped the light fantastic.

Dorph What food did she eat there, Porph?

Porph Eggs and crumpets, I think.

Dorph What animals did she bewitch to sickness and death?

Porph My cat. No, my little fish.

Dorph How can she fly through the air, Porph?

Porph She swims. She swims through the air.

Dorph Has the Devil set a limit to her period of evil-doing?

Porph Any day now.

Dorph That's right, Porph. Good girl. No, wait a minute. Were you her accomplice in evil?

Porph Me?

Dorph Things are looking bad for you, Porph. Were you her accomplice?

Porph No. Yes. No, I –

Dorph But you do know her.

Porph You see, I –

Dorph You know her.

Porph I'm not sure if –

Dorph You know her. She's your best friend, Porph. You must never leave her.

Porph No. No. No I –

Dorph Are you lying to me, Porph?

Porph No I swear that I don't know her. I'm telling you the truth. May God punish me if I'm not. I don't know her. I don't know her. I don't.

Lights fade up. Dorph slowly lowers her head into the bath. Porph scrambles to the top of the stairs. Then, as if in slow motion, Dorph 'ducks herself' three times into the water. Each time, Porph goes to scream but, although she can move her arms about and tear at her hair, no sound comes out of her mouth. The third time Dorph doesn't re-surface. Porph is released.

DORPH! DORPH! Dorph! Dorph, swim. Dorph. Swim in the air, Dorph. Dorph. Please. Don't let this – Come on, Dorphy. Swim. Swim for Britain. Swim up, Dorph. Swim up through the air. Dorph. Dorph. Dorph. (*Trails off.*)

Pause.

The dastardely man came, Dorph. He asked me lots of questions. I couldn't answer them, Dorph. I'm in critical danger, Dorph. Do something. Come on, let's sing. Sing ourselves to sleep.

When I was just a little girl
I asked my mother what shall I be
Shall I be something, shall I be something else
Here's what she said to me
Que sera, sera –

She falters.

I can't hug you into life, Dorph, I just can't. I can't make you mine. I've gone and lost the thing that was most precious to me. The game's up now, isn't it, Dorph? You'll never be happy and healthy and American as apple pie.

I'm wild again
Beguiled again
A simpering, wimpering child again
Bewitched, bothered and bewildered am I
Couldn't sleep and wouldn't sleep
Then love came and told me I shouldn't sleep
Bewitched bothered and bewildered am I.

Blackout.

SCENE FIFTEEN

Persephone is standing over the bath

Persephone Dora. Oh my God, Dora. Come on now.
Don't do this to me. (*She lifts her out of the water and
tries to revive her*). We're nearly there now, Dora.
There's no need for all this. Come on, Dora. Please,
please, Dora.

Dora gasps for air.

Persephone That's it. That's my girl. No, soldier. My
brave little soldier. Come on, Dora. Come back to me.

Dora She died.

Persephone What?

Dora She died.

Persephone Who?

Dora Anne Dorphan.

Persephone Shush, it's all right. Calm yourself.

Dora In 1647 Anne Dorphan was drowned for being a
witch.

Persephone Shush. Sshh. No more dates. I'm sick of dates.

69

Dora Do you know why, Persephone? For having more wit than her neighbours.

Persephone I know. I know. Oh you scared me, Dora.

Dora Don't be clever, Dora. My father always said, don't be clever.

Persephone No, you must always, always be clever.

Dora I couldn't remember the year. Something snapped. And I couldn't remember the year.

Persephone It doesn't matter what year it is.

Dora I wanted to know, though. I really wanted to know.

Persephone We'll find out. We'll find out. Hang on a minute. I saw a paper. They left us a paper for the polishing. Here it is. (*She gets the paper out of the box.*)

Dora What's the year? Tell me the year. TELL ME THE YEAR!

Persephone 1958. (*Reads.*) Doris Day is voted the world's favourite actress by the Hollywood Press Association. There you go, Dora. There you go.

Dora (*pause*) Who's Doris Day?

Persephone I don't know – some actress.

Dora She must be good . . . 1958, you say?

Persephone Yes.

Dora And I came in 1922?

Persephone Yes.

Dora Thirty-six years?

Persephone Yes.

Dora Thirty-six years?

Persephone We can face it, Dora. We can face this. We've got the mettle. We can stare this in the face. But you mustn't leave me. You must never try this again. You're not leaving me now. Dora, I didn't ask to be put with you. But put with you I was, and you're not taking the coward's way out.

Dora I was tired.

Persephone Being tired has nothing to do with it. Dora, you're a sergeant-major. A bloody sergeant-major. The Royal Fusiliers. In charge of. In charge of – help me out here, Dora.

Dora Polishing?

Persephone Yes, in charge of bloody damn well polishing. Guns at the ready. (*She wields her cleaning rag.*) Come on, Dora. Caesar or nothing. Come on now.

Dora We're old now, Persephone. We're too old.

Persephone Well long live old people, that's what I say. Vive la bloody France. What are the words to the 'Marseillaise'? I want us to sing while we work. To hell with them. Come on, Dor, the 'Marseillaise'. Isn't that what Joan of Arc sang when she was being frazzled to a crisp?

Dora I don't think so.

Persephone Well, she should have done the bloody frog. Come on Dora. Age cannot wither us.

Dora Nor polishing stale our infinite variety.

Persephone Absobloodylutely. Come on, Dora. Let's dance. We're the flappers. The original bona-fide flapper girls. The limbs are slower but boy, can we flap.

Dora I can't.

Persephone Of course you can. We're only just getting going. Let's kick up a stink. They made us mad when we were twenty, and now we're young again. Let's dance for Caesar, for Joanie and for all the bloody nuts in here. Let's dance for us, Dora. Old witchy hags that we are. Come on.

Dora Persephone. I'll make a soldier of you yet.

Persephone Not bloody likely. Come on, Dor. Let's dance.

Music: Doris Day, 'It Had to Be You'. They dance like two old ladies at a tea dance, supporting each other as they each in turn stumble and regain their balance.

SCENE SIXTEEN

Dora What's the year, Persephone?

Persephone 1972.

Dora I thought so. Our Golden Jubilee. Well, it's time. We're ready.

Persephone For what?

Dora To come out.

Persephone Where?

Dora To come out of here. They're letting us out.

Persephone We're coming out of Dymphna's? That's nice, isn't it?

Dora Yes, isn't it?

Persephone Do you want to do the bath or shall I?

Dora I fancy the stairs for a change.

They polish.

Persephone When will it be?

Dora Any day now.

Persephone At the Dorchester?

Dora No, no, just a quiet affair – no need for speeches.

Persephone No, there's nothing to say really, is there?

Dora No. They've arranged some council accommodation for us. Separate or together, whichever you prefer.

Persephone Oh together, I think, if you don't mind. What will we wear?

Dora I think it has to be white, don't you?

Persephone Yes. Satin and lace and calico and butter muslin veils.

Dora And long, long gloves. There'll be food.

Persephone Champagne and oysters?

Dora No, tea and a battenburg.

They finish polishing.

Persephone I don't know if I can be bothered.

Dora No, perhaps we should just stay in.

Persephone Yes, I think it's raining. We could come out another day.

Pause.

Dora You know, I think we'd better. If we don't now, we might never.

Persephone You're right.

They get ready to go.

Dora One thing.

Persephone Yes?

Dora Persephone is such a mouthful. I think I might call you Porph. In the next bit.

Persephone Very well. Then I shall call you Dorph.

Dora We'll be new people.

Persephone Anything's possible.

Dora We could grow pot plants and potter about.

Persephone And listen to nice music.

Dora It's quite exciting really.

Persephone Yes.

They stand uncertainly.

Dorph Are you ready, Porph?

Porph Let's get cracking, Dorph.

Dorph Right.

Dorph Let's go.

They hold hands.
   They swim through the air.
   They repeat the same airswimming routine, although now they are much older and slower.

Lights fade

IN FLAME

For Elizabeth 'Molly' O'Keefe
and Ida Noreen Jones,
my grandmothers,
and Sophie Winter, my friend

In Flame was first presented by St Elmo Productions, produced by Matthew Byam Shaw and Grant Parsons, at the Bush Theatre, London, on 13 January 1999. The cast was as follows:

Clara / Clootie Rosie Cavaliero
Frank / Mat Ivan Kaye
Annie / Gramma Marcia Warren
James / Arthur Tom Smith
Alex Valerie Gogan
Livvy Emma Dewhurst

Director Anna Mackmin
Designer Tom Pye
Lighting Sue Baynton, Flick Ansell
Choreographer Scarlett Mackmin
Composer Andy Cowton

The play was revived at the New Ambassadors Theatre, London, produced by Matthew Byam Shaw, Act, Lee Dean and ATG, on 4 September 2000. The cast was as follows:

Clara / Clootie Rosie Cavaliero
Frank / Mat Ivan Kaye
Annie / Gramma Marcia Warren
James / Arthur Jason Hughes
Alex Kerry Fox
Livvy Emma Dewhurst

Director Anna Mackmin
Designer Tom Pye
Lighting Jenny Kagan
Choreographer Scarlett Mackmin
Composer Andy Cowton

Characters

Clara / Clootie

Frank / Mat

Alex

Mother / Gramma

James / Arthur

Livvy

Act One

SCENE ONE

Thackley, 1908.
  Clara kneels listening to a wall. She can't quite believe what she's heard. Listens again. Then moves along to hear something else.
  Frank enters. He is a burly, good-looking man in his early thirties. He watches her. Suddenly she notices him.

Clara Oh!

Frank Don't mind me.

Clara I'm listening to the wall.

Frank So I see.

Clara (*suddenly suspicious*) You don't live in Thackley.

Frank No. I'm just passing through.

Clara Oh right.

  Pause.

Do you want to have a listen?

Frank Why not.

Clara This is a particularly good wall. Although they've most of them got sommat to say.

  He comes over.

Frank Here?

Clara Lower down. Can you hear?

Frank What?

81

Clara Sounds.

Frank Not a sausage.

Clara Wait a bit.

Frank What am I supposed to be listening out for, exactly?

Clara Shufty over. (*She listens next to him.*) There's all sorts here. Ladies singing and dancing. Music playing. You know. Lutes. A bit of poetry. (*She moves to a different place.*) Over 'ere there's a baby crying. (*She moves again.*) And over 'ere there's a man shouting his head off. An army in the distance. Drummin'. Marching. Battle. Bloodshed.

Frank What does bloodshed sound like?

Clara You know, moaning and wailing. Dying really slow.

Frank That's a lot of sounds for one little wall.

Clara Of course. It's all the secrets of this place, you see, when the people die, the secrets pass into the stone.

Frank Like osmosis.

Clara I don't think so.

Frank Let's have another listen.

Clara Did you hear that?

Frank What?

Clara A low rumbling.

Frank I think that was my stomach.

Clara (*sharply*) It's gone now anyway. You've got to be on your toes.

Frank Do you listen to walls a lot?

Clara I do.

Frank Must be exhausting.

Clara It is actually, 'specially 'cos you hear more sad things than happy things.

Frank Why?

Clara Because the sound of them lasts for longer.

Frank I wonder why I couldn't hear anything.

Clara You mustn't have the knack. Or else you didn't want to hear.

Frank I don't have your talent for wall listening.

Clara No. Only trouble with me is I hear all these things but then I just forget them.

Frank In one ear and out the other?

Clara That's right. I'm very good at hearing. But I'm even better at forgetting. That's all you're good for, Gramma says.

Frank Who's Gramma?

Clara She's my all and I'm her all except for Livvy. Our parents are dead.

Frank Oh. I forget everything too. All the time.

Clara It's good to forget things sometimes. Like Dilly Barley's dog. You can kick it and bite it and throw stones at it and the next time you see it, it wags and wags. It's a stupid dog.

Frank Yes.

Clara Gramma says that when you're born, the first instant of being a little baby you have a perfect memory. You remember everything about God and clouds and all the people who ever lived and all the happiness and sadness and recipes for cake and things and then after that it's just one long forgetting and forgetting and forgetting. Every day. Until you've forgotten everything and then you're ready to die so you can be born again and remember everything that you've ever forgotten.

Frank Is she very wise, your Gramma?

Clara Very. She's got a big oracle.

Frank Has she?

Clara Yes. It's like a telescope. Do you want to meet her?

Frank Ah. I don't know.

Clara You might have already met her.

Frank I don't think so.

Clara Sometimes you know people a long time before you meet them. And then you meet them and it's a surprise because you already know them really well.

Frank Is that so?

Clara (*she has taken a real shine to Frank*) Yes. Like you. I think maybe I've known you for ages. But we've only just met.

Frank That's nice.

Clara Yes. I'm Clara.

Frank Pleased to meet you again.

Clara What are you going to do for me now?

Frank I have to do something?

Clara Yes. Something special, since you're just passing through.

Frank I don't think I do anything special. No. Nothing that special.

Clara Oh.

Frank Sorry.

Clara I felt sure you could.

Frank No. For you I would. I certainly would. But I've got nothing up my sleeve today . . . I'll be off then.

Clara Maybe you've just forgotten it.

Frank What?

Clara The special thing you do. Maybe it's slipped your mind.

Frank I'm nothing special, Clara.

Clara Oh yes you are.

Frank Really I'm not.

Clara If you remember it, come back.

Frank What?

Clara Your special thing. I'll wait.

Frank Ay. I'll do that. (*He goes to exit.*) Clara's a very pretty name. It suits you.

Clara beams. Lights fade on her.

SCENE TWO

Alex's mother Anne shuffles on. She is in her early sixties. She has had a mild stroke which slightly restricts her movements. She also has Alzheimer's Disease. She is in a nursing home.

85

Mother

> I could have danced all night
> And still have begged for more
> I could have spread my wings
> And done a thousand things
> I've never done before –

James, her care assistant who is in his early thirties enters during this.

James That's right, Annie. You raise the rafters.

Mother I pissed myself.

James Oh. Don't worry, petal, we'll soon have you sorted out. Just sit yourself down, lovey.

He starts to clean her up. She continues to sing, perhaps with more gusto.

Mother

> I never knew what made it so exciting
> Why all at once my heart took flight
> I only know when he began to dance with me
> I could have danced, danced, danced all night –

James (*during this*) Woops-a-daisy. There we go, pet. Now just wipe between your legs, Annie. Try and keep still. There's a good girl. Shall I put some talc there to dry you off? Don't want you getting sore. There, that's better.

Mother I was a dancer.

James Were you now?

Mother Tap dancer. Lovely pair of pins. Right up to my neck.

James We'd better get you some dry knickers, Annie.

Mother She did all the same steps as him.

James What?

Mother (*impatiently*) Ginger Rogers.

James Ah yes, Ginger Rogers and Fred Astaire. The same steps as Fred Astaire. Yes.

Mother But she did them backwards. On high heels. The men didn't do the hard stuff. It was all, one, two, swivel your head and present. No tricksy stuff. I liked dancing on my own the best.

James I bet you did. Right little rocker.

Mother You always had to smile. I didn't like that so much. But I miss the tap, tap, tap. My feet couldn't keep still. Even in bed they had a life of their own.

James That's great, Annie. We'll have to get you up and tapping. Entertain the troops.

Mother No, no, no. Not after she was born.

James Ah well, I've hung my dancing shoes up as well.

Mother I saw her. Ginger. She became a right bloater in the end, you know. Not even the dancing can save you.

James No, you're right there, Annie.

Mother Are you sure this is where I live now?

James Oh yes. You live here all right.

Mother What a doghole.

James No sitting on the fence for you, Annie, is there? We'd better get you spick and span for when Alex comes.

Mother Alex?

James Your daughter, Annie.

Mother Now you keep away from me. I'm not in the habit of giving strange men my knickers.

James That's a very wise policy, Annie. I'll leave some fresh out.

Mother (*sadly*) These shoes won't tap. No matter how hard you try.

James They're Hush Puppies, Annie.

Mother What?

James Hush Puppies.

Mother I don't know any.

James No, your shoes.

Mother I'm allergic to cats.

James Never mind. You keep singing, eh?

Mother Hum.

> *James exits.*
> *She suddenly lights up with a memory.*

I was magnificent. I was bloody magnificent.

SCENE THREE

*Alex's flat. Alex is looking through some old
photographs.*
*Clootie enters in a flurry. She is slightly younger than
Alex, plump and attractive.*

Clootie Sometimes I want to push people out of the way. I'm not talking about nudging. I'm talking about shunting them. Right off the pavement.

Alex Hello Clootie.

Clootie And sometimes I want to push strangers under trains. That's bad, isn't it?

Alex Yes.

Clootie I mean I don't think I ever would.

Alex No.

Clootie Do you ever feel like that?

Alex No I don't.

Clootie I think I might be an evil person.

Alex I brace myself. On station platforms. Just in case.

Clootie Perhaps I've got a syndrome.

Alex No you haven't.

Clootie Like a screaming in church and pulling emergency cords in a non-emergency-situation-type syndrome.

Alex You've had a bad shift. You didn't get good tips.

Clootie I think I've developed road rage.

Alex You can't drive.

Clootie Pavement rage, then. Sometimes the way people walk really fucks me off.

Alex You're over-tired.

Clootie I work in a pie and cider restaurant. How on earth did that come to pass?

Alex You should look for something else.

Clootie All the people who eat there are mad. Serial killers. With rotting genitalia.

Alex You could do lots of things.

Clootie They only employ me because I make people feel better about ordering pudding.

Alex That's not true.

Clootie I mean I went to university. The world was once allegedly my oyster.

Alex You just haven't found your niche.

Clootie I can't do any more courses, Alex. Or anything that involves a gym.

Alex Don't worry. It'll come to you.

Clootie Yeah, maybe. How was your day, plum?

Alex Okay. I had to put my mother's house on the market.

Clootie Shit.

Alex They think I'll get a good price.

Clootie Good.

Alex I need the money to pay for her now.

Clootie 'Course you do.

Alex You disapprove. I know you do.

Clootie No. No, I don't.

Pause.

Alex I don't look like her, you know. There's not one trace of her in my face.

Clootie You look the spit of your dad.

Alex I was always more like him.

Clootie You've done the right thing, Alex. She couldn't look after herself.

Alex She used to cut my fringe. Right up to when I was sixteen or seventeen.

Clootie I wouldn't let her loose with the scissors now if I were you.

Alex No . . . I went to the house today. And she's still there somehow. Giving me little shocks.

Clootie What are those photos?

Alex I found them in her bedside table. I don't know who they are.

Clootie Let's see. Ah! The long lost relatives.

Alex This one's got a name on the back. Livvy Unwin. Thackley, 1908. That's Yorkshire, isn't it? It's more likely to be my dad's family.

Clootie Ask her tomorrow.

Alex Questions tend to freak her out a bit.

Clootie Sometimes they're better with things from ages ago.

Alex Do you think she looks like me? Livvy Unwin? I think she does.

Clootie Maybe. If she had a fringe. She's probably your great-great-aunt and she probably died of diphtheria two weeks after this was taken.

Alex Don't say that.

Clootie How was your mum today?

Alex Aggrieved.

Clootie And how was nurse James?

Alex He asked after you again.

Clootie I love him. He is my prospective saviour.

Alex You should say something to him then.

Clootie I'm too busy raising depression to an art form.

Alex Clootie.

Clootie I might.

Alex I've got to do some work.

Clootie You're so glamorous.

Alex I'm not. You mistake having responsibility for glamour.

Clootie Well I must get on with things too. Cultivate my own bile in a petri dish or some such. Night, night, star.

Alex Sleep well. (*She's still looking at the photos. She sighs*) . . .Livvy Unwin. Livvy. You do look like me. I've got a picture somewhere just like this. We'd gone to Weston-super-Mare! Yes. And there was no sign of the sea. All day the tide had gone out. There was just hundreds of worm casts. I'm staring at the camera, as if to say: 'Where the fuck's the sea? Why have you brought me to this place of worms?' I'm holding a very big spade and a ridiculously small bucket. And I look like you. This one you look nice. Like you're about to say something.

Livvy appears behind her during this, watches her. She is beautiful but in an unpredictable way.

Livvy
My frame was not hidden from you when
I was made in that secret place.
When I was woven together in the depths of the earth,
My eyes saw your unformed body.

Alex Or laugh. Yes, you were about to laugh. What were you laughing at, Livvy Unwin?

Alex gets up and leaves during the next. She is totally unaware of Livvy's presence.

Livvy I can't remember. I can remember that day so clearly. It was beautiful. The best day of my life. But I can't remember the thing that made me laugh. Isn't that funny?

SCENE FOUR

Thackley, 1908.

Clara Livvy! Livvy! Livvy! Livvy! Livvy!

Livvy Clarty-clugs. Where have you been? Gramma's been worried.

Clara I've been on my travels.

Livvy You haven't been listening to walls again?

Gramma enters during this. She is in her early sixties.

Clara No. Well. Only a bit. But Livvy, I met a man. He came right up to me and breathed fire for me. All over me, but I didn't burn.

Gramma Don't tell fibs, child.

Clara I'm not, Gramma.

Gramma Where did you meet this man, Clara? And I want the God's truth.

Clara In Reggie Copson's field by the cowshed. Near to where they're setting up Thackley Fair.

Gramma I see. For future reference, I think you'd better steer clear of Reggie Copson's field. And while you're at it you'd best leave men alone especially if they start up any fire-breathing shenanigans. For if a man breathes his fire on you there's no turning back. Now go and help your sister with the tea.

Clara You don't believe me.

Livvy Yes she does. We do believe you, Clara.

Clara I remembered it specially and you don't believe me.

Livvy There now, don't get all worked up, Clara.

Clara No one ever believes me because I'm an idiot.

Gramma Happen I know what occurred in that field today.

Clara What?

Gramma You had an Epiphany.

Clara A what?

Gramma Epiphany.

Clara I don't know about that.

Gramma The Holy Ghost came down on you in Reggie Copson's field.

Clara I don't think so. What does the Holy Ghost look like? Does he have a moustache?

Gramma The Holy Ghost can assume any shape or form.

Clara Is it a good thing if the Holy Ghost comes down on you in a field?

Livvy It's the best thing that could possibly happen. It means you're blessed. It means you'll come to no harm.

Clara That's good, isn't it Gramma?

Gramma No more than you deserve. Now help Livvy with the tea.(*She goes to lie down.*)

Clara Who'd have thought it, Livvy? That I would have an Epiphany in Reggie Copson's field by the cowshed?

Livvy You're a special girl. Come on, we've got raspberries for tea.

Clara runs off followed by Livvy.

SCENE FIVE

The nursing home.

Mother (*getting into bed/chair at nursing home*) Bury me then. Bury me in the sand. Go on. Then you and your dad can run and play in the sea. Ganging up on me. The pair of you. Wasps buzzing about my face. Sand in my crannies. And the radio's gone off the station. Weston-super-bloody-Mare. The donkeys have got mange. Poor fuckers. And I can't move my limbs. I can't move an inch. I don't like it.

Alex enters during the last.

Alex What don't you like, Mother?

Mother Oh. It's you.

Alex Are you tired, Ma? You look tired.

Mother It's terrible here at night.

Alex Is it?

Mother Shouting and wailing. Wandering about like bloody Banshees. Her in there. She just shouts, 'Hurry up,' every few minutes. 'Hurry up, hurry up,' all night. In the end I told her, 'Why don't you hurry up and peg it, you old bat. Give us all some peace.'

Alex And did it shut her up?

Mother Did it, my arse.

Alex Mother.

Mother (*looks at Alex*) You never do what I tell you.

Alex And you never do what I tell you. (*Pause.*) I found these photos in your room. Do you recognise any of them?

Anne looks at them intently, fixes on one.

I thought she looked a bit like me. Livvy Unwin. Is she someone in your family?

Anne knocks them all to the floor except the picture of the girl.

Mother Never seen them before. Ugly fuckers.

Alex You don't have to swear at me, Mother. Let's put them away. Give me that one.

Mother It's mine.

Alex I'll put it with the others. You don't know who they are. Give it back to me.

Mother You stole it from me. Bitch.

Alex All right, Ma. Keep it. It's fine. Keep it.

James enters.

James Here we all are then. How are we doing?

Mother I can smell sulphur.

James Good for you. We like it when Alex comes, don't we Annie?

Alex Anne – her name's Anne.

Mother Annie. Annie. Annie.

Alex All right, that's enough Ma.

James You've been on good form, haven't you? Showing a bit of leg for the lads.

Alex What?

James You were telling us all about your dancing days, weren't you Annie – Anne? We didn't realise we had a dancing queen in our midst.

Alex My mother doesn't dance. You are a fibber, Mother.

Mother What would you know about it?

James It's never too late to learn, is it Annie?

Mother I was magnificent. Gold shoes. Ruffles.

Alex And where was this, Mother? Bromley High Street?

Mother You know nothing about me . . . She's not even married you know.

Alex Here we go.

James Oh, they're all terrible matchmakers in here. All my ladies are worried about me, because I'm on the shelf, isn't that right Annie? They've taken to knitting me a trousseau in the vain hope that I might get hitched one day.

Mother My daughter's a cardigan.

James Is she now?

Alex Cartographer, she means, I think. I'm a cartographer. You know, maps.

James That must be really interesting.

Alex Well, not really. It's all done by computers these days.

Mother Daddy would never use a map.

Alex No that's right, Ma . . . It's a bit of a family joke, that I became a cartographer.

James Yeah?

Mother You got him in the end though, didn't you?

Alex What, Mother?

Mother Don't think I don't know your little games because I do.

Alex That's enough now, Mother.

Mother Had him wrapped round her eye-teeth.

Alex I'm not having a spat with you today, Mother. I'm not in the mood.

Mother Sugar and spice, my arse.

Alex I won't come back if you start this again. Then you'll have no one.

James That's it now, Annie.

Alex Oh it's all right, James. I've got to be going anyway. You can have too much of a good thing. Bye, bye then, Mummy. I'll probably see you tomorrow.

They move away from Anne.

Mother Tuesday's child is full of shit. Hah! I know your games. I can see what's underneath, Missey May.

James Alex?

Alex I have got to be going.

James She doesn't mean it.

Alex Maybe not.

James If you ever want to just –

Alex I'm fine really. Thanks.

James I'm always here. For you too. You know that.

Alex Yes. I know.

James And hi to Clootie.

Alex Sure.

Anne is staring at the photo. All animosity has left her. Alex exits.

James That's a lovely photo, Annie. Who's that pretty lady then?

Mother (*proudly*) That's my daughter.

James Yes, she is pretty, isn't she?

Mother Beautiful. Lovely girl.

James Your daughter.

Mother Yes.

James Do you think she'd fuck me? Your daughter?

Mother I don't see why not. Why don't you ask her nicely, dear?

SCENE SIX

Thackley, 1908.
Clara runs on and gets on the bed with Gramma.

Clara Tell me where you found me again, Gramma?

Gramma Washed up on the beach. Flotsam and jetsam. That's what you were. But I thought, 'No. I can take that one home. Find a use for her.'

Clara Are you very wise, Gramma?

Gramma As wise as they come.

Clara I want to be wise like you.

Gramma You have to be very, very old to be wise. Old as Methuselah. You need to have suffered and endured.

Clara Do you think I will be wise one day?

Gramma Sometimes it is better to live in ignorance, Clara. There is no fun involved in being wise. If you want wisdom you must be miserable almost all of the time. I think you will never attain wisdom, Clara. But it is also a blessing to be an idiot and to be happy.

Clara Why do you speak in riddles, Gramma?

Gramma It gives the impression of wisdom, dear child. And it is the prerogative of the aged.

Livvy enters. Clara stamps her feet.

Clara Livvy!

Livvy Clarabelle!

Gramma That girl will never be a lady if she persists in this incessant stamping.

Clara I like to stamp.

Livvy Perhaps she doesn't want to be a lady.

Gramma You two will be the death of me. Now Livvy, we must decide on a course of happiness for you. Arthur Willis has set his cap at you and I think you could do a lot worse –

Livvy Gramma, Arthur Willis is a calamity.

Gramma Ay, I know right enough what he is. But being a fool has never stopped anyone being a husband.

Clara Arthur Willis got struck by lightning.

Livvy No, it narrowly missed him.

Clara It made his head sizzle.

Livvy He won't make me happy, Gramma.

Gramma There's no point worrying about happy or not happy. Live in a straight line, young lady. I can do no more for you and there's this one to think of. He's got two left feet and a tendency to make horses bolt but he's devoted to you and as long as you keep him away from the mangle, you could muddle through.

Clara Arthur Willis nearly chopped off his thumb.

Livvy Arthur Willis is lucky to have any digits left at all. What if I want more than muddling through with Arthur Willis, Gramma?

Gramma Nothing ever came of wanting more, young lady.

Clara Arthur Willis fell off Minnie Culver's roof.

Gramma Think of your poor mother, Livvy.

Clara Then he had the galloping runs.

Gramma A life of desperate wandering is no life.

Clara (*stops suddenly*) Our mother upped and walked into the sea.

    Pause.

Gramma Hush now, child. Livvy, you could do a lot worse. At least look kindly on the chap. He'd look after you.

Livvy Arthur Willis doesn't do a very good job of looking after himself.

Clara I'm not a child any more.

Gramma No, and I'm an old woman and I can't worry about the pair of you until the day I die.

Livvy All right, Gramma. I'll walk out with him if it will make you happy, but I can't make any promises.

Clara Arthur Willis is very urgent.

Livvy Ay, that he is. Come on, Clarts, let's go and do some stamping.

Livvy and Clara exit.

SCENE SEVEN

A bar. Mat is sitting at a table, drinking. He is very good-looking, younger than Alex.

Alex I feel sick.

Mat What's up, baby?

Alex I killed a pigeon.

Mat I bet he had it coming to him.

Alex It flew into my windscreen.

Mat There are some fucking kamikaze pigeons about, I tell you.

Alex It was lying on its side staring up at me. I thought it was stunned but it was dead.

Mat Alex. Have you seen the state of some of the pigeons knocking about at the moment? Fuckin' desperate. Pigeons have really let themselves go.

Alex I hate seeing dead things in the road.

Mat Too much compassion can kill you, you know.

Alex (*she smiles*) I know. How's the world of High Finance?

Mat Scintillating. How's the world of Mapmaking?

Alex I've got to do this lecture. 'Mapmaking from the Renaissance to the New Millennium.'

Mat Blimey.

Alex I'm not getting very far.

Mat You'll be great.

Alex I was thinking about you today. How you should have been a Renaissance Man. Eating, drinking and colonising the world. Slaying the fire-breathing dragons.

Mat Nah.

Alex Why not?

Mat They had to wear tights, didn't they?

Alex Oh come on, you're not averse to a bit of Lycra.

Mat I think you have serious fire-breathing tendencies. It's very sexy.

Alex And you want to colonise me?

Mat Yes I do.

Alex Ah, but then you take on responsibilities. You have to cultivate your new-found territory.

Mat But I want my colony to be self-governing.

Alex I don't think you can have it both ways.

Mat Is this a revolt?

Alex No. Not at all.

Mat No one person can give you everything you need.

Alex And what percentage of your needs do I fill?

Mat One hundred per cent. When I'm with you.

Alex And when I'm not with you? You don't think of me at all.

Mat Yes I do. But I control it.

Alex I don't know how you do it. Keep all the parts of your life so airtight. I admire you.

Mat I like to juggle things.

Alex That's what I like about you. You're very slick.

Mat And you give me a run for my money.

Alex Keeping your life in little boxes though. It must get tricky.

Mat I'm a demon at storage, me.

  Alex smiles.

Do you know what I love about you? I never know what you're thinking.

Alex It's a family trait. The one thing my mother taught me. That and invisible mending.

Mat Actually I do think about you quite a lot. You've got under my skin. I didn't mean that to happen.

Alex I know.

Mat How is your mum?

Alex Oh. She's in her favourite place. Occupying the moral high ground.

Mat I love my mum. She taught me everything I know. I can't do wrong in her eyes, but I've told her if she starts to smell I'm bunging her in a home.

Alex Why are you so flippant all the time?

Mat Why are you so serious?

Alex I'm not . . . Maybe I am. Sometimes I wish I could –

Mat What?

Alex I don't know. Splurge. Clootie – the girl I live with. She's in a mess. She's pissing her life up a wall but she makes me feel, I don't know, half-baked sometimes.

Mat I like you the way you are.

Alex But not as much as you like Katherine.

Mat Don't try and catch me out.

Alex I'm not.

Mat I was too young when I got married. It was a mistake.

Alex I have no problem with being the Other Woman. It suits me, Mat. I'm used to it. Ask my mother.

Mat She has been a bit arsey lately, Katherine. I don't know why. She won't talk to me.

Alex Mmm . . . The music here is terrible. It's getting on my nerves.

Mat I like it.

Alex Really?

Mat Yeah. A bit of Latin. I respond to that. Everyone should have a bit of Latin in them. A bit of fire, a bit of passion. Don't deny the Latin in you, Alex.

Alex Must be where I've been going wrong . . . It's my birthday next Thursday. Will you be able to meet me?

Mat You, my darling, are going to be cosseted.

Alex You don't go in for cossetting do you, Mat?

Mat Start getting your hopes up.

SCENE EIGHT

Livvy and Clara.

Clara Livvy, when I'm dead, can I come back and haunt you?

Livvy Don't talk about sad things, Clarty.

Clara It's not always sad to die, Livvy.

Livvy Well, it would be sad for me if you died. Anyway I'm older than you so I shall probably die before you.

Clara But if I do die, can I haunt you, please?

Livvy Why would you want to do that?

Clara Because I would miss you.

Livvy You won't scare me, will you?

Clara No. You won't be able to see me.

Livvy Then how will I know it's you?

Clara (*considers this*) Well I think I will probably stamp a bit. And maybe howl.

Livvy That would be good. Then I'd know for sure it was you and I wouldn't be scared.

Clara Can I practise? How I'm going to haunt you?

Livvy You'd better had. So I can prepare myself.

Clara does a howling and stamping dance. During this Arthur enters and is very shocked by Clara's behaviour. Clara finds this funny.

Arthur You are an evil girl, Clara Unwin, trying to frighten a fellow like that. My heart, Livvy, it's going nineteen to the dozen. I haven't a strong constitution, my mother says. I can't withstand too many more shocks like that. I feel quite faint.

Livvy You'd better sit down, Arthur. Find your breath. Clarty, don't laugh at Arthur. I'd have thought you'd be used to shocks though, Arthur, you've had more than your fair share of them.

Arthur My mother says she's never known anyone more afflicted than me, Livvy. Did you notice I had a slight limp, Livvy, when I arrived?

Livvy I can't say I did, Arthur.

Arthur Yes, indeed, Livvy. I thought it might be polio at first, but no – a blood blister the size of a fist on my foot. It just appeared overnight.

Clara You probably trod on something.

Arthur If I wanted your opinion I'd ask for it.

Livvy You really are afflicted, Arthur.

Arthur Indeed I am. But I have some good news too.

Clara I could burst the blister for you, Arthur.

Livvy That's enough now, Clarty. What's your good news, Arthur?

Arthur I've got myself a good apprenticeship.

Livvy Well, I'm pleased for you, Arthur. Who is it with?

Arthur (*very pleased with himself*) Samuels the butchers.

Livvy Are you sure that's a good idea, Arthur? With your history might it not be better to work somewhere with fewer knives involved? All that chopping, Arthur, are you sure?

Arthur Thank you for your concern, Livvy but mother says I'll be a natural. Which brings me in a roundabout way to what I really wanted to ask you.

Clara I could get Gramma's crochet needle and burst the blood out of it, Arthur.

Arthur What I'm meaning to say, Livvy,, and please hear me out. Bear with me now. Since I'm going to be more in the way of a steady chap, what with my job and everything, I feel it's time to settle down. Stop staring at my foot, Clara Unwin, you can't see it there, it's on the other side anyway – and although my mother says you're a bit flighty, I mean she feels sorry for you on account of first your father and then your mother dying and all, but she thinks that Suki Drivers is a better bet on account of having sturdy hips, but I said to my mother – will you get off my foot – Suki Drivers is a carthorse by compare of Livvy Unwin. I think you'd be a neat wife, not that I'm talking of getting wed yet but I wondered if maybe, you might see your way to – my prospects are good and I love babbies, so I do – what is this damn girl doing clinging to my leg – (*He walks around trying to shake her off.*) – where was I – yes, well the fair is coming to Thackley next week and although last time I did injure myself somewhat on the coconut shy, I'm not a coward and I wondered if you might – GET OFF MY LEG RIGHT NOW YOU IDIOT GIRL – LIKE TO GO WITH ME – whether you might like to, like to go with me?

Pause.

Livvy Pick me up at noon next Saturday. Come on Clarty.

They exit.

Arthur What? Really? Yes. Yes. Noon next Saturday. It's a date. (*He exits.*)

SCENE NINE

Alex and Mat.

Alex I'm binding you. The thread cutting your wrists. I'm going to bind you all over. I'm going to inscribe you with my name. I'm going to lick my name out in your sweat. I'm going to pass my thread through you. I'm going to pull you. I'm going to reel you in. I'm going to well up inside you. I'm going to run through your veins. Till the blood in your veins throb with me. I'm going to breathe inside you. I'm going to ignite you. Kindle you to flame.

Mat I love you, Alex.

Alex smiles.

SCENE TEN

The nursing home. Late at night.
  Anne is slumped over in her chair.

James Annie, you need a bit of a hitch-up, don't you, darlin'?

Mother I can't be bothered.

James Can't be bothered to sit up straight. Dear me, Annie. You have to be able to sit up straight in this life. Didn't your mother teach you that?

Mother All such a bother.

James You need someone to re-charge your batteries, don't you, old girl?

Mother What?

James You need to be handed a new lease of life. You don't want to be old. You want to be brand new, don't you sweetie?

Mother It'll never happen.

James It might, Annie. You see, every seven years your body renews itself. All the cells shift a gear. When you're growing up, you can shoot up an inch overnight. But when you're fully grown it doesn't stop happening, you know. Just the results aren't so easy to notice. We're all renewable, you know.

Mother Oh yes, lovely.

James If you concentrate hard enough, you can feel it inside you. Like your blood suddenly pumps harder. But it only happens every seven years.

Mother That's a shame.

James It is a shame.

Pause.

But do you know something, Annie? With me, I feel like nothing ever settles. Inside of me is always re-arranging. Sometimes, Annie, the veins in my arms hurt me.

Mother Oh dear. (*Anne starts to inspect her own arm.*)

James It's not a nice feeling.

Mother No.

James Do you understand me, Annie? Perhaps you do. Your brain's all knotted up, isn't it? Can you feel it tangling up? All the memories swelling and swirling about? Can you feel everything that you've lost?

Mother Only on Sundays.

James Yes that's right. On the Sabbath. Pain is always more acute on the Sabbath.

Mother Is this my arm?

James Yes, Annie.

Mother Are you sure?

James Let's have a look. Yes it appears to be your arm, madam. Must have lost its label, that's all.

Mother No sensation.

James I know. Poor Annie. (*He strokes her arm.*)

Mother Not a thing.

James starts to pinch her arm.

James What about now? Do you feel it now?

Mother Dead as a dodo.

He pinches harder.

James What about now?

Mother No. I want an abortion.

James No, no, don't upset yourself. What if I chinese burn it, Annie? No, wait a minute. That's kids' stuff, isn't it, Annie. You want to cry out with the pain, don't you?

Mother Yes.

He gets out a box of matches.

James You've got to concentrate now Annie. I'm going to hurt you now. I'm going to burn you. You're going to feel this. I'm going to singe your skin. I'm going to really, really hurt you. (*He lights a match and holds it up to her arm.*)

Mother (*suddenly alarmed*) You shouldn't play with fireworks.

Pause.

James No, of course you're right, Annie. But sometimes the temptation is very strong. (*He blows out the flame.*)

Mother I love sparklers.

James Yes. Yes. I bet you do.

Mother Holding the sparklers in my hand. Spinning with the sparklers in my hand.

James We'll have to get you sparklers, then. That's what we'll have to do.

SCENE ELEVEN

Alex's flat.
   Alex enters. Music: Peter Sarstedt, 'Where do you go to my lovely.' Clootie is drinking wine.

Clootie Hi, Alex, how was the married man?

Alex Fine.

Clootie Will I ever meet him?

Alex I don't think so.

Clootie Will he leave his wife?

Alex Eventually. If I want him too. Which I don't.

Clootie You've got it all worked out.

Alex Oh, I've worked long and hard on my mission statement.

Clootie Did you have sex?

Alex Yes. Thank you. How was your evening?

Clootie Oh, much better than yours. I've spent the evening in the company of Peter Sarstedt. He really is thrilling company. He's sung 'Where do you go to, my lovely?' to me twenty-seven times now.

Alex I hate this song. (*She goes and turns the volume down.*)

Clootie So do I. It's a wonder to me that this song was a hit. And do you know what, you never really discover where his lovely does go to – when she's alone in her head. But then again you don't really care either. In fact I defy anyone to like the woman in this song. I don't think she's lovely.

Alex Clootie. Why have you rearranged all the furniture?

Clootie Oh yes. I hope you don't mind. I had an urge to become more south-facing.

Alex Well, if it makes you feel better –

Clootie My mother swears by furniture-moving as therapy. She's feng-shuiing her way towards Paradise. Have we got any paracetamol?

Alex You shouldn't keep taking them.

Clootie I have no immune system. You know that. He robbed me of my immune system.

Alex Not Nigel again, Clootie. Please.

Clootie He took everything, Alex. Even the bloody shower curtains.

Alex I know.

Clootie He only ever has baths.

Alex I know. You're exhausting me, Clootie.

Clootie No, but Alex, I've realised tonight, I am so very nearly over him.

Alex Good.

Clootie I hope he's enjoying wonderful power showers on an hourly basis.

Alex It will get easier, Clootie.

Clootie I can't decide what I find worse though. The fact that he was having sex with other men. Or the fact that he was having it in toilets. What do you think?

Alex I really don't know. Both things are bad.

Clootie Yes, yes they are, aren't they? But the location does make a difference. I wonder if he'd been having sex with another man in – a meadow, say, would I find it any easier to cope with? I find the image of the toilet very troubling, you see.

Alex Yes.

Clootie I imagine the sound of the cistern filling and re-filling and the drip, drip, and the smell, of course. I've got it all in my head in glorious technicolour, Alex. I wish he'd chosen somewhere more aesthetically pleasing.

Alex You have to stop this, Clootie.

Clootie Yes, yes, I do. 'We are hard-pressed on every side but not crushed.'

Alex What?

Clootie St Paul to the Corinthians. I've had him out tonight too. He's very good when you're feeling low,

St Paul but not quite as good as Elvis Presley for some reason. Why is it that I still want a boyfriend, Alex? After all this. I don't think I can be fully evolved. I must have some sort of chemical imbalance.

Alex Why don't you ask James out?

Clootie Because I can't. I haven't got the necessary – what-do-you-call-it.

Alex But you like him.

Clootie Yes. I do. A lot.

Alex He's lovely. He cares for old people. He's nice-looking but –

Clootie – but not totally out of my league, I know.

Alex I didn't mean that.

Clootie But I can't imagine asking him out, Alex. I can imagine say waking from a coma and finding him right there holding my hand, but I can't ask him out. It's humiliating. He'll say no. He'll probably howl in derision at me.

Alex Of course he won't. He likes you. He laughs at all your jokes. He always asks after you. You should get your wonderbra on and get down there.

Clootie You don't understand, Alex, I'm not like you, the prospect of happiness renders me utterly paraplegic. I'm a Catholic. I've been brought up never to expect anything good.

Alex You're being ridiculous, Clootie. It's a match made in Catholic heaven. Now why don't you come with me tomorrow?

Clootie I don't think so.

Alex Well, just to see my mum then. My mum would like to see you. And it would take the pressure off me.

Clootie It would be nice to see her.

Alex She always really liked you. 'Clootie always says thank you.'

Clootie Yes, well, I was brought up to be grateful.

Alex That's settled then. I'm looking forward to it. (*She goes and switches off the record.*)

SCENE TWELVE

Thackley, 1908.
  Arthur and Livvy process on with Gramma close behind.

Arthur I didn't know as Gramma Unwin would be coming with us to the fair, Livvy.

Livvy Gramma wouldn't let me come unchaperoned to the fair with an urgent young man like you, Arthur.

Gramma What's he saying?

Arthur Nothing . . .We haven't seen you at Samuels the Butchers this week, Gramma Unwin.

Gramma No, well I wanted to make sure you had all your fingers, Arthur, before I go buying any more of their pork sausages. Now and don't you be getting too close to that young girl. And while we're at it, if you've any sharp objects in your pockets you'd better be giving them to me now. We don't want this day ending in tears.

Livvy Leave him be, now Gramma.

Gramma I shall walk behind you two. But I'm watching you, Arthur, so no funny business with my grandchild.

Arthur No, Gramma Unwin.

   Clara enters.

(*sotto voce*) Not the idiot girl as well.

Livvy Don't call her that.

Clara Will you take me on all the rides, Arthur?

Livvy Don't be pestering Arthur now, Clarty.

Arthur I can go on no rides with you, Clara, for I have a queasy stomach.

Clara Arthur Willis will never make anyone happy.

Gramma Come with me now, Clara and we'll find a use for you. Remember what I said now, Arthur Willis.

Arthur You've nothing to worry about with me, Gramma Unwin. Livvy is safe in my hands.

   Gramma and Clara exit.

Livvy Well.

Arthur You look very beautiful, Livvy.

Livvy Thank you, Arthur.

Arthur What would you like to do? I've got my first week's wages with me, Livvy, and I don't mind telling you I intend to spend at least a third on you. So name it, Livvy. Anything.

Livvy I don't mind, Arthur.

Arthur Can I kiss you then, Livvy?

Livvy Why don't we wander about a bit first, Arthur, take in the sights.

Arthur Whatever you want, Livvy. This is your day. But I am hoping you'll see your way to letting me kiss you at some stage of the proceedings, Livvy. I've talked to me mates and they said it's not too much to ask of you now that we're officially courting. I wouldn't have said anything but I'd have just worried the whole time about it, when to make a move and so forth and Mother says it's better to get things out in the open if they're on your mind. So any time you want me to kiss you just say the word, Livvy. I'll be ready for you.

Livvy Thank you, Arthur. I'll bear that in mind.

Frank enters, as Fabrizio, with a camera on a tripod. As he speaks he sets up the camera.

Fabrizio Buon giorno! Ah bella bella Signorita! The Great Fabrizio at your service. Take my card. (*Looks at card.*) No. No. Wrong card. Scusa.

Arthur No thank you.

Fabrizio I am here, madonna, for one night only. Sad news, I know. No please. It is all I can do. One night. For you at the most a week. Then back to Verona. No tears, please. I cannot stand to see the ladies cry.

Arthur She's not crying.

Fabrizio For now I am at your convenience. I will do all I can do for you, madonna.

Arthur We don't want anything, thank you very much.

Livvy Arthur.

Fabrizio Please sir. I must ask you to hold your horses. Please. Rein them in. Two minutes of your time is all I ask. Madonna, here you see the humble box that is the tool of my trade. With this I capture the present. Poof! Beautiful, no? I give you something to remember for the rest of your life. A whisper of happy times. My life's duty is to capture rare moments of beauty. Life is hard, yes? But there are moments, wonderful moments, eh madonna?

Livvy Yes.

Arthur How much for one photograph?

Fabrizio All I ask is uno, duo, tres, quattro, half a crown. Half a crown! Look at this woman, sir. Look at her. You are a lucky man. Shake my hand. Shake it. (*Arthur does.*) Later I buy you a pint. She is a rare creature. I should know. I have travelled the world. I have seen beauty, oh yes I have, I have been to the Far Indies and seen the birds of paradise. I have held them in my hand, the most fantastico creatures in this world. See? I weep as I remember. What do you say, Arthur? Half a crown only for a photograph of this beautiful lady?

Livvy is laughing.

Arthur Come on now.

Fabrizio Oh, lady, pretty lady. You don't wanna walk away from me, huh. It will break my heart if I cannot photograph you. For you, I will waive my fee. Only one shilling for I must capture you with my humble box. What's your name, pretty lady? No, don't tell me. I guess.

Arthur That's it, we're going.

Fabrizio Vittoria? No. Emilia? No. Don' tell me, now. I am a magician. I can see inside your head. Beatrice? No. Jane? No. Of course not. I insult you with such a name. There, see, I smite myself for such ignorance. I have it, I have it, Lucia! No. Consumpta? No –

Arthur Livvy. Come on, now.

Fabrizio LIVVY! LIVVY! Of course. I knew it. Livvy. Perfecto. Livvy – lives. Livvy – full of life. Perfect.

Arthur We're leaving now, thank you very much, erm, er –

Fabrizio I am the Great Fabrizio of Florenza, at your service Arthur.

Arthur Well, Great Fabrizio. Look here, old chap, it's very kind of you but we won't be requiring your services –

Livvy No, Arthur. Get Gramma and Clara. I'd like a photograph of us all.

Arthur But Livvy –

Livvy You said this was my day. And it'll be a nice memento for us. Please, Arthur. Go and get them. I'll wait here. Quickly.

Fabrizio My advice to you, Arthur. Always do what the women say. It make your life much easier. Take it from one who knows.

Arthur Very well. Will you be all right?

Livvy Of course.

Arthur Well, I shall run, which I don't mind telling you is something my mother told me to avoid at all costs.

Livvy I'll be waiting.

Arthur exits.

Livvy Where will I stand, for the photograph?

Fabrizio Permit me to show you, madonna. You are a true beauty, if I may say so. Like the female bird of paradise.

Livvy I thought the female birds of paradise were very dowdy. It's the male birds that are beautiful.

Fabrizio Indeed, you are right.

Livvy The male birds have resplendent tail and head feathers, of azure and gold and vermilion but they only display them when they want to win a mate.

Fabrizio You know a great deal about them.

Livvy I read a lot. I would like more than anything to travel.

Fabrizio I have been to the farthest corners of the globe.

Livvy It must be a real comedown to have to photograph at Thackley Fair.

Fabrizio Not when Thackley has such a bird of paradise.

Livvy And when the birds of paradise show their plumage they also dance for their mate, don't they? While she looks on.

Fabrizio That's right.

Livvy And you have seen them.

Fabrizio Of course. I will remember that dance until the day I die.

Livvy Show me.

Fabrizio What?

Livvy Show me how they dance.

Fabrizio You want me to show you how they dance.

Livvy Yes. Just roughly. To give me some idea.

Fabrizio Of course. For you, I will do this . . . (*He is improvising.*) First of all they let down their tail feathers, a wiggle, thus. Then they mark out their territory, backward, forward motion, thus. Then they display their head feathers. Then they begin to vibrate. Side to side.

Up and down. An orgy of colour. But they do not look at their mate once. No, they are proud fellows. Then the dance begins.

Fabrizio does a funny, strange, jerky dance with mad head movements and strange throat noises. Livvy watches amused.

Fabrizio That is more or less it.

Livvy That was very illuminating. Your name isn't Fabrizio is it?

He shakes his head.

Livvy What is it?

Fabrizio (*he drops the Italian accent*) Frank.

Livvy And you're not from Verona or Florence, are you?

Frank I'm from Skipton.

Livvy And you haven't travelled to the far-flung corners of the globe.

Frank I've never been outside Yorkshire.

Livvy And you've never seen a bird of paradise have you, Frank?

Frank Not till today.

Clara enters.

Livvy Here she is. This is Clara.

Frank (*slight falter*) Clara? And I am the Great Fabrizio. Can I give you my card?

Clara I know you.

Frank I don't think so, signorita.

Livvy Have you been on the rides, Clarty?

Clara No. I've been listening to the walls. There's some pretty good walls here.

Livvy Clara, we didn't bring you to the fair so you could listen to walls.

Frank If she wanna listen to the walls, she should listen to the walls.

Clara Yes Livvy. I'm sure I know you.

Livvy He's only just come to Thackley, Clara. The Great Fabrizio only makes very brief forays into the public eye.

Frank This is correct. What you say. Is correct.

Clara Can you keep secrets?

Frank Can I keep secrets! She wanna know, if I, the Great Fabrizio can keep secrets! Come here. I am world renowned for my secret-keeping ability. Any secret you tell me will go no further than between you, me and the goalpost. Even if I travel the world I will not breathe a word. I would rather have my hands cut off than tell your secret. No I would die first.

Livvy You don't have any secrets, Clarty-Clugs.

Clara Of course I do. You can't live and be a lady unless you have a secret to tell.

Frank What she says – it is true. I think you are very wise.

Clara (*delighted*) Am I?

Frank If I tell you this, it is true.

Clara I'm going to tell you my best secret.

Livvy Clara.

Frank No, no, is too much. Too great an honour. Even I, the Great Fabrizio, must sometimes know when to draw the line.

Clara No, please.

Frank I don't know if my heart can stand it.

Clara Livvy, please turn your back.

Frank Yes. This is a necessary precaution.

Clara Go further off. Now.

Livvy All right, Clara.

Frank Please to whisper. For security reasons it is always best to whisper secrets.

Clara (*with pointed look at Livvy*) Good idea. (*She whispers in his ear.*)

Frank Perhaps I think a little bit louder.

Clara whispers again – a stage whisper.

Clara I had an Epiphany in Reggie Copson's field by the cowshed.

Frank Yes, yes. I knew it. I could tell at a glance. There now, your secret is safe.

Clara I hope I can trust you.

Frank It is etched on my heart. A special moment has passed between us, no?

Clara We're friends now because you know my secret.

Frank And what about Livvy? Do you think she will share a secret with me?

Clara I think you've got enough to do with safeguarding my secret.

Livvy I don't have any secrets.

Frank I don't think that is true.

Clara She's certainly not as good as me at having secrets, Great Fabrizio.

Frank No, she is very bad at secrets, Livvy, you know why? Because her heart is in her face.

Arthur and Gramma enter.

Arthur She's here all the time. Clara Unwin, we've been high and low for you.

Frank Ah! Scusa, scusa ladies, we must prepare for the big moment. If I can just move you over here. And you, madam, what may I call you?

Gramma You can call me what you like. And there's no need to manhandle me. I don't hold with foreigners I'll tell you now, and Arthur was right about you, but I should like to have a photograph so let's get this over and done with.

Frank I defer to you, great, wise lady.

Arthur Where shall I stand? Next to Livvy?

Frank As you wish. Now everybody, a big smile for the Great Fabrizio.

Gramma I'm not going to smile.

Clara Can I stamp?

Livvy No, you must be still, Clarty.

Frank Yes, Arthur, great gusto, but you are obscuring the lovely Livvy.

Arthur Less of the lovely, from you. I'm paying for this.

Frank (*he looks at Livvy*) No, I ask no fee. This is a pleasure for me.
   And ready?

Flash

Yes. Very good. Perhaps a little less fierce this time from the great lady.

During this dialogue Frank takes photos.

Livvy Don't scowl, Gramma.

Gramma I'll 'ave you know I'm troubled with wind.

Arthur I suffer terrible from wind. My mother says I was born with a twisted colon.

Flash.

Clara Can I see it, Arthur?

Livvy It's on the inside, Clara.

Arthur I was a breach baby. I didn't breathe for a good minute when I was born. I was purple for the first week of my life.

Gramma It's a wonder they didn't put you out of your misery straight off.

Flash

Clara You're still a funny colour, Arthur.

Livvy He's not a funny colour, Clara.

Gramma He's sallow. All the Willises are sallow.

Frank Arthur, can you smile?

Arthur I'm beginning to feel very unwell.

Gramma Dose of salts is what I would recommend for you, Arthur Willis.

Flash.

Clara You can kill someone with salt.

Arthur Can you?

Clara Yes. It's called salt killing. Can I have one on my own?

Gramma Vanity is a terrible sin, Clara Unwin.

Livvy No, let her, Gramma.

Arthur I need to put my head between my legs.

Gramma Yes, best place for it, lad.

Frank All the ladies I take on their own, yes?

Gramma I bet you do.

Clara Me first.

Frank Beautiful. The camera loves you. There is something very noble in your brow, Clara. Smile for me. With all your teeth. Good girl.

Flash.

Clara I think I love the Great Fabrizio.

Gramma Come and sit here, before your heart takes flight all together now, Clara.

Clara Was I beautiful, Gramma?

Gramma From the day you were born.

Frank And you, madonna?

Gramma No, I don't want my face out wandering the world without my people beside me. I think that's us done.

Arthur Yes, we should be heading off now.

Clara What about Livvy?

Gramma She's not bothered, are you?

Arthur We could get saveloy and chips, Livvy.

Clara Yes please.

Livvy I thought you had a queasy stomach, Arthur.

Arthur Must be hungry, that's all. I've a very fast metabolism, my mother says.

Gramma Come on then. Let's be having you.

Frank No! Please. I will take the lady's picture. Please. I have only a few pictures left. I must finish them today.

Arthur It's getting dark.

Frank But Livvy has her own light. Please, Livvy, permit me?

Clara Say cheese, Livvy!

Frank No, say, formaggio!

Gramma She's not saying filth. If she says anything it will be the Lord's word.

Clara Livvy has all the psalms by heart. She says them to me till I fall asleep.

Gramma Ay, that's it, Livvy. Give us a psalm. (*pointedly at Frank*) There's evil all around.

Livvy (*intently to Frank who stops looking through the camera lens to watch her*)
  I praise you because I am fearfully and wonderfully
    made,
  Your works are wonderful, I know that full well.
  My frame was not hidden from you when I was made
    in that secret place,
  When I was woven together in the depths of the earth,
  Your eyes saw my unformed body

Arthur Are you sure that's from the Bible?

Clara He's forgotten to take the picture. The Great Fabrizio forgot to take the picture.

Gramma It's the Lord's word, all right.

Livvy You didn't take my picture.

Clara Livvy went all shimmery. Did you see her? She went all shimmery.

Arthur I'm going for my saveloy and chips.

Frank (*from now on Frank drops his Italian accent*) Yes, she did.

Gramma Hold your horses, Arthur, you can buy me a skate and chips. I might even stretch to a pickled egg.

Arthur Are you coming, Livvy?

Livvy I'll be right there.

Gramma You can take my arm, Arthur Willis. I'm fit to drop.

Arthur Do you think my arms are the same length Gramma Unwin?

Gramma You've enough deformities to sink a thousand ships, Arthur Willis. Now let's be off.

Arthur All right, all right. Livvy?

Livvy I'm right behind.

   Gramma and Arthur exit.

Livvy You didn't take the picture.

Clara You were full of fizz, Livvy.

Frank I didn't need to take the picture.

Clara Sparks flew off you, Livvy.

Livvy But I want something to remember.

Clara You went like a sherbert dip in my mouth.

Frank You will remember.

Livvy Take it anyway.

Clara I want to go fizzy too.

Frank Smile then.

Clara (*starts to spin on the spot*) Look! I'm spinning. Am I going fizzy?

Livvy I don't want to smile.

Clara (*spinning*) I'm whizzing and whizzing in the sky.

Livvy I want to laugh.

Clara Look at me, Great Fabrizio! Look at me!

Frank At whose beauty the Sun and Moon stand amazed.

Clara I can shimmer too!

Livvy I want to laugh! I want to laugh!

> *Livvy and Clara are both laughing, Clara spinning round and round on the spot. Frank takes Livvy's picture. Blackout.*
> *Interval.*

Act Two

SCENE ONE

The nursing home.

James Who's been a naughty girl, then?

Mother Stop manhandling me.

James Thinking of emigrating, were you?

Alex What's wrong?

James Annie's been on a walkabout.

Mother I went to the fair.

Alex No you didn't, Mother.

Mother How do you know? I went to the fair on a motorbike.

James It's all right. A lot of them go wandering at night. She didn't come to any harm. Did you, Annie?

Alex Why did you go wandering off, Mother?

Mother I've lost something. I just can't find it.

Alex What is it? Tell me. What have you lost?

Mother (*agitated*) I don't know. I don't know.

James Don't worry, Annie. Let's sit you down.

Alex It's all right, Mum, I'm here. You don't have to worry.

Mother (*she looks at James*) He tried to burn me. I was very very scared.

James No need to worry now, Annie. You're safe. You're safe now Alex is here.

Mother (*looks at her for the first time. With pleasure*) Alex!

Clootie enters.

Alex Yes and look who's come too!

Anne looks confused.

Clootie Hello Anne. Don't you look well.

She kisses her.

Alex Annie. Apparently she prefers Annie now.

Clootie Ah. Annie. All right, Annie? Hi, James.

James Clootie. Lovely to see you again.

Mother Who are you?

Alex Mum, don't be silly. It's Clootie.

Mother Who?

Alex Clootie.

Mother Suzy?

Clootie No. Clootie.

Mother Ruby?

Alex Clootie. Clootie. Her name's Clootie.

Mother Clootie? What sort of name is that?

Clootie A bloody stupid name, Annie.

James It's a nice name.

Mother Clootie? No.

Alex We were at school together, Ma.

Clootie I was named after a cake.

James No!

Mother Alex?

Clootie My mother's idea.

Alex What, Ma?

James What kind of cake?

Mother Who's Annie?

Clootie A clootie dumpling.

Alex You are, Ma.

Clootie A suet and raison dumpling.

Mother Oh fuck it.

Clootie My sentiments exactly.

Alex Clootie's a great name. It's better than Alex. Alex is too hard.

Clootie Clootie MacBride. I mean my parents seriously disliked me.

James You could have been a very successful folk singer.

Alex Clootie's a lovely name.

James Alex suits you. It's not hard, I mean, you're not at all hard.

Clootie Yes, I can see it now. Clootie MacBride and the Dumplings. I shall wear a kaftan, and play the harp and sing songs of lost love and lost hair.

James Are your parents Scottish?

Mother Lost.

Clootie No. They're from Tunbridge Wells.

Mother Lost.

James Oh.

Alex All right, Ma.

Mother I wish I was young. My whole life ahead of me. (*She starts to cry.*)

Alex Don't cry, Ma. Please. I hate it when you cry.

Clootie You don't want to be young, Annie. Being young is rubbish.

Alex We're not young any more. We're in our thirties.

Mother I used to be brand new.

Alex I've got a photo of my mum on her honeymoon and she looks like Audrey Hepburn. Don't you, Ma?

James She's still a stunner, aren't you, Annie? Sets all our hearts fluttering.

Clootie Oh God, sorry, Annie these are for you. (*She hands her a bunch of flowers.*)

Mother I can't abide carnations.

Alex They're chrysanthemums, Mother.

Mother I wanted wild flowers.

James These are very pretty, Annie.

Mother Snapdragons. Hollyhocks. Poppies. And cornflowers. And lots of fern. It stretched nearly to the ground.

Clootie What did, Annie?

Mother It was too heavy to carry. Over ten pounds. It was a burden really. My dad helped me carry it up the aisle. Then I handed it to Margery Evans. She nearly buckled under the weight.

Clootie Ah, your wedding bouquet. How lovely.

Mother Margery Evans was a scrawny bint, though. She became a nun not long after. Only life she was fit for.

Alex Mother, I think you're making this up.

Mother I couldn't throw it. They always want you to throw it. I couldn't, it was too heavy. I wanted it wild though.

James Shall I take those, Annie?

Alex Mother, you're such a terrible fibber. I've got her wedding photos. You had a posy, didn't you?

Mother How do you know? You weren't there. You don't know anything about me.

James I'll put them in a nice vase for you.

Clootie No, we can do it.

James No, no, it's one of my main accomplishments. Hours of training at nursing school. Back in a tick. (*James exits.*)

Mother (*to Clootie*) It was because of her, you see.

Clootie Was it?

Mother I had to have a long one. She was already quickening inside me. I had to cover her up. You can't let on about the quickening.

Alex (*pointedly*) Clootie?

Clootie I can't do it.

Mother What?

Alex Yes you can. For God's sake, Clootie. He really likes you. He laughs at everything you say.

Mother It's all a leap in the dark, dear. You spend your whole life leaping.

Clootie He is so nice. He's devoted his life to old people. He must be gay.

Mother So very, very dark.

Alex (*exasperated*) Clootie.

Mother Can't see a bloody thing.

Clootie We hate homosexuals, don't we, Annie? They should be bludgeoned.

Mother Yes, dear.

Alex Clootie.

Mother And vegetarians.

Clootie He's coming back.

Alex Do it.

James enters with the vase of flowers.

James There we go then.

Alex Don't they look lovely?

Mother Lovely. Are they mine? Who are they from?

Clootie They're from me, Annie.

Mother Who are you?

Clootie Oh dear. I feel a bit of a conversation loop coming on. I'd better be going. Bye, Annie. God bless.

Alex Clootie?

James Well, we'll see you again, Clootie.

Clootie Yep.

James Bye then.

Clootie Bye. (*She goes to exit, turns.*) I hope you don't mind me asking, James.

James What?

Clootie Do you like tapas?

James Sorry?

Clootie Tapas. You know. Spanish. Food. On plates. I just love tapas.

James Oh.

Mother Tapas.

Clootie Do you?

James What?

Mother Tap. Tap. Tap.

Clootie Like Tapas?

James Yeah, I don't mind.

Clootie There's a new place opened on King Street. Do you want to go? Next Thursday? Maybe?

Alex I've heard it's really good.

James Oh. Thursday. Sure. Why not? I'm working the night shift but I don't need to be here till midnight.

Clootie Great. Shall we meet there about seven?

Mother I know what I lost.

Alex Do you, Mum?

James Whatever. Yeah. Great. Are you coming, Alex?

Alex I'm not sure yet.

Clootie But we could go anyway?

Mother Tap.

James Why not?

Mother Tap shoes. I lost my tap shoes.

Clootie What?

James Annie's a little Cyd Charisse.

Clootie So that's a date?

Alex (*laughing*) No she's not.

Mother Will you find me my tap shoes dear?

Clootie Yes?

Alex Yes.

James Yes.

Mother That's good.

    Blackout.

SCENE TWO

Thackley, 1908.
    Frank and Livvy.

Frank I've thought about you all week.

Livvy I know.

Frank Livvy.

Livvy Show me your hand, Frank.

Frank Why?

Livvy I'm going to read your future.

Frank You can do that?

Livvy Oh yes. Didn't I tell you, I've got mystical powers?

Frank It doesn't surprise me.

Livvy Let's see. (*She takes his hand.*) Oh dear.

Frank What?

Livvy I see itchy feet.

Frank Where?

Livvy It's written all over your palm. Itchy feet.

Frank You're wrong.

Livvy I see paths leading you away.

Frank Where to?

Livvy Far-flung places.

Frank How far-flung?

Livvy Very. The furthest-flung you can get.

Frank I'll take you with me. Where do you want to go?

Livvy I want to go everywhere.

Frank What does it say in my hand? Where are we going to go?

Livvy The road leads you north. To the sea.

Frank That'll be Scarborough. Yes. Do you fancy a trip to Scarborough?

Livvy No, I don't think it's Scarborough. More exotic than Scarborough.

Frank Whitby then. Filey at a push. No, let's have a look, I think it's definitely Whitby.

> *Livvy laughs.*

Livvy It could be Whitby.

Frank Wait a minute. (*He smells his hand.*) I can smell kippers. Smoked kippers. It must be Whitby. Smell.

Livvy Mmm. Definitely something fishy.

Frank That's it then.

Livvy I don't think you're taking me with you.

Frank Of course I am.

Clara enters.

Livvy Clara!

Frank (*Italian accent*) Hello, Princess.

Clara Great Fabrizio! I've found some new walls. I thought maybe we could go and listen to them together.

Frank Of course! But first I've got some pictures here and there's a certain princess in them who looks very, very beautiful.

Clara Is that me?

Frank I don't know any other princesses. Now I'll give them to you but you must look at them very quietly. No stamping. Because if you're too noisy when you look at photographs they start to disappear. And we wouldn't want that, would we?

Clara No.

Frank Sit a little way off.

Livvy Where we can see you, Clarty.

Clara (*a little reluctantly*) All right. But we can go and listen to some walls later?

Frank My ears are itching for some walls, princess.

She takes the photos and sits down and looks at them.

Frank (*to Livvy*) Now let me do you. No, not your hand. Hands are for beginners. I like to chart the whole person. Stand there that's it. Be still. Now let's see. (*He moves around her slowly. He never actually touches her though.*) We'll just do from the waist upwards. From the equator. This will tell us all we need to know. We don't need to stray down into the tropics. Not today anyway.

Livvy Frank!

Frank This is our first continent. Your back. Oh yes. This is a beautiful place but largely undiscovered. This is, tell me where –

Livvy Asia.

Frank Yes, Asia. And down the vertebrae. Into the arch of your back. The small of your back. This is a frightened place. A little island.

Livvy Timor Island.

Frank Yes. Look at these. I love these. The hairs on your forearms. Up through the grasslands. The pampas. Oh. This is a smooth warm place. Your belly. This is –

Livvy Italy?

Frank More exotic.

Livvy Brazil?

Frank Perfect. And upwards. It's getting very hot now.

Livvy Frank, I'm watching you.

Frank This bit is definitely South America. I've always wanted to go to South America.

Livvy It's too far. And it's a dangerous place. Unpredictable.

Frank I'm definitely going there one day though. But for now I shall lose myself here. Your face. Your face is like the whole world. No, the sun. You see. You turn, and I can only orbit round you.

He turns her around as if she were a globe while he moves slowly round her.

I want to hold the sun in my hands.

Livvy You want to eclipse me?

Frank No, I'm definitely a sun worshipper. (*He pulls her into him.*) Livvy, I don't need to travel the world.

Livvy But you promised me kippers.

Frank I'll just pop to Whitby then. But I'll come straight back.

Livvy All right then.

They are about to kiss. During the last Clara has stopped looking at the photos. She watches Livvy and Frank. Then she gets up.

Clara I'm not beautiful. You lied to me. I'm not beautiful like Livvy. I'm ugly. I can see that in the pictures. And you're not the Great Fabrizio. Your name is Frank. And I have met you before. You said we'd never met, but you came and breathed your fire on me and now you only want to breathe your fire on her. And I told you my secret and now you only want to hear her secrets. I hate you. I hate you both. You both lied to me.

Livvy Clara. No. You are beautiful. I'm sorry.

Clara I'm the idiot girl. And I'm ugly. See. Look at the photos. He's made me look ugly. I hate you, Livvy. (*She throws the photos down and runs out.*)

Livvy No wait. Please, Clarty. I'm sorry. Please wait. Frank, I'm sorry. I'll have to go after her.

Frank No, Livvy. Don't go.

Livvy But I have to see if she's all right.

Frank She'll be all right. Come here. Please. They all ask too much of you. I want to look after you.

Livvy I don't know.

Frank Hush. Don't speak. This is our time. I love you, Livvy. Do you love me too? Please Livvy.

Livvy Yes. Yes. I do.

He kisses her tenderly.

SCENE THREE

The nursing home.

Alex Here we are then, Mother. (*She gets the tap shoes out and places them before her.*) Nothing to hold you back now. And I've brought you another treat. Raspberry Royale. That's what you wanted, isn't it? They had Sherry Trifle too but you turned your nose up at that last time. Ah. We're going for the silent treatment, are we? (*Pause. The next is very chatty, light, conversational.*) Well. It's my birthday today. I didn't get your card. Second post, maybe. Thirty-six today. I don't look it? Thank you very much. I use extremely expensive eye cream. Guaranteed to cover that 'not-quite-as-fertile-as-I-used-to-be-look' that's creeping up under my eyes. Anyway, I'm meeting Mat later. Did I tell you about him? I don't think you'd approve. He's an acquired taste. And he's married. I fell right into that cliché. Very good in bed though. We get up to all sorts.

143

Your mind, if you had one, would boggle. He never holds my feet though . . .

Pause.

Come on, tuck in. Can't let a good Raspberry Royale go to waste. Raspberries fit for a queen. Come on. You don't have to watch your figure any more. Open wide and let the choo-choo train in. (*Pause. The tone is sharper suddenly.*) Eat up, mother. It's a treat. Come on.(*She feeds her during the next.*) Oh dear, it's all down your front, Mother. You look a right old mess, don't you? (*She looks at her.*) You're very quiet today. Now you haven't got your audience.

Livvy enters.

But I can see you're thinking. It's all going on in there, isn't it? Pickfords must have been, Mother. The careful movers. Packed you away with the crocks and the glassware. But it's all right because I know what you're thinking. Slugs leave trails, you see.

Livvy No.

Alex comes right up close to her.

Alex I was a little girl. You were the one who turned it into a competition. I was just a little girl. Sweetness and light, my arse. You play dirty, don't you, Anne?

Livvy Tell her.

Alex Well it doesn't matter. He's dead now. My dad's dead. I still dream about him though. It's a recurring dream. We're at Weston-super-Mare and we're burying you in the sand. And then we just leave you. We run off together and we have ice-cream. Neopolitan flavour, because I can never choose. And I wake up and I feel safe and then I realise that we've forgotten you, you're

still there buried in the sand and I feel guilty for the rest
of the day.

Livvy She knows but tell her anyway.

Alex What's so ironic, what you don't realise, Ma, is
I still want to help you. I'm here with my spade. And
I'm ready to dig.

Livvy Good.

Alex But you're not interested are you?

Livvy It's nearly time.

Alex Just answer me one thing, Mother, why does this
feel like a punishment? You being ill, and helpless. Tell
me what I've done. Come on. (*Alex sighs.*) Well, you
win. (*As an afterthought she kisses her on the head.*)

> She leaves.
> During the next Anne has great difficulty speaking.

Livvy Put your shoes on then. Here, let me give you a
hand.

Mother Th–, th–, th– THANK you, d–, d–, dear.

Livvy They look lovely.

Mother You're a g–, g–good girl, Alex. But your fr–, fr–,
fr–fringe needs c–cut–cutting.

Livvy Are you ready?

Mother Just about.

> She gets up with great effort. Her one arm is senseless
> as if she's had another stroke. They go to leave. An
> afterthought.

Mother You know I l–, l–, l–, l–, love you, Alex, don't
you?

Livvy Yes, of course.

They go to exit. Anne's movement is very laboured.
Anne exits.

SCENE FOUR

Frank enters. He laboriously composes his letter.
Livvy lingers to listen to him. Perhaps she takes out a
letter and reads it as he speaks.

Frank Dear Livvy, Sorry for my delay in writing to you.
By the time you read this letter, I will be gone. No. Long
gone.

Forgive me. I'm not very good at goodbyes.

You were right. I'm off on my travels again. I don't
know where. Further than Yorkshire this time I hope.
Ha. Ha.

I won't forget you.

I'm sorry Livvy. I never meant to be more than what
I seemed. Does that make sense? No.

I never meant to get your hopes up. Better.

I'm a bad sort all together and you're better shot of
me.

Regards to your family. Take care of yourself.

     Yours, etcetera,

      The Great Lorenzo.

P.S. I got tired of Fabrizio. The great Lorenzo has got
a real ring to it, don't you think?

He exits.

Livvy Frank? But we haven't picked a name yet. I
wanted us to pick the name together.

She sinks down.

SCENE FIVE

Thackley, 1908.
   Livvy sits silently. Gramma and Arthur stand around her.

Gramma You foolish, foolish girl. You've thrown your life away. And where is he? Vanished into thin air. Well, I can do no more for you now. I've done my best for you for your poor mother's sake. But no more. And what have you to say for yourself? No, it's as well you're silent. For we don't want to hear what you have to say. As for Clara, I don't know what you've done to her but you've broken that poor simple girl's heart.

Arthur That's enough now, Gramma Unwin.

Gramma Ay, I shan't waste my words on her. For she's surely lost. What were you thinking of, girl? To let the first chap that comes along turn your head. And don't think, madam, that I don't know who it was, for I do.

Arthur Who was it, Livvy?

Gramma No, we shan't speak of him, Arthur. Not in this house. With his fancy words.

Arthur Was it –

Gramma No, Arthur, don't speak of it.

Arthur But I reckon –

Gramma Arthur, be silent.

Arthur But I only want to –

Gramma Arthur, I've warned you.

Arthur But can I just –

Gramma Arthur I must beg of you to hold your tongue.

Arthur No, I don't want to know who –

Gramma Are you a complete fool, Arthur Willis? Hush up. We won't speak of what's past . . . Now my girl, Arthur here has something to say to you and you'll listen hard to what he has to say and you'll be grateful for what he has to say for I wouldn't be saying what he is saying if I were in his place but he's told me he wants to say it and I cannot stop him although you don't deserve such good treatment, so listen up hard and good, young lady, to what he has to say and don't say anything till he's said it.

   Slight pause.

For God's sake speak up, Arthur Willis, for the suspense is killing us.

Arthur Oh sorry, Gramma Unwin, am I to speak now?

Gramma Of course you're to speak if you still have something to say.

Arthur Livvy, I –

Gramma Not that she deserves to be called by her own name.

Arthur Livvy, I know as the baby's not mine –

Gramma No, that baby is lost before it's born.

Arthur And I know as you maybe don't love me.

Gramma She's in no position to love or not love.

Arthur And I know as we never really got started.

Gramma She was too busy getting started elsewhere. And look where getting started got you, young lady. You

should have stopped getting started before getting started
stopped you.

Arthur ENOUGH! Gramma Unwin. I must speak and
you must be silent.

Gramma There's no need to get uppity with me, Arthur.

Arthur I'm not getting uppity, Gramma Unwin, but
nothing will stop me from saying what I have to say. My
mother says I shouldn't, Livvy, that I will bring shame
upon my own head, but I'll still have you. Ay, and bring
up this baby as my own. I'll stand by you and look after
you, Livvy, and all I ask is you stand by me, too.

Gramma And you can't say fairer than that, young lady.
And it's more than you deserve.

    Arthur ignores her and takes Livvy's hand.

Arthur I know I'm a fool, Livvy. But with you I think
I could learn to be wise. I love you, Livvy. I love you till
I'm fit to burst. And then I love you still more. You don't
have to say anything. Just a nod, a look, Livvy to say
you'll be mine.

    Silence.

Gramma (*quietly*) Ay, come on lad, you've said it. Now
we must leave her be.

    They exit.

Livvy You are not lost, child. You will always know
who your mother is. I'm saving up my words for you.
You shall have a different story every day, child, so that
you will be born wise and full of memory. You will have
an extraordinary pair of lungs. You will chatter all day
and all night and no one will ever tell you to be quiet.
(*She touches her stomach. Quietly*) Livvy – lives. Livvy –
full of life.

She smiles. Clara enters (perhaps she has witnessed this last confession).

Livvy Clara? Where have you been, Clarty-clugs? I've missed you.

Clara is silent.

Livvy Don't be like that, Clara. I want us to be friends.

Clara I've been listening to walls.

Livvy Why don't we bake a cake together? That would be nice.

Clara A funny thing's happened.

Livvy What's that?

Clara The walls have started telling me the future as well. They tell me what's going to happen. They tell me what I should do.

Livvy About what?

Clara just looks at her and then she exits.

Livvy (*calls after her*) No wait, Clara. Please. I want to talk to you. He's gone now. Please. Help me with the cake?

Lights fade.

SCENE SIX

Alex's flat. Mat sits as Alex enters.

Mat Nice smells.

Alex I'm baking a cake. You know you're in your thirties when you have to make your own birthday cake.

Mat Ah, babe. Never mind, I've got a prediction for you.

Alex Oh yes.

Mat You are going to have a great birthday. I can feel some serious cosseting coming your way tonight.

Alex I didn't know you were psychic, Mat.

Mat Oh yeah. It's the family business.

Alex You work in the City.

Mat I'm a futures broker. I deal in the future. My mum's clairsensitive though.

Alex What's that?

Mat She can sense things before they happen. She can't see them, that's clairvoyant, she feels them. In her bones.

Alex That's weird.

Mat It's all bollocks, mind.

Alex You don't believe in it.

Mat Oh. She's in touch with something all right. There's no rest from it. She has manifestations when she's on the bog. It's just she never finds out anything useful. The dead are not a very effective channel of communication.

Alex Why not?

Mat They don't have their finger on the pulse. They never told her that my dad was gonna sling his hook. Which was a bit fucking remiss of them in my opinion.

Alex Perhaps you take after your dad.

Mat Why do you say that?

Alex Hook-slinging. Perhaps you come from a long line of hook-slingers?

Mat We'll have to wait and see, won't we?

Alex Can't you see that far into the future, Mat?

Mat You can never see things for yourself, that would ruin it.

Alex I'd like to know what was going to happen. The gift of hindsight as foresight. I'd like that.

Mat Nah. That's no fun. It's gotta be all up for grabs.

Alex I suppose so.

Mat Well, come on then, Birthday Girl, make your wish.

Alex (*smiles*) I'm only allowed one?

Mat Of course.

Alex Right.

Mat Go on then.

Alex I've made it.

Mat What is it?

Alex I'm not telling.

Mat Oh come on.

Alex No. You just want to know if it involves you.

Mat Course I do.

Alex Well, I'm not telling you.

Mat Which means it does involve me.

Alex When are you going to have your shower?

Mat It involves a very clean me?

Alex You know I only fornicate with shiny, happy people.

Mat Your wish is my command. I won't be long. (*He kisses her.*) You taste vanillery.

Alex Cake mixture.

Mat Can I lick the bowl?

Alex Clean yourself up, Mat.

He exits.

I wish I knew what to wish.

Mat (*off*) What?

Alex Nothing.

SCENE SEVEN

The tapas bar. James and Clootie.

Clootie You're lucky. You believe in people. You help people.

James I'm not lucky. Really I'm not.

Clootie But you care for people.

James No, that's a modern myth. Carers don't actually care. We confine and we contain. We make people sit in the corner and be quiet.

Clootie It's still better than working in a restaurant.

James Most people I know would rather be in a restaurant than a nursing home.

Clootie I don't want to spend my life serving other people dinner. I've got enough problems.

James Like what?

Clootie You don't want to hear all my woes.

James Why not? I'm a professional. I won't be shocked.

Clootie Oh. I don't know. Other people seem to flow through life while I get caught up in the eddies. Like Alex. She was definitely cut on the bias.

James Change. People can do that. That's what I believe in. People's ability to transform themselves.

Clootie (*quietly*) Maybe.

James Are you okay?

Clootie No, not really, James. I can't remember the last time I was okay.

James Oh.

Clootie You see, nine months ago I was going to get married and then my fiancé was arrested for cottaging, oh, you can laugh, it is funny, I know. Now he's come out as a fully fledged homosexual. He holds musical soirées for thin middle-aged men in black leather with handlebar moustaches. Apparently all my friends could see it coming from a mile off but I lived with him for six years and I didn't have one fucking iota of an idea . . . I'm sorry, I didn't want to even mention this tonight. In fact I practised not mentioning this in the mirror before I came out. Sorry.

James Sometimes we hold on to pain for a reason.

Clootie What reason would that be, James?

James You tell me. (*Pause.*) Look at this.

Clootie What is it?

James It's a bone.

Clootie Oh. Yes.

James From my best friend's foot.

Clootie Do you think he might be missing it?

James He's dead.

Clootie Sorry. Shit. I didn't mean to be flippant.

James He killed himself. He went to Hampstead Heath. He doused himself in petrol and then set himself on fire. This is all that was left of him. I carry it with me.

Clootie Oh my God. Hampstead Heath. Why?

James (*impatiently*) I don't know. He lived near there.

Clootie No, sorry. I didn't mean, 'Why Hampstead Heath?' I mean, I suppose Hampstead Heath is as good a place as any. Big open space, etc. No I meant, 'Why did he – ?'

James I don't know. Despair's the usual reason, isn't it? . . . Daniel. We went travelling together all through South America. He was twenty-four when he died.

   Pause.

Clootie Why take it around with you? Like a fetish.

James To remind myself.

Clootie Of him?

James No. Of the alternatives. You always have to be aware of the alternatives.

Clootie I feel a bit sick.

James I think it's a good way to go. In flame.

Clootie I'm a Catholic. We don't hold with burning.

James Do you know what the Parsees do? They bury their dead in the sky. They put the bodies on top of a tower and let the vultures pick them clean. I like that. It's – honest.

Clootie Do you think working with old people has made you a little bit morbid, James?

James Maybe. Do you think serving people dinner has made you a little bit bitter?

Pause.

Clootie All I want is to be more than who I am right now.

James You're too hard on yourself.

Clootie I really like you, James.

James Thank you.

Clootie I want to breathe again. I want to live in the present and breathe more than enough air.

James You will.

Clootie Will I?

James Of course. You're a good person. You deserve a whole lot of air.

Clootie Will you kiss me? Will you kiss me then?

James What?

Clootie I really like you. I'm out of practice but I know I really like you.

James Clootie –

Clootie I just want to – be with someone for a minute. I'm so tired of myself.

James Clootie, I –

Clootie Just for a minute? It doesn't have to last. I'm not looking for lasting commitment.

James Please don't –

Clootie I'm not that repugnant, am I?

James No, of course not.

Clootie Don't tell me you're gay. Now that would be the last screaming irony.

James No, I'm not.

Clootie I have put on a bit of weight lately.

James I'm in love with Alex. I love Alex.

Clootie Oh. Yes.

James I'm really sorry. I thought it was obvious.

Clootie (*quickly*) Yes. Yes it was. Sorry. I'm so stupid. I knew it. Exposing this much cleavage always goes to my head.

James When I'm with her, I live in the present. I just don't know how to tell her, Clootie.

Clootie Yes. Yes. Of course.

James She robs me of my voice, my breath. She has such a glow about her. I'm sorry. That all sounds wanky.

Clootie No, no. You've certainly blossomed into metaphor.

James But do you know what I mean?

Clootie Yes. Yes. She shimmers.

James It's such a relief to say these things out loud. I do really like you, Clootie.

Clootie Yes.

James I need to tell her. I'm crawling up the walls with not telling her.

Clootie Then you must. What's the use of having a secret unless you share it?

James I could do.

Pause.

Clootie She's at home now.

James Really?

Clootie Yes.

James Do you think I should?

Clootie What's the alternative? You have to think of the alternative, James.

James You're right.

SCENE EIGHT

Livvy enters. She is mixing a cake. She wipes her brow with her apron. At the same time Alex enters in a different part of the stage with her cake. She makes the same gesture with her hand to her brow. Livvy continues to mix as Alex sets the cake down and puts candles in the cake. Their gestures should almost echo one another.

Livvy It's so hot.

Pause.

This is your first story, child.

They both hear a noise at the same time.

Alex Mat?

Livvy Frank?

The doorbell goes in Alex's flat. At the same time Livvy is gripped with stomach pains. Alex puts down her cake as Livvy drops the bowl she is mixing.

Clarty! Clarty! Please help me. Clarty, get Gramma.
Please, Clarty. (*She staggers about and then falls gasping
to the ground.*)

SCENE NINE

Alex's flat.
  James followed by Clootie enters.

James Alex. Hi. You look lovely.

Alex James. Clootie. I didn't expect you back so soon.

Clootie No, change of plan, Alex. Happy birthday. I'm
afraid I couldn't get him gift-wrapped at such short
notice.

James It's your birthday?

Alex What? Yes.

James Happy birthday. If I'd have known –

Alex No, don't worry. Well, I'll get out of your way.

Clootie No, no, Alex. James wants to look inside your
head. Just for fun, for a laugh. Ha, ha, ha, ha.

James (*flustered*) Clootie, – I just wanted a brief word, it
won't take long, Alex.

Clootie
  Where do you go to my lovely
  When you're alone in your bed
  Tell me the thoughts that surround you
  I want to look inside your –

God, this song is seminal, isn't it? You know, I think I'm
in love with Peter Sarstedt. I love the fact he had only
one hit and sank without a trace. I identify with that.

Alex Are you drunk, Clootie?

James I think she is.

Clootie Oh, listen to him, Al. He's such a boring old nurse. He's been totting up how many units of alcohol I've had all evening.

Alex Have you had a good time? Was the tapas nice?

James Yes it was fine.

Clootie Fine! Jamie, that tapas was out of this world. It was definitive tapas, Al, tapas with knobs on, and me and Jamie here got on like a towering bloody inferno.

Alex Clootie, are you all right?

Clootie I'm fine.

James She's fine.

Clootie I'm seething but I'm fine. Do you know that feeling, Al? I don't expect you do. What about you, Jamie? Come seethe with me and be my love and we will all the whatsits prove.

Alex Shall I make some coffee?

Clootie No, coffee's for pouffs, Al.

James Can I just have a quiet word with you, Alex. In private?

Mat enters wearing a towel.

Mat We having a party?

Clootie Yes, we bloody well are. You must be Mat. I've heard all about you and I have to say on first viewing I'm not disappointed, Mat. I'm especially loving your towel arrangement.

Alex This is Clootie. The girl who's sharing with me at the moment.

Mat Nice to meet you, Clootie. Want a drink?

Clootie Oh yes, I do, Mat. A beer please. He's marvellous, isn't he, Al? I can see what you mean. He's like a gladiator.

Alex Yes, well. I think you'd better rein yourself in, Clootie.

Clootie Oh Mat, sorry, this is James. Step forward, James. Don't be shy. Me and James have just had a date, Mat.

Mat All right, mate? Did it go well?

Clootie Fabulous, Mat.

Mat Do you want a beer?

James I've got to get back to work, actually.

Clootie Oh no, James, you must accomplish your mission first. James here has something rather precious to impart to the group.

James No, Clootie. It's okay.

Alex Clootie.

Clootie Oh no, I've got to tell Mat. This is great, Mat – you'll love this. You see, James here wined and dined me tonight. Tapas, no less. Got my juices going, I can tell you. Then he told me he was in love with Alex.

Mat What?

Clootie It's classic, isn't it? Boy, we laughed. I nearly had a hernia.

James I'm sorry, Alex.

Alex All right, that's enough now, Clootie.

James I wanted to tell you. But not like this. I didn't realise you were –

Mat Who is he exactly?

Alex James is a nurse. He looks after my mother.

Clootie They've seen each other every day for the past eight months, Mat.

Mat He's a nurse?

Alex This isn't my fault, Clootie.

Clootie (*turns on Alex for the first time*) You knew how he felt. It was obvious.

James Alex, I want you to forget about all this. It really doesn't matter. It was a mistake. A misunderstanding.

Mat Let me get this right. He's a nurse?

Alex No, wait a minute, James.

Clootie Geriatric, yes.

Mat Have you slept with him, Alex?

Alex Don't get all territorial with me, Mat. Save that for your wife.

Mat I've always been straight with you, Alex.

Clootie What did you think, Alex, you'd get rid of two lame ducks in one go?

James I'm not a lame duck, Clootie.

Mat No, you're a fucking nurse.

Clootie I told you how much I liked him. This was a big deal for me, Alex.

Mat He shovels old ladies' shit for a living, love, I think you're better off without him.

James What would you know about it?

Mat Hark at Florence Nightingale. Keep your hair on, Florence.

James Alex. I can't get you out of my head. I think about you all the time.

Mat You're not her type, Florence. Too lame. And there's definitely something of the duck about you.

Alex Shut up, Mat.

James Yes, shut up.

Mat Ooh. Quack, quack.

James Alex, I think I should leave.

Alex No, James, we should sort this out.

Clootie You're in your element now, aren't you, Alex? With men falling for you left, right and centre.

Alex Don't blame me because you've fucked up your life. Because your fiancé ran off with another man.

Mat He what?

Alex I'm sick of you, Clootie. I'm sick of picking you up when you're down.

Clootie You don't pick me up. You trample all over me.

Alex You shouldn't assume people are happy just because they don't moan as much as you.

Clootie Next to you I'm invisible.

Mat You're pretty audible though.

Alex I'm thirty-six. I have no children. My lover is married.

James You're thirty-six?

Alex What?

James I mean, you really don't look it.

Alex Oh yes, I feel great, James, I'm at the pinnacle. I've peaked. I'm thirty-six and my mother is dying.

Clootie You don't like your mother. You never have done.

Alex That's not true.

Clootie Well, look after her then.

Alex I can't. She needs full-time care. Doesn't she, James? Doesn't she?

Clootie Don't ask him, he's a fucking nutter. He's got this bone he carries around. He's probably got jars of pickled baby at home. And he's got scars all up his arms. I didn't like to ask, well, you don't, do you?

James You bitch.

Clootie You're welcome to him, Alex.

James Did you set me up with her, Alex?

Alex I didn't do anything.

James I thought I made it obvious, how I felt.

Clootie Of course you knew, Alex. I bet he dribbled all over you.

Mat She plays things close to her chest though, don't you, Alex?

Alex All right. All right. So what if I knew. He likes me. They all like me, isn't that right, Clootie? I'm very desirable. Right up there in the pecking order. But open me up and I'm full of shit. Is this what you want to hear, what you all want to hear?

James I love you, Alex.

Mat You're on a losing wicket, mate.

Alex Oh yes, Mat, and you're speaking from such a position of strength. We're not having a good time, Mat. Let's face it, we're just not.

   Pause.

Mat (*coolly*) No. You're right. I think we'd better call it a day.

Alex What?

Clootie I thought he was going to leave his wife, Alex.

Mat You don't want me, Alex. I'm just a bit of rough to you. Who earns a fuck of a lot of money.

Alex No, I –

Mat There was a moment back there when I could have wavered for you. But I don't like being underestimated either, you see.

Clootie You tell her, Mat.

Mat Besides I'm beginning to feel a tad underdressed.

Alex I want you to leave Katherine.

Mat I can't do that.

Clootie You mess people up, Alex. It's a great talent of yours.

Alex Do you love me?

Mat Katherine's pregnant.

Alex What?

James Jesus.

Mat Which makes everything different. I'm sorry. But we both knew –

Alex And when were you planning to tell me that?

Mat I was waiting to find the right moment.

Clootie Oh dear. I don't think you've found it yet.

Mat Why don't you shut up, you fat cunt?

Clootie I'm not fat.

Mat I'm going.

Clootie Oh stay, Mat. Aren't you going to fuck her till she's senseless? For old time's sake.

Mat lashes out and hits Clootie. She is knocked to the ground.

Mat I'm sorry. I don't know you, but you had that coming to you from such a long way off.

Pause.
James goes to help her up.

Clootie I'm fine.

Mat I'm sorry, Alex. (*He kisses her lightly on the forehead*) Mind how you go on the roads, eh? (*He exits.*)

Alex I can't breathe in here.

Clootie I'm crap at parties. I always end up on the floor.

Alex Get out, please.

Clootie Don't worry, I'm going. (*She exits.*)

James You knew I felt this way, didn't you?

Alex Yes.

James You deserve better than him.

Alex No, James, I don't deserve anything.

James I want to be with you.

Alex James –

James I think we could –

Alex I would never find someone like you attractive. I'm sorry.

James Right. Yes.

Alex I'm sorry. James?

James What?

Alex Was I wrong to put my mother into care?

James I can't answer that.

Alex Please.

James You entrusted your mother to my care, Alex. And I could do anything to her. There are hours and hours when I could do anything to her. I don't, but things go through my head. When you look after the dispossessed, they drag you down, you see.

Pause.

Anyway. I've got to get back – see to – yes.

He exits.
  Alex is left. She stands a minute and looks at the cake. She starts to light the candles.

SCENE TEN

In another part of the stage Alex's mother shuffles on. She stops. Suddenly she notices that she is wearing tap shoes. She tries out a few steps as Alex lights the candles. She looks up at the audience, smiles a huge smile. She is transformed; there is no sign of her stroke. She launches into a tap routine. Music: 'I Could Have Danced All Night'. She is all smiles. Alex finishes lighting her candles. Alex gets up and walks out. The tap routine finishes. Lights fade.

SCENE ELEVEN

Lights up on Livvy as before; she is collapsed on the ground. Clara is standing over her.

Livvy Clara. Please help me. Please get Gramma for me. I'm burning up, Clara.

Pause.

Please. My baby. I'm losing my baby.

Clara I hate you, Livvy.

Livvy No, Clara.

Clara And the walls told me what to do.

Livvy Clara –

Clara I'm going to haunt you till you die.

Livvy No please, Clara. GRAMMA! GRAMMA! HELP! HELP ME PLEASE!

Clara begins to stamp. She drowns out Livvy's cries. Her stamping becomes ryhthmic, like a dance. Livvy

collapses completely on the floor. At the same time,
Alex comes back on. She has a large packet of
paracetomol. She kneels on the floor at the same time
as Livvy and calmly pushes the pills out of their
blister packets. She counts them out.

Livvy Suddenly I am rising above myself.

Gramma What's happened, Clara?

Livvy I can see myself – (*She looks at Alex.*) – so small
and lost down there.

Clara The stones are crying out to me, Gramma. Make
the stones stop.

Livvy And Gramma and Clara around me –

Gramma We're losing her, Clara.

Livvy – as if from a great height.

Gramma Do something, Clara. We must do something.

Clara I'm sorry, Gramma. I didn't mean to. I didn't
mean it. The walls told me to.

Livvy I want the child to live so much.

Gramma I don't know what to do, Clara.

Clara Make her have an Epiphany, Gramma. Make her
blessed.

Livvy I'm shooting up and up.

Gramma My poor lost girl, come back to me.

Clara Make her come back, Gramma.

Livvy The land cannot hold me.

Clara We must breathe on her. Breathe her back to life.
Do it, Gramma. Breathe her full of fire.

Gramma It's no good, Clara.

Clara I'm sorry, Livvy. I didn't mean it, Livvy.

Alex picks up a handful of pills.

Livvy I am being swallowed by the sky.

Clara I love you, Livvy.

Gramma Pray, Clara. We must pray for her.

Clara Holy Ghost come down on my sister. Please.

Livvy I'm leaving myself behind. (*Livvy walks past Alex towards the birthday cake.*)

Clara Please! I didn't mean her to die. Livvy live Livvy live Livvy live Livvy live Livvy live Livvy live Livvy live –

Livvy blows out the candles. She watches the next.

No. (*a small whine*)

Alex sits up abruptly. Anne speaks as if to a child. .

Alex Mother?

Mother I'm here, Alex.

Alex I want my mother. (*She starts to cry. Throughout the next she doesn't respond directly to Anne.*)

Mother Shsh. Shsh. It'll be all right. Everything will be all right.

Alex I'm sorry. I'm sorry. I'm sorry.

Mother It's all right. None of it matters. Not a bit of it matters.

Alex I'm sorry.

Mother I know you are.

Alex I don't know what to do.

Mother We'll get that fringe cut for a start. That'll make you feel better.

Alex I'm lost. Please help me.

Mother Put them all back in the box. That's it. I won't stand for it. What would your father say.

Alex I'm sorry. (*She picks up the pills and puts them back in the box.*)

Mother That's it. That's better. Go and wash your face. Don't listen to any of them. They can all go to hell. There. Now. It'll all feel better in the morning.

Alex Yes.

Mother Off you go then.

Alex I'm sorry.

Mother Off you go. There's a good girl.

   Alex gets up slowly and walks off.

Livvy Come on then, Annie. Are you ready?

Mother/Gramma Ready as I'll ever be.

Clara No wait, Gramma. You mustn't go too. You haven't heard my secret yet.

Mother/Gramma No time for secrets now, Clara. I'm exhausted. Let's have a bit of hush.

Livvy Here sit here, Annie.

Mother/Gramma It's all the dancing you see. It's worn me out. (*She lies down.*) That's better. Take the weight off my poor old feet.

Livvy That's it, you rest now.

   Mother/ Gramma shuts her eyes as if to sleep. Livvy exits.

Clara No, you can't leave me. You can't both leave me. Gramma.

She shakes her. Gramma doesn't respond.

Gramma. Listen to me, Gramma. Please. I've got a baby too. I've got Livvy's baby inside of me now. And my baby will live. My baby will live for Livvy. (*Clara exits.*)

SCENE TWELVE

The nursing home.
Anne is lying in her bed as James enters

James Well, I asked her nicely, Annie. And she wasn't having any of it. I'm just not glossy enough, Annie. I'm a bloody fool. So I wondered if maybe I could fuck you instead. In for a penny, in for a pound, eh? It's just you and me, kid. Come on, get up, old lady. Let's be having you.

He realises something is wrong. Feels for her pulse. Anne is dead.

Shit. Shit. Shit.

Pause.

The things women do to avoid sleeping with me. Don't you worry yourself, Annie. You're fine now. Just fine. You've renewed youself, Annie. All your molecules have re-arranged themselves. You've changed gear, haven't you? Now you'll be brand new again.

Pause.

I wonder if I might have the pleasure of this dance? We can dance the night away. You'd like that, wouldn't you? Right little rocker. We just need the finishing touches. (*He exits and gets two sparklers out and lights them.*)

I bought these for you. But I was just waiting for the
right moment. Annie you are absolutely the person
I want to be with now. You are my dream date for this
evening. There. Look at them sparkle, Annie. Do you
want to hold them? No, you need both your hands for
dancing. I know.

You look magnificent, Annie. Let's dance. (*He lifts her
limp body.*) We're spinning, Annie. We're spinning with
the sparklers.

He exits with her.

SCENE THIRTEEN

Alex's flat. Some time later.
Alex collects the framed photograph of Livvy Unwin.
She places it. Clootie enters.

Clootie I didn't expect you to be here. I just came to get
my things together.

Alex Tie up all the loose ends. Go ahead.

Clootie I'm sorry about your mother.

Alex I have no idea what to say when people say that to
me.

Clootie That's okay.

Alex I didn't love my mother, Clootie, but she was still
my mother.

Clootie Yes.

Alex I nearly lost it completely, you know, that night.

Clootie I'm sorry for the things I said.

Alex You shouldn't be sorry if you meant them.

Clootie I was drunk.

Alex But you know what you said.

Clootie Yes.

Alex I hate you for that night, Clootie. But you were right, what you said, some of the things you said, you were right.

Pause.

You look better.

Clootie I feel better. Sorry.

Alex Why should you be sorry?

Clootie shrugs.

Can you keep a secret?

Clootie No, I'm terrible at secrets, you know that.

Alex I'm pregnant.

Clootie Oh my God.

Alex Mat's parting shot. I'm not going to tell him. Anyway I haven't decided what to do about it yet.

Clootie Oh.

Alex I've offended your Catholic sensibilities.

Clootie No. No. Anyway I'm giving up being a Catholic. I'm going to get hypnotherapy for it . . . You must do what you think best.

Alex I want to feel like I – deserve it . . . I've taken my mum's house off the market. I want to spend some time – I've been going through all her things, you were right. Livvy Unwin was my great-great-aunt.

Clootie What?

Alex The girl in the photograph, she died in 1908, the year the photograph was taken. Ectopic pregnancy.

Clootie How did you find out?

Alex There were letters and stuff. Family papers. My great-grandmother was mad apparently. Clara.

Clootie Well that's what happens to women, isn't it? They go mad or they die in childbirth.

Alex Looks like I'm heading for the double whammy.

Clootie You'll be all right, my lovely. I'd better get started.

Clootie exits. After a moment Livvy appears. Alex looks at her picture as Livvy speaks to her. At the same time Clootie re-enters as Clara and sits as in the first scene.

Livvy You are not lost.

Alex Clootie?

Livvy You will always know who your mother is.

Alex touches her stomach.

I've been saving up my words for you.

Alex takes the picture and sits next to the wall. She curls up to it as if she were listening to it.

This is your first story.

SCENE FOURTEEN

Frank walks past Livvy and Alex towards Clara.

Clara You came back!

Frank I remembered it.

Clara What?

Frank The special thing I do.

Clara I thought you might.

Frank Lie down, Clara.

Clara Oh yes. That's right.

Frank It's a pretty name, Clara. So pretty. (*He starts to fuck her quite gently.*) Am I hurting you?

Clara No.

Frank I don't want to hurt you.

Clara No. I like it.

He gains momentum.

You're breathing all over me. Yes. Breathing like fire. I've been waiting for something like this for so long. Yes. I like it. You make me feel wise.

He comes. Gets up.

Frank I've got to be going.

Clara Oh. All right.

Frank Goodbye, Clara.

Clara Goodbye.

He exits. (She sits there. She stares ahead.) Won't tell anyone about this. Nobody at all. (*She looks at the walls.*) Shsh. Shsh. Shsh.

Lights fade.

MARTHA, JOSIE
AND THE CHINESE ELVIS

Martha, Josie and the Chinese Elvis was first presented at the Octagon Theatre, Bolton, on 15 April 1999. The cast was as follows:

Martha Anny Tobin
Josie Ann Rye
Timothy Wong Paul Courtenay Hyu
Lionel Malcolm Hebden
Brenda-Marie Debra Penny
Louise Melanie Ramsay

Directed by Lawrence Till
Designed by Dominie Hooper
Choreography Lorelei Lynn
Lighting Nick Johnson
Sound Thomas Weir

Characters

Brenda-Marie Botting

Martha Clear

Josie Botting

Lionel Trills

The Chinese Elvis (Timothy Wong)

Louise

Act One

SCENE ONE

We are in Josie Botting's front room. It is a respectable lower middle-class front room – perhaps it's still a bit seventies in décor, but not tatty. There are some rather tired Christmas decorations up. There are four exits: one to the front door, sliding glass doors that lead to the patio and garden, an exit that leads to the kitchen and one that leads upstairs. There is a window with net curtains. There are one or two family photographs – not excessive – which show Josie with her two daughters, Brenda-Marie and Shelly-Louise. There is a mirror on one wall. It is 6 January (Feast of Epiphany).

Music: Elvis Presley, 'Suspicion'.

Brenda-Marie is a podgy young woman of twenty-two, with learning difficulties. Brenda-Marie leans against the window staring out. She blows against the frame and writes the word SNOW *on the window.*

She pays no attention as Martha Clear enters the living room. She is an Irish woman in her mid-forties with very long hair (in a plait down her back) who suffers from obsessive-compulsive disorder. She comes through the door, shuts it and turns the handle five times.

Martha *(under her breath)* One, two, three, four, five.

Brenda-Marie Snow.

Martha then taps the door in sequence from the top.

Martha One, two, three, four, five.

Brenda-Marie Please God.

Martha repeats the sequence.

Martha One, two, three, four, five.

Brenda-Marie Please snow.

Martha One, two, three, four, five.

The music starts to fade. Martha gets out her cleaning utensils ready to start work. Again her movements are very ritualistic.

Martha Look at this mess. One, two, three, four, five. One, two, three, four, five. In the name of the Father, Son and Holy Ghost.

Brenda-Marie Come on God, snow! We want some snow. Bloody well snow, God!

Martha It's too cold to snow.

Brenda-Marie gives Martha a black look. Martha starts to polish the furniture.

Martha One, two, three, four, five.

Brenda-Marie Six! Six! Six!

Martha (*covers her ears*) No! No! Get away from me, child of Satan.

She returns to the first point that she was polishing. Frantically she begins again.

Martha One, two, three, four, five.

Brenda-Marie You're a nutter, Holy Jo. You always miss out the six. One, two, three, four, five, SIX! Even I know that.

Martha You evil girl! One, two, three, four, five –

Brenda-Marie Six.

Martha No that's not right. I'll have to start all over again. Yes. Un, deux, trois, quatre, cinq

Brenda-Marie (*she shouts delightedly in English*) Six, Holy Jo, six!

Martha If you say that particular number one more time, I shall scalp you.

Brenda-Marie Sorry, Holy Jo.

Martha And don't call me that. One, two, three, four, five.

Brenda-Marie Why do you count, Holy Jo?

Martha Because if I didn't evil would happen, Brenda-Marie. In this world today evil is everywhere. It's imminent. And from the most unexpected quarters. On the way here, I was almost flattened by an emergency ambulance. Would you credit it? One, two, three, four, five. And all that's as nothing compared to the incident of evil involving my kettle. My life savings were in that kettle.

Brenda-Marie Why did you keep your life savings in a kettle, Holy Jo?

Martha I never drink hot beverages. Hot beverages are an invitation to Satan.

Brenda-Marie What's his favourite?

Martha What?

Brenda-Marie I bet he likes cappucino.

Martha I'm not speaking to you, naughty girl.

Brenda-Marie Why did you have a kettle then, Holy Jo? If you don't drink hot drinks?

Martha In case of emergency.

Brenda-Marie What sort of emergency?

Martha I don't know. In case a child was about to be born in the vicinity.

Brenda-Marie Why do you need hot water then?

Martha To prevent contamination.

Brenda-Marie What sort of contamination?

Martha One, two, three, four, five. Now don't rile me, Brenda-Marie. I had a kettle because it was a cunning place in which to keep my life savings. What do you expect to find in a kettle, Brenda-Marie?

Brenda-Marie Water, Holy Jo.

Martha Exactly. Who would expect to find four hundred pounds in a kettle, I ask you that?

Brenda-Marie The robber who nicked yours.

Martha That was a sore day for me, Brenda-Marie. To discover that my kettle had been ransacked. I felt violated, I don't mind telling you.

Brenda-Marie You should have put the money in the bank.

Martha Banks are not to be trusted any more, Brenda-Marie.

Brenda-Marie Neither are kettles.

Martha Do you know what I was going to do with that money, Brenda-Marie? I was going to fly to Graceland. To see where my King is buried. Memphis, Tenessee. What a beautiful sound those words have.

Brenda-Marie I thought you were going to Lourdes where they throw all them sick Catholics in the holy water.

Martha Of course I was hoping to include Lourdes in my itinerary. And they don't throw them in. They dip them in.

Brenda-Marie Like chicken nuggets.

Martha Nothing would have stopped me, Brenda-Marie. A pilgrimage to Graceland . . . hopefully taking in the healing waters of Lourdes on the way back.

Brenda-Marie And now you're going nowhere. You're staying in Bolton and being me and me Mam's cleaner.

Martha Mmmm. One, two, three, four, five. One, two, three, four, five.

Brenda-Marie Why don't you cut your hair, Holy Jo?

Martha returns to polishing. Josie, Brenda-Marie's mother, enters. She's absently looking at the post.

Josie And why don't you mind your own for once, young lady?

Martha Ah, Mrs Botting, do you want me to take these decorations down?

Brenda-Marie No, leave them, Mam.

Martha Feast of Epiphany. They have to come down today.

Brenda-Marie Last year we didn't take them down till February, did we, Mam?

Martha But that's terrible bad luck, Mrs Botting!

Josie I've known worse.

Martha I beg your pardon?

Josie I've had such a run of bad luck, I'm getting to embrace it, Miss Clear, welcome it with open arms.

Martha Yes, well, we'll leave them for now then . . .
I was just wondering if I might wash the walls today,
Mrs Botting.

Josie We're not having this battle again, Miss Clear.

Martha If you could just see your way to letting me
spring clean the kitchen cupboards?

Josie It's not spring yet. Nowhere near.

Brenda-Marie It's going to snow soon.

Martha Then the carpets. I could wash the carpets –

Josie I've warned you about this –

Martha At least let me bleach the bin –

Josie Whatever floats your boat –

Martha And the doors! The tops of the doors!

Josie You're on an hourly rate –

Martha (*close to tears*) It's not the money! I just want
it all right!

Josie (*softening*) You're getting excessive again, you
know.

Martha I know.

Josie I've told you – a quick spray and a light dust and
I'd be none the wiser. You're the only cleaner I know
that actually cleans. You'll wear yourself out, you know.
And the rest of us in the process.

Martha I know, Mrs Botting, I'm terribly sorry.

Josie Tell you what, you can do a double shift at the
beginning of next week.

Martha I don't want your pity, Mrs Botting.

Brenda-Marie You've missed a bit over here, Holy Jo.

Josie Brenda-Marie!

Martha (*rushes over*) You put that smear there! One, two, three, four, five. I'll have to start over now. Right from the beginning.

Josie Leave it! Please! Thing is, I've got a client coming over at very short notice.

Martha Oh. I see.

Josie And I need you to get me a few things from the shops.

Martha (*suspiciously*) How many things?

Josie One or two.

Martha How much will it come to? It's just that certain numbers – I won't be able to buy it, if it comes to certain numbers.

Josie Just do your best. My client will be here for an hour and we will need complete privacy.

Martha (*deferentially*) Oh yes. For his counselling session, of course.

Josie That's right.

Martha It's a wonderful thing you do there, Mrs Botting.

Josie Someone's got to do it.

Brenda-Marie (*proudly*) My mam counsels odds and sods.

Josie But mostly sods . . . I've left the money and the list in the kitchen, on the side.

Brenda-Marie You could get a haircut while you're at it, Holy Jo.

Josie (*sharply*) That's enough of your lip today, Brenda-Marie.

Brenda-Marie You're all at me. All the time. You're all on at me.

Josie Bren, love –

Brenda-Marie I wish my sister wasn't dead. Shelly-Louise never went on at me.

Martha (*crosses herself*) God rest her soul.

Josie Brenda, don't talk about Shelly-Louise.

Brenda-Marie Why can't I talk about her? Just because she's dead. She's still my sister.

She runs upstairs. Josie takes the post from the mantel and sits down heavily.

Martha A Mother's loss is always the worst, Mrs Botting.

Josie What would you know about it?

Martha I'd better get going, then.

Josie I'm sorry – (*looking at the cards*) It's just – it's my birthday, Miss Clear.

Martha Oh! Many happy returns, Mrs Botting!

Josie They don't seem to agree with me – birthdays. Must be genetic.

Martha And what's the lucky number?

Josie The big four-oh.

Martha Ah! Life is just beginning for you, then.

Josie Do you think?

Martha smiles.

Martha I'll pop back in just over an hour then.

Martha goes to the door, she knocks five times (a bit more surreptitiously this time) and turns the knob five times. In the meantime Josie opens her cards.

One, two, three, four, five.

Josie God help us.

Martha Sorry about this, Mrs Botting.

Josie You go ahead.

Martha repeats the whole ritual at double quick speed and exits very speedily

Martha One, two, three, four, five. Goodbye, Mrs Botting.

She exits

Josie Don't step on the cracks.

Josie arranges her one or two cards (she tries to spread them out perhaps).
Brenda-Marie comes back in.

Brenda-Marie Sorry, Mam.

Josie Me too, pet.

Brenda-Marie Do you like me card?

Josie Work of art!

Josie sits back down

Brenda-Marie I thought I might practise me ice-dancin' for you.

Josie I just want a little sit-down before Lionel comes, love.

Brenda-Marie I'll do it quiet, Mam.

Josie All right, love.

*Josie shuts her eyes. Brenda-Marie goes over to the
window and perches on the ledge – her commentary
box. She takes a hairbrush to use as a microphone.
She speaks quietly at first and then gets carried away.
She doesn't move during her commentary – she is
imagining it.*

Brenda-Marie And here we are in the Olympic Stadium
in Heidelburger. It's snowing outside. (*She gestures
outside.*) Brrrr. And onto the rink come our first
contestants. Here they are, Brenda-Marie and Shelly-
Louise Botting, the sisters from Bolton. Tonight they're
skating for – (*She pauses.*) – Canada. As Brenda-Marie
told us earlier, 'We don't want to skate for Britain
because then we're bound to come fifteenth because after
Torvill and Dean all the British couples come fifteenth
and Barry Davies says they've made a very good effort
when really they haven't, they've been shit and landed on
their bum loads of times –'

Josie opens one eye and looks at her.

Sorry Mam . . . Shelly-Louise and Brenda-Marie are in
top position after their short programme where they
completed all their compulsory elements with ease.
They're skating their free programme to a medley of
Elvis songs.

The doorbell goes.

Josie I'll go.

*Josie rouses herself from the chair and makes her way
to the front door.*

Brenda-Marie And they're skating perfectly together.
Brenda-Marie has stronger technique but Shelly-Louise is

a lovely little skater. See her launch like a rocket into the air in that triple salcho.

We hear Josie greet Lionel offstage. Josie enters with Lionel, a short, dapper, balding but kindly-looking man of about fifty.

Lionel Hello there, Brenda-Marie.

Josie Say hello to Lionel, Brenda-Marie.

Brenda-Marie I'm in the middle of a routine, Mam.

Lionel I'll get myself ready then.

Josie I'll show you up.

Lionel and Josie exit.

Brenda-Marie Now Brenda-Marie lifts her high in an inverted star lift. Delightful landing into the triple lutz. Low into the triple salcho. Side-by-side triple toe-loop. Now the laid back spin into the camel spin. These girls are really doing Bolton and Canada proud. And now for the finale. Flying split triple twist. Brenda-Marie flies fifteen feet across the ice. In her multicoloured dress she's like a human rainbow. And she's coming in to land now. Will she hold onto it? Yes! The landing's good. The crowd's on its feet. The judge from the Ukraine is crying. And there they hold up the marks. Marks for technical merit. Six from the US of A. Yes! Six from Hungary. Six from Australia and New Zealand and the Isle of Man. But oh no! Five point nine from the Belarus. The crowd's up in arms. They're booing, they're jeering, they're attacking the Belarus lady. She deserves it. She's like Holy Jo. She never gives us six.

Josie enters again.

Brenda-Marie The Belarus lady only gave us five point nine, Mammy.

Josie What does she know? Silly cow.

Brenda-Marie (*delighted*) Exactly.

Josie You'll have to let Mammy work now, Brenda-Marie.

Brenda-Marie I know, I know. I'm going to my tent.

Josie Don't get cold.

Brenda-Marie I never get cold, Mam.

Josie smiles. Brenda-Marie runs outside. Josie looks around the room. Perhaps she straightens a Christmas decoration. She takes some deep breaths. The door knocks. Her demeanour changes sharply.

Josie I can't hear you. Use a firm hand.

Lionel knocks again

Yes?

Lionel's voice from behind the door

Lionel May I come in, madam?

Josie Who is it?

Lionel It is I, Miss Geraldine.

Josie (*mock surprise*) Ah, Geraldine. You'd better show yourself then. Let me give you the once-over.

Lionel enters wearing a French Maid's outfit.

Josie You forgot to curtsy.

Lionel Oh, I do beg your pardon, Madam Josie. (*He curtsies.*)

Josie I can't abide a sloppy curtsy.

Lionel Sorry, madam.

Josie Look at the state of you.

Lionel Sorry, madam.

Josie Waste of space.

Lionel Yes, Madam, sorry madam.

Josie Not fit to lick my feet.

Lionel If you say so, madam.

Josie Will you ever learn?

Lionel No, I don't suppose I will.

Josie Petticoat, Geraldine!

Lionel Has it slipped again, Madam?

Josie A bad case of subsidence where your undergarments are concerned I fear, Geraldine.

Lionel Am I a slut, madam?

Josie A nice girl is always in control of her gusset.

Lionel I am a terribly naughty slut.

Josie Slut of the week. That's what you are.

Lionel Yes, madam.

Josie When it comes to sluts, you take the biscuit.

Lionel Thank you, madam.

Josie And we know what happens to sluts, don't we?

Lionel They have to be punished.

Josie You naughty, dirty slut. I'm going to have to punish you good and proper.

Lionel Yes, I'm afraid you will have to, madam.

Josie Do you think I've got time for this?

Lionel No, no. You bend over backwards for us girls, madam.

Josie Don't be cocky, Miss Geraldine. It doesn't suit you.

Lionel No, madam.

Josie Get down on all fours, trollop!

Lionel Please, madam, be merciful –

Josie Adopt slave position! That's not a request, that's an order, bitch.

Lionel (*kneeling down*) Whatever you say, madam!

Josie Geraldine, in light of your unpardonable sluttishness, I'm going to have to beat you.

Lionel I think you probably are.

Josie I'm going to have to paddle you and straddle you.

Lionel I think it's unavoidable.

Josie I'm going to have to feather you, leather you, smother you and mother you.

Lionel I do deserve it. Unquestionably.

Josie I'm going to have to whack you, tack you, tie you up and smack you.

Lionel Do it, madam! Do it! Beat me, beat me, tie me up and beat me!

Josie Oh, Lionel, I can't be chuffed.

Lionel Madam!

Josie Stop calling me that.

Lionel You can do it!

Josie I can't! I feel ridiculous. I just – can't – dominate – any more. I've lost the will.

Lionel Don't say that!

Josie Oh get up, Lionel. You're not a pretty sight down there, love.

Lionel What's brought this on?

Josie I'm forty today and I've decided I'm packing it all in.

Lionel No!

Josie It's like ballet dancing, my body just can't take it any more.

Lionel (*protesting*) But – you're beautiful – magnificent. You're not just a dominatrix – you're an artist, a word-smith – you're operatic, you really are.

Josie Oh yes, the Dame Nelly Melba of the domination world, that's me.

Lionel You are! A lashing from you is like an aria, I tell you.

Josie You're a good man, Lionel. But let's face it – you only come for the frocks. You should get yourself a wife with a full wardrobe. It'd be cheaper in the long run.

Lionel You can't do this, Josie. You're renowned for your transformation work.

Josie I can't be bothered with the dressing up any more. I'm going to get rid of all the stupid cossies.

Lionel But the hours you've put into them – the fabric alone – look at this for quality!

Josie Don't suppose the Sally Army would have much call for them.

Lionel I don't like hearing you like this.

Josie I'm tired, Lionel. Through and through.

Lionel I'll put some Elvis on for you. (*He goes over to the record player.*)

Josie I need more than a bit of Elvis.

Lionel Come on, Jos, it's your birthday.

Josie We're friends aren't we, Lionel? Not just – you know.

Lionel Of course.

Josie There's something I need to tell you –

Lionel What?

Josie I don't know who else to – Brenda-Marie's too – and there's no one else – not now.

Lionel What is it?

Josie It's just – when I go, I don't want to be buried –

Lionel I don't like this morbid talk –

Josie – and I don't want to be cremated, either.

Lionel I won't have it.

Josie I want to be frozen!

Lionel You what?

Josie I read about it. Cryogenics they call it. As soon as you die they freeze you. Then they put you in a casket. With dry ice and stuff. At minus one hundred and eighty degrees. They suspend you in animation. That sounds nice, doesn't it? And then you lie there for hundreds of years in the ice until they wake you up again. I'd like that.

Lionel They wake you up – from the dead? How do they do that?

Josie Well – they thaw you out and warm you up,
I suppose.

Lionel How long does it take?

Josie I don't know – perhaps it depends how much you
weigh. Like a turkey.

Lionel You what?

Josie You know, with cooking a turkey, twenty minutes
a pound and twenty for luck.

Lionel So once they've defrosted you, you're alive again?

Josie They have to repair you first – all the damage – so
you're brand new. You get to wipe this life out and start
afresh.

Lionel I don't know if I'd want to go through it all again.

Josie No. That's what I want. Definitely. Another go at it
all.

Lionel Another crack at the whip.

*Brenda-Marie hovers in the doorway. She listens to
what is said.*

Josie Oh no nothing like that next time. I'm not interested
in the body for my next life. I want a sit-down job that
involves some serious thinking. That'd suit me down to
the ground.

Brenda-Marie enters.

Brenda-Marie Can I be frozen too, Mam? So that next
life I can be International World Ice Dancing Champion?
Lionel, I love the ice-dancin' more than football. Me
mam says we're going to get the sky television so I can
watch the ice-dancin' to the content of me heart. Do you
like being one of me mam's nappy men?

Lionel Yes I do, Brenda-Marie.

Brenda-Marie 'Naughty, naughty boy. Mama's going to smack your bum into next week.' (*She laughs, delighted.*) I'm going to be a domino lady like me mam.

Josie Dominatrix, love.

Brenda-Marie That's what I said. You've got loads of hair on your legs, Lionel.

Josie That's enough now, Brenda. Calm down. You'd better get yourself changed, Lionel. My cleaner'll be here any minute

Lionel Back in a jiffy. (*Lionel exits upstairs.*)

Brenda-Marie If I were 'im, Mam, I wouldn't wear the tights.

Josie No, you're right. It doesn't do him any favours.

Brenda-Marie It's a shame he can't have some of the hair off his legs on his head, Mam.

Josie Then he wouldn't be such a baldy coot.

Brenda-Marie I like the nappy men when they wear the maid clothes.

Josie Yes . . .

Brenda-Marie And the nurse isn't so bad.

Josie No, no . . .

Brenda-Marie But when they dress like babbies they look plain stupid, don't they Mam? I mean I'm young for me age, aren't I? But I don't wear the nappies any more. If I was a big man I wouldn't want me Mam to smack me bum any more.

Josie You're a clever girl, Brenda-Marie.

Brenda-Marie I don't think I've got difficulties in the learning like they all say. It's the meaning of some things I don't understand.

Josie Nor me, love. We've got meaning difficulties, Brenda-Marie. That's what we've got.

Brenda-Marie laughs. Pause

Brenda-Marie Mam?

Josie What, love?

Brenda-Marie You know, sometimes I can feel the ice dance welling up inside me.

Josie Can you, love?

Brenda-Marie Yeah.

Josie The day it comes out will be something special.

Brenda-Marie You're telling me!

Lionel re-enters in a suit.

Lionel Now Brenda-Marie –

Brenda-Marie Your legs look heaps better in them slacks, Lionel.

Lionel Now, what would you say to a party this evening for your mam's birthday?

Brenda-Marie Oh yes! We never have parties.

Josie No, no, Lionel. I don't want a party. I'm too old for that sort of thing.

Brenda-Marie We've never had a party since our Shelly-Louise went on up to heaven.

Josie It's a ridiculous idea. We've got no friends.

Lionel Too late. It's arranged. I'm coming and Brenda-Marie is coming and I'm going to invite someone else.

Josie Who?

Lionel It's a surprise.

Brenda-Marie I love it when someone's coming.

Josie No, no, Lionel, really, I don't want a party. I can't bear fuss.

Lionel Don't be silly! Get your glad rags on. I'll be back here around seven.

Brenda-Marie It's like Advent. With the calendar.

Josie I've got no food for a party.

Lionel A bit of tinned ham will do. You must have that.

Josie No, no, you have to have those other things. Crudities.

Lionel We don't need food.

Brenda-Marie Opening all the doors on the calendar. Waiting for the really important person to come.

Josie I'm really not bothered, Lionel.

Lionel You're forty today, Josie. We must celebrate. Now go and have a lie-down. And I'll see you later.

Martha enters with shopping.

Martha One, two, three, four, five . . . I'm sorry, Mrs Botting. I got overwhelmed by the numbers on my bus ticket.

Brenda-Marie Holy Jo's got this thing about numbers, Lionel.

Martha (*seeing Lionel*) Oh, I beg your – one, two, three, four, five.

Josie This is Mr Lionel Trills. Miss Martha Clear.

Lionel Enchanted, Miss Clear. (*He holds out his hand to her.*)

Martha One, two, three, four, five. I'm afraid I don't shake hands, Mr Trills.

Lionel Ah. No, no, of course not.

Martha Not that I'm implying that your hands are contaminated in some way.

Lionel I hope not.

Martha Although people these days barely wash their hands, you know.

Brenda-Marie My mam makes me wash mine after I've done a wee.

Josie Too much information, Brenda-Marie.

Martha I wash mine thirty-five times a day.

Lionel Being a dry cleaner I would say that I washed mine more than the average.

Martha That's very refreshing to hear, Mr Trills.

Josie Far be it from me to interrupt this little hygiene summit –

Martha Oh yes. The shopping! I beg your pardon, Mrs Botting. One, two, three, four, five – (*She hands it to her.*)

Lionel Miss Clear. We're having a party this evening to celebrate Josie's birthday. Perhaps you'd like to come.

Josie Lionel. We don't want to make this into an event.

Martha I don't go out normally after the hour that follows five.

Lionel You surprise me, Miss Clear. I had you marked down as a party animal.

Josie Yes, you look a right little raver, Miss Clear.

Martha Oh no, no, no. I'm more of a home-bird.

Brenda-Marie Someone else is coming who's special but we don't know who it is, Holy Jo.

Lionel Well that's settled, then.

Josie No, it's not.

Brenda-Marie I'm going to get ready. Mam, will you help me?

Josie We're not dressing up.

Brenda-Marie I am. Come on.

Lionel See you later.

Josie I'm not coming, Lionel.

Lionel Now don't be silly. Off you go and get dolled up. I'll see myself out, Josie.

Brenda-Marie (*exiting*) Yes! Come and doll me up, Mam.

Josie All right, all right . . .

Brenda-Marie drags Josie out.

Martha I must be on my way, too.

Lionel Can I drop you off anywhere, Miss Clear?

Martha Oh no, I don't think so.

Lionel Reall,y it's no trouble.

Martha No, no, Mr Trills. Thank you all the same. One, two, three, four, five.

Lionel As you wish, Miss Clear. But I will see you later.

Martha I don't really, one, two, three, no, I don't really go to, four, five, parties.

Lionel Nor do I, to tell the honest truth. I never had a party when I was small.

Martha I went to a lot of wakes.

Lionel My mother didn't like people rucking up the carpet.

Martha I can see her point.

Lionel I think you have to be taught how to party from a tender age.

Martha I wouldn't know.

Lionel So tonight we can both let our hair down!

Martha That won't take very long in your case, Mr Trills.

Lionel Whereas in yours it may take all night . . . It must take an age to wash.

Martha It's the drying that's really wearing. A normal hair-drier just doesn't have the stamina.

Lionel Do you know what you could do? Pop it in a trouser press.

Martha That really doesn't appeal, Mr Trills.

Lionel Oh forgive me, Miss Clear, I didn't mean to offend you. Your hair is truly remarkable.

Martha And yours is truly absent. Now if you don't mind.

Lionel I don't. There were a few years when I did. When I used to hang upside down from doors and the like.

Martha I beg your pardon?

Lionel To stimulate the follicles.

Martha looks scandalised

But now I've grown to rather like it.

Martha Good for you.

Lionel It's a funny thing, but you can always tell how I'm feeling from my head. If I'm particularly chipper my pate gets a lovely sheen to it. Like a polished apple. A Worcester Pearmain or a Russet Gold. But if I'm feeling under the weather, it looks grey, my head. Positively grey. What colour would you say it was now? (*He lowers his head in her direction.*) Not quite a Granny Smith but possibly a Golden Delicious?

Martha I would advise you to invest in a hat.

Lionel Oh no, Miss Clear, I like to air my head.

Martha One, two, three, four, five. Yes, well –

Lionel Do you find bald men unattractive, Miss Clear? No, it's all right – you can tell me.

Martha Really, Mr Trills, I'm amazed by your, one, two, three, four, five – but since you ask I've always preferred a full head of hair in a man.

Lionel (*sadly*) Yes. I see.

Martha I'm sure there are women who favour men who are challenged in the hair department, such as yourself.

Lionel I think I can say from experience that a woman prefers to have something to run her fingers through.

Martha But I could imagine a situation where a lady might get equal pleasure from say, taking a duster and some Mr Sheen . . . and giving your head a good old buff and polish.

Lionel I wish that I had encountered such a lady, Miss Clear, I really do.

Martha Well, we all have our crosses to bear.

Lionel Indeed.

Martha After you, Mr Trills. (*She gestures towards the door.*)

Lionel No, after you, Miss Clear.

Martha No, please.

Lionel No, I insist.

Martha Mr Trills, it is absolutely essential that you leave before I do. Believe me.

Lionel Enough said, Miss Clear. I do admire a woman who doesn't mince her words.

Martha My words are never minced.

Lionel No indeed, your words are tenderised with a large hammer. Well. It's been a pleasure. I look forward to seeing you later. In your glad rags, mind.

Martha Goodbye, Mr Trills.

He exits.

Glad rags. I'd catch my death. (*She shuts the door rapidly behind him. She raps the door and turns the doorknob rapidly.*) One, two, three, four, five. One, two, three, four, five. One, two three, four, five.

She exits through the door. We hear her repeat the procedure on the other side of the door as lights fade.

One, two, three, four, five. One, two, three, four, five. One two, three, four, five.

SCENE TWO

Music: Elvis Presley, 'Party'.

Josie enters. She has changed, but she hasn't made a big effort with her appearance. She brings various party food and arranges it. She sings absently along to the record. She opens a packet of nuts that sprays all over the floor. She begins to cry. As she is crying, Brenda-Marie enters. Brenda-marie is wearing an improbable party dress and heavy make-up.

Brenda-Marie Don't do the crying, Mam. You know I hate the crying.

Josie I'm not crying. Switch that silly record off for me.

Brenda-Marie You shouldn't cry over spilt peanuts.

Josie It's me tear ducts. I go out into the wind and my eyes pour. But then it's a cold wind at the moment.

Brenda-Marie It's going to snow, Mam. Any day.

Josie Let's get these nuts picked up. I don't know, having a party at my age.

Brenda-Marie You're still young, Mammy.

Josie What would I do without you, Brenda-Marie?

Brenda-Marie You'd be lost, Mam.

Josie You're right there, love.

Brenda-Marie I have to fill up the space for two in your heart.

Josie What do you mean?

Brenda-Marie When we lost our Shelly-Louise . . . I bought you a happy birthday present.

Josie You don't have to go spending your money on me.

Brenda-Marie It were dirt cheap. (*She hands her a crudely wrapped package.*)

Josie Thank you, love.

Josie opens the present. Inside is a snow-scene.

Brenda-Marie If you don't want it, I'll have it.

Josie No. No. This is just what I needed.

Brenda-Marie You can shake it, Mam, and the snow falls. See, that's like our house. And I'm like that girl outside, dancing in the snow. Shake it again, Mam. Make it snow again.

Josie What a beautiful present!

Brenda-Marie And then if I'm away for a short while and you're missing me, you can shake it and see me dance in the snow.

Josie Where are you going?

Brenda-Marie Haven't decided yet, Mam. I'll send you a postcard.

Josie Yes, or I'll worry.

The doorbell goes.

Josie There's the front door.

Brenda-Marie I wonder if it's the special person.

Josie It's probably just Lionel.

She goes to the front door. Brenda-Marie shakes the snow-scene.

Brenda-Marie Brenda-Marie Botting is doing the Dance of the Ice Queen. Look at her go. She's bloody brilliant.

Martha enters the porch. She quickly does her door routine – just the doorknob this time, and she counts silently. She calls back to Josie.

Martha I can't seem to shake that man, Mrs Botting.

Josie Lionel?

Martha He seems to be struggling with rather a large box of alcoholic beverages.

Josie I'll give you a hand!

Josie exits again. Martha enters the lounge.

Martha I think he's intent on getting us all intoxicated.

She takes off her coat. She's looking very dressed up, in a rather bizarre crochet-dress. Her hair is done very elaborately.

Brenda-Marie Holy Jo! You look like Mortitia.

Martha I assume this is not a favourable comparison.

Brenda-Marie We didn't think you'd come. Me and me mam.

Martha Well I was in two minds myself. More than two minds.

She spreads out a small scarf on the sofa and sits on it.

Brenda-Marie Were you in six minds, Holy Jo?

Martha I'm not going to rise to you this evening. If I feel the urge to count, I shall do so silently.

Josie enters.

Martha Counting like prayer can be silent.

Brenda-Marie Your dress is full of holes.

Josie It's a lovely dress, Miss Clear. Very you.

Martha Thank you, I made it myself.

Brenda-Marie It could be a tablecloth.

Josie I never mastered crochet myself. One of my life's many regrets.

Brenda-Marie Where's Lionel?

Josie He's in the kitchen putting some bottles in the fridge. Why don't you offer Miss Clear a crisp, Brenda-Marie?

Brenda-Marie slouches over to the table and takes the crisps.

Martha Thank you very much, Brenda-Marie.

She takes a wet one from her bag, hastily wipes her hands, then takes some crisps.

Brenda-Marie How many crisps have you got there, Holy Jo? I'd say about – six.

Josie That's enough, Brenda.

Martha throws the crisps back, visibly stiffens, counts silently to herself, resumes in her normal voice

Martha You know Mrs Botting. I read a most disturbing report the other day. About Bombay Mix.

Josie Did you really?

Brenda-Marie What's Bonbee Mix?

Josie It's what you get in Indian restaurants isn't it? Like Indian crisps.

Martha Apparently they examined some of this Bombay Mix under the microscope and found five different types of men's urine in it.

Josie How many different types of men's urine are there?

Martha It was the urine of five different men, I believe. Not different types of urine.

Brenda-Marie Five different men weed in the Bombay Mix?

Josie It's a wonder nobody noticed.

Martha They didn't urinate in the mix. They went to the bathroom, failed to wash themselves after doing their business, then plunged their hands into the bowl when it was proffered to them.

Josie That's criminal, that is.

Martha That's why I steer clear of restaurants.

Brenda-Marie Do you want a nut, Holy Jo?

Martha Thank you. (*She takes a nut, puts it to her mouth, hesitates.*)

Josie You're all right. I haven't had five different types of men round here today.

Brenda-Marie We've had all sorts of men come round here though, haven't we, Mam?

Martha (*startled*) What?

Josie She means – door-to-door salesmen. Plagued we were at one time.

Martha smiles and pops the nut in her mouth.

Brenda-Marie You dropped them nuts on the floor earlier, didn't you, Mam?

Martha nearly chokes. Josie goes to her aid. Lionel enters with a hostess trolley of drinks.

Josie Yes, but my floor's good enough to eat off, thanks to you, Miss Clear. Ah, drinks, Lionel, about time.

Lionel I think you're in desperate need of lubrication, Miss Clear.

Martha I'm all right. Please don't fuss. Just a little water, please.

Lionel Water to start with. But I've got a treat for you ladies. I've made my special cocktail. It's called a catastrophe.

Brenda-Marie I want a catastrophe!

Lionel And you shall have one, my sweet. One for Josie first. Our birthday queen.

Josie Thank you, Lionel. Ooh, that'd put hairs on your chest.

Brenda-Marie You need a drink that puts them on your head, Lionel.

Lionel (*handing her a drink*) Yes, well, we're still working on that recipe. Brenda-Marie.

Josie Don't drink it all down in one. Your head'll be spinning.

Lionel Can I tempt you, Miss Clear?

Martha No, thank you, I'm fine with the water.

Brenda-Marie Lionel. When's the special person coming?

Lionel Any minute.

Brenda-Marie Ooh!

Lionel You look very lovely this evening, if you don't my saying, Miss Clear.

Martha Don't get fresh with me, Mr Trills. I know your sort of old.

Josie Miss Clear. Lionel paid you a compliment.

Martha I've had men pay me compliments before and I know where it leads.

Brenda-Marie Where?

Martha Men just want one thing.

Josie Don't I know it.

Martha They want you to clean up after them.

Josie But our Lionel's very hygienic. The only thing he might want to get his hands on are your dresses.

Martha What?

Lionel (*quickly*) It sounds to me like you've had your fingers burnt where men are concerned, Miss Clear.

Martha A lot more than my fingers, I can tell you.

Josie Were you married once, Miss Clear?

Martha No, it never got to that. It was all very short-lived. The summer of love.

Josie A holiday romance?

Martha Funeral.

Josie What?

Martha I met him at my Uncle Padraic's wake.

Josie How romantic.

Martha I thought he had the look of Gene Pitney about him or I wouldn't have bothered.

Lionel Gene Pitney was small, wasn't he?

Josie Oh yes. He was a dwarf.

Brenda-Marie What did Gene Pitney do to you, Holy Jo?

Martha He did unmentionables, Brenda-Marie.

Brenda-Marie Go on.

Martha Don't press me on this now, Brenda-Marie.

Brenda-Marie Go on, tell me, Holy Jo. What did he do?

Lionel He stepped on her blue-suede shoes.

Brenda-Marie giggles.

Martha This is a difficult memory for me, Mr Trills, I'd appreciate a little respect.

Lionel I'm sorry Miss Clear.

Martha Suffice to say, Mrs Botting, he did the dirty on me. With an altar boy from Our Lady of Pity. I should have known. He had skulduggery written all over his face.

Brenda-Marie That must have looked funny.

Josie It must have been very hard for you, Miss Clear.

Martha It's one of the main reasons I came over here, Mrs Botting. To escape the skulldugger. Since that escapade I've given men very short shrift, I don't mind telling you.

Lionel But we're not all skulduggers, Miss Clear.

Martha No. But I've come to terms with it, Mr Trills. Some women are not born to be brides.

Josie You're right there.

Martha Spinster is such a lonely word, though, don't you think, Mrs Botting?

Lionel It's no worse than bachelor.

Martha (*with feeling*) Oh yes, it's much worse, Mr Trills.

Much, much worse. But you were blessed Mrs Botting. I never hear you mention Mr Botting. Has he passed on?

Josie Passed out more like. We were married in Oldham. Home of the tubular bandage.

Martha (*interested*) Oh?

Josie Yes. Some women get the Spanish steps and the Trevi fountain. I got ten minutes in the back of a Ford Capri . . . Suffice to say, I wasn't blessed for very long, Miss Clear.

Martha But long enough to have a beautiful daughter.

Brenda-Marie I'll never be a bride.

Lionel Of course you will, Brenda-Marie.

Brenda-Marie All I want is to be a bride for a day and for everyone to throw confetti at me because that's like love and money and stars all over you all at once. But no one will ever throw confetti at me.

Lionel Of course they will.

Brenda-Marie No, I've been left on the ledge.

Josie On the shelf, I think you mean, love.

Brenda-Marie No, it's too narrow for a shelf. It's definitely a ledge.

Josie Some young man will snap you up.

Brenda-Marie No one will marry me. I'm too simple.

Lionel Ah, but simplicity in a woman is much sought after, Brenda-Marie. I'm often asked what are the top three qualities you look for in a woman, and I say, 'Good looks, sweet breath and gentle simplicity,' every time. And you have those qualities in abundance, Brenda-Marie.

Brenda-Marie Yeah, but I'm not marrying you, Lionel. You're far too old for me. And I could never marry one of the nappy men.

Martha The who?

Lionel Happy men.

Josie (*overlapping with Lionel*) Clappy men.

> *Pause*

Lionel You know, happy-clappy men.

Josie It's one of her peculiar turns of phrase. Your prince will come one day, Brenda-Marie.

Lionel Another catastrophe, Josie?

Josie Make it a double.

Brenda-Marie I want a Coca-Cola. With lots of ice.

Lionel Coming up. Miss Clear?

Martha I think I'd like half a catastrophe. Just to try.

Josie Don't go mad.

> *The doorbell rings.*

Lionel And there's the bell! Aha! Are you ready for this now, ladies?

Brenda-Marie Hurray! The surprise person is here.

> *Lionel exits to the front door.*

Martha I very much hope this is going to be legal.

Brenda-Marie I don't.

Josie I don't think I can bear any excitement.

Brenda-Marie It might be Father Christmas. He always comes at the end of Advent.

Martha It's probably just a fellow dry-cleaner.

Josie Lionel works on his own.

Martha But he probably moves in dry-cleaning circles.

Lionel re-enters. He is brimming with excitement.

Lionel Are we all set then, ladies? Let's just dim the lights for a bit of ambience.

Brenda-Marie I think it might be Father Christmas calling round early, like.

Lionel Oh no, someone much more exciting.

Josie So long as it's not the Vice Squad, we'll be all right.

Martha Why would it be the Vice Squad, Mrs Botting?

Josie No reason. Come on then, Lionel. The suspense is killing us.

Lionel He's ready for you.

Martha So it is a he.

Brenda-Marie I think I might faint when the surprise man comes in.

Josie Take a deep breath, Brenda-Marie. No man is worth fainting over.

Lionel Hold on to your seats then, ladies, I give you our special mystery guest. (*He goes to the door and does the thumbs-up.*) Ready when you are, Mr Wong.

The Chinese Elvis enters. He is a young Vietnamese man who is fully kitted as a young (Jailhouse Rock-type) Elvis. He launches into his act with gusto: Elvis hip thrusts and gyrations and curling lip, but it's obvious that he's nervous. He brings a small tape recorder for his backing music – perhaps he plugs

*a microphone into it. When he speaks he has a strong
Manchester Accent. The Chinese Elvis gives Lionel a
signal to switch on his music.*

Chinese Elvis
Well since my baby left me
I've found a new place to dwell
Down at the end of Lonely Street
At Heartbreak Hotel,
I'm so lonely, baby
I'm so lonely
I'm so lonely
That I could die.

Good evening, Ladies and Gentleman. My name is
Timothy Wong and I will be your Elvis for the evening . . .
(*'e clears his throat to make his presentation, which is
rather bad.*) His name was Elvis Aaron Presley. His
records have sold over one billion copies around the
world. He made thirty-three hit movies. He became one
of the highest paid performers in the history of Las
Vegas. His name was Elvis Aaron Presley. His is the story
of a raw talent and humble beginnings rising to huge
success and an unbelievable stage charisma. His name
was Elvis Aaron Presley.

Martha We know what his name was.

Lionel Carry on, lad. You're doing grand.

Chinese Elvis Um . . . Elvis Aaron Presley. Umm. Sorry
about this.

Josie Just cut to the chase, lad.

Chinese Elvis Yes. Well. Tonight I bring you a taste of
that Elvis magic into your front room. Where two or
three people are gathered in the name of Elvis, his magic
can live on.

Martha Oh yes, I like that.

Chinese Elvis Yes, madam, Elvis lives on through me and people like me. Think of your requests now. I will undertake any of the King's hits. The thin years or the fat years. Because this night is for you and you alone. A private audience with the King of Rock and Roll.

> Now if your baby leaves you
> And you gotta tale to tell
> Just take a walk down Lonely Street
> To Heartbreak Hotel, where you'll be
> You'll be so lonely, baby
> And I'll be lonely,
> We'll be so lonely
> That we could die.

Thank you very much. (*a la Elvis*)

> *A pause. Lionel and Brenda-Marie clap ferociously. Martha and Josie look sceptical.*

Lionel Fantastic! That was great!

Brenda-Marie Elvis is alive!

Josie He doesn't look much like him, does he?

Brenda-Marie And he's a Chinaman!

Josie He don't sound too bad, though.

Lionel Josie!

Martha I don't know if I hold with these Elvis impersonators.

Josie No, nor do I.

Martha At the end of the day, there's nothing like the real thing.

Josie No.

Lionel Ladies, please, a bit of respect for Elvis.

Brenda-Marie I like him.

Chinese Elvis Do you think I could use your toilet? I'm busting. It must have been all that standing about in the cold.

Josie Go ahead.

Lionel Here we go, Tim, I'll show you the way.

Chinese Elvis Give you a minute to think of your requests.

Lionel exits with the Chinese Elvis.

Josie I read about a Chinese Elvis who was up for aggravated bodily harm.

Martha No!

Josie He worked in a Chinese Elvis restaurant and he used to duff up the customers.

Martha No!

Josie Yes! He went prawn crackers!

Martha You don't think it could be the same one?

Josie I think he was older.

Lionel re-enters.

Lionel Josie what are you like? You ought to give the poor kid some encouragement. He's in tatters up there, you know.

Martha Has he ever been involved in a fracas?

Lionel What?

Josie You know. He's never caused a public affray?

Lionel No. Not as far as I know.

Martha No kind of kerfuffle whatsoever?

Lionel No, what do you mean?

Josie You read terrible things, Lionel. In the papers. We were just checking.

Lionel I thought it would be a nice surprise.

Josie How do you know him?

Lionel He's from that Kissagram company round the corner from me. I dry-clean all their outfits. They've got a few Elvis's.

Brenda-Marie Are they all Chinese?

Lionel What?

Martha I bet not. Elvis comes in all shapes and sizes these days. Norwegian, African, I even heard that you can get an Eskimo Elvis.

Brenda-Marie An Elvis that lives in an igloo!

Josie They have conventions.

Martha They sky-dive out of aeroplanes.

Josie It makes a mockery of the King.

Brenda-Marie I think it would be lovely. Lots of Elvises falling out of the sky. Like snow.

Lionel Well I'm very sorry, ladies. I'm sorry to disappoint you. I thought you'd enjoy it, Josie. Really I did.

Josie Oh yes, yes, Lionel. It was a lovely surprise. A touch of Las Vegas in my own front room, what more could I want in life?

Lionel I can ask him to go now.

Martha No. Not now he's made the effort.

Lionel I mean, I thought you loved Elvis.

Josie Oh, I do love Elvis. Elvis has helped me get through many a dark hour, I can tell you.

Martha Me too.

Josie I didn't know you were partial, Miss Clear.

Martha Call me Martha, Mrs Botting. I'd go as far as to say that Elvis has been the saving grace of my life, Mrs Botting.

Josie Elvis has always been there for me, too. More than any other man.

Martha Mrs Botting, as a Catholic I pray for the Second Coming, but do you know what I hope and God forgive me for saying this, Mrs Botting, I hope when He comes again that He'll be wearing rhinestones and singing 'Love Me Tender'.

Josie What an interesting image you've conjured for us there. He's a long time in that lavatory, Lionel. What's he doing?

Lionel I don't know.

Martha I hope whatever he's doing that he washes his hands afterwards.

Lionel He might have lost his bottle. Apparently he's only just starting out as an Elvis. If you want him to stay you'll have to be a bit more encouraging to the lad.

Josie I didn't mean to be discouraging. He's got a nice voice. It took me by surprise, that's all. I hope he's all right.

Martha I hope there hasn't been some sort of tragic accident. We all know how Elvis died, God rest his soul.

I hope this Chinesey fellow wasn't so disheartened by our lack of enthusiasm that he has decided to end it all in a bizarre Elvis copy-cat suicide.

Brenda-Marie How did Elvis die?

Josie On the toilet, love. You do have a tendency to look on the black side, Miss Clear.

Martha Stranger things have happened, Mrs Botting. And the Chinese are all for a bit of hara-kiri.

Lionel That's the Japanese.

Josie You'd better check on him all the same, Lionel.

Brenda-Marie No, he's coming! The Chinese Elvis is still alive!

Chinese Elvis re-enters.

Josie Ah, you had us all worried there, love.

Chinese Elvis Sorry. I got caught short.

Lionel This is the birthday girl. Josie, this is Tim.

Josie Elvis. You must call him Elvis. I'm sorry we weren't more encouraging before, Elvis.

Chinese Elvis That's okay. I'm a bit of a beginner, to tell the truth.

Josie But there's a lot of potential there, I can tell you.

Chinese Elvis Do you think so?

Martha Oh yes, and we don't hold with Elvis Impersonators as a rule.

Brenda-Marie I'd like to see you fall like snow, Chinese Elvis.

Josie He hasn't got time for that. Well, is it request time?

Chinese Elvis Oh yes, Josie. What can I sing for you? For your birthday.

Josie Let's see now.

Brenda-Marie Marie's the name of his latest flame! Let's have that. Only you can sing, Brenda-Marie's the name of his latest flame, if you want, Elvis.

Chinese Elvis I don't do that one.

Martha What about 'Love Me Tender'? That's my favourite.

Chinese Elvis I only know the first verse.

Josie But I thought you said you could do the full complement.

Lionel He's only just getting going. Give the lad a chance.

Josie I know what I'd like. Come here. (*She whispers in the Chinese Elvis's ear.*) Can you do that one?

Chinese Elvis I'll have a go. Number Fourteen, Lionel . . . Ladies and Lionel. Here's a little song that's going out to our birthday girl, this evening. This is from Elvis to Josie to say 'happy birthday'.

He leaves the room, closes the door. The music starts and he operates his own smoke machine. Smoke emerges from under the door.

Martha An Elvis impersonator who doesn't know any of the songs, I don't know.

Brenda-Marie Shush, Holy Jo.

Chinese Elvis
Maybe I didn't treat you
Quite as good as I should have –

225

Lionel (*over the singing*) Lovely choice, Josie.

Josie I'll have another catastrophe now, thank you Lionel.

Chinese Elvis
    Maybe I didn't love you
    Quite as often as I could have
    Little things I should have said and done
    I just never took the time –

The door knocks

Chinese Elvis
    You were always on my mind
    You were always –

Lionel pauses the music.

Lionel Is that the front door?

Josie We're not expecting anyone else, are we, Lionel?

Lionel No.

Brenda-Marie It's another mystery guest. Shall I go?

Josie It's probably kids messing about.

Martha Perhaps it's another Elvis.

Josie Perhaps we're to be thronged with Elvii this evening.

Chinese Elvis Shall I carry on?

Josie Yes, Elvis, if you would. I was loving every minute of that.

Chinese Elvis
    Maybe I didn't hold you
    All those lonely lonely times
    And I guess I never told you

I'm so happy that you're mine
If I made you feel second best
Girl I'm so sorry I was blind
You were always on my mind
You were always on my mind.

*During the last three lines, Brenda-Marie re-enters,
followed by Louise. Josie and Louise stare at each
other. It is as if everyone is suspended in time for a
minute except the Chinese Elvis, who continues to
sing. The words overlap with the music.*

Chinese Elvis
Tell me , tell me that your sweet love hasn't died –

Brenda-Marie I don't know who it is. But I think it
might be Audrey Hepburn.

Josie Oh my God!

Lionel What is it, Josie?

Chinese Elvis
Give me, give me one more chance
To keep you satisfied, satisfied –

Brenda-Marie She said you'd want to see her.

Martha Are you all right there, Mrs Botting?

Brenda-Marie (*suddenly, with awe. She walks around
her sister*) I know who you are. I know what happened
to you. They froze you, didn't they? Then they thawed
you out. And warmed you up. And now you're alive
again! You're alive!

*From now on the characters speak after each sung
line.*

Chinese Elvis
Little things I should have said and done–

Brenda-Marie Is it her, Mam?

Chinese Elvis
  I just never took the time –

Brenda-Marie (*euphoric*) It's her, isn't it, Mam?

Chinese Elvis
  You were always on my mind –

Lionel Who is it, Josie? Josie?

Chinese Elvis
  You were always on my mind.

Louise Mother?

Josie Shelly-Louise?

Louise Happy birthday, Mother.

Martha Holy Mary, Mother of God! It's a miracle.

Chinese Elvis
  You were always on my mind.

  Pause.

Chinese Elvis (*a la Elvis*) Thank you very much.

  *Blackout. Original Elvis version of 'Always on My
  Mind' takes over.*

  End of Act One.

Act Two

Incidental music: Elvis Presley, 'It's Now or Never'.
Louise looks out of the window. She blows on the
window and starts to write HELP *as the Chinese Elvis*
enters. He wears an Elvis GI costume. He doesn't see
Louise at first. She watches him.

Louise Boo!

Chinese Elvis (*jumps*) Oh! Sorry.

Louise What's the matter? Look like you've seen a
ghost.

Chinese Elvis No, I didn't realise you were –

Louise Nice costume. Sexy.

Chinese Elvis Oh. Thanks. I like to change a couple of
times in my act. Give people their money's worth.
Especially 'cause I'm not on top of all the songs yet.

Louise Style over content. Much more important.

Pause. He doesn't know how to take her.

Chinese Elvis Where is everybody?

Louise Brenda-Marie's in her tent. She won't come out. I
don't know about the others. I think I've scared them all
off.

Chinese Elvis Oh, right.

Pause.

Well, I suppose I'll go and find Lionel.

Louise No, don't go. It's nice to have some company. Sorry, I haven't introduced myself. I'm the dead daughter. I'm Shelly-Louise.

Chinese Elvis Pleased to meet you.

Louise Except I've changed my name to Louise. I felt I couldn't grow old with a name like Shelly-Louise.

Chinese Elvis I see.

Pause.

Louise Oh! And I'm not dead. I was never dead.

Chinese Elvis Right. Great. You look well.

Louise Yeah. I just left, you see. I'd had enough. But my mother told everyone I was dead.

Chinese Elvis Oh . . . What did you die of?

Louise That's a good question, Elvis. I don't know. I'll have to ask her . . . I've been away for four years. I thought they'd be pleased to see me.

Chinese Elvis It must be a shock.

Louise Suppose. Anyway, why don't you sing something?

Chinese Elvis Like what?

Louise I don't mind. Come on. I don't want to be blamed for wrecking the party.

Chinese Elvis I don't know them all.

Louise I'll help you out.

Chinese Elvis I'm not sure.

Louise Oh, come on. We'll tempt them all back in here. Here we are. Number five. 'Suspicious Minds'. Come on. Work your magic, Elvis.

Louise helps herself to a drink

Chinese Elvis (*tentatively*)
We're caught in a trap
I can't walk out –

Louise That's it, Elvis.

Chinese Elvis
Because I love you too much, baby –

Louise Give it some welly, Elvis. Come on.

Chinese Elvis
Why can't you see
What you're doing to me
When you don't believe a word I'm saying.

Josie watches through the patio doors. Louise sings backing vocals.

Chinese Elvis
We can't go on together with suspicious minds –

Louise
Suspicious minds –

Chinese Elvis
And we can't build our dreams
On suspicious minds –

Louise (*prompts Chinese Elvis*)
So if an old friend I know –

Chinese Elvis
– I know
Stops by to say hello
Would I still see suspicion in your eye?

Chinese Elvis
Here we go again
Asking where I've been –

231

Louise
Ahh. Ahh. Ahh.
You can't see –

Chinese Elvis
The tears
I feel I'm crying –

Louise
Yes I'm crying –

Chinese Elvis/Louise
We can't go on together
With suspicious minds
Suspicious minds
And we can't build our dreams
On suspicious minds –

Josie enters. They don't notice her at first. She has changed: dolled herself up, put on make-up.

Louise (*prompts Chinese Elvis again*)
Oh let our love survive-
Oh dry the tears from your eyes
Don't let a good thing die
'Cos you know honey I would never lie to you.

Chinese Elvis
Ooh, Ooh, yeah, yeah
We're caught in a trap –

Chinese Elvis sees Josie and stops singing.

Chinese Elvis Josie! You look- (*He can't find the right word.*)

Josie Thank you. Transformation is my speciality. Besides I felt I needed my war paint on. (*She goes and pours herself a drink.*)

232

Louise We've got a question for you mother. How did I die? Elvis and me really want to know.

Chinese Elvis (*switching off his music*) I think that's enough of that one.

Josie Don't do this, Shelly-Louise.

Louise Let me guess. Was it a freak accident? Did I electrocute myself with my hairdryer? No? Oh I hope it was something romantic. Did I drown at sea? Fling myself off Beachy Head? Come on, what did you tell everyone? How did I die?

Josie You choked on your own vomit.

Louise (*taken aback*) What?

Josie You heard me.

Louise (*trying to hide her hurt*) That's a terrible way to go, don't you think Elvis?

Chinese Elvis Yeah, yeah. I don't know.

Josie She said I made her sick, Elvis, sick to her stomach.

Chinese Elvis Right.

Josie She left me a note. A Post-It. Said she hated me. Said she'd never come back.

Louise Did I get a funeral?

Josie It was the Monday. The Monday after I said you'd died. Four months after you'd gone. I got up and I went to Blackpool for the day.

Chinese Elvis I love Blackpool.

Josie I think Blackpool's one of the most depressing places on earth.

Louise Did you wear black?

233

Josie I wore navy. Black wouldn't have been quite right.

Louise And you cried for your poor dead Shelly-Louise?

Josie Something like that.

Louise What about Brenda-Marie? Didn't she want to go to my funeral?

Josie I told her your body had gone for medical research.

Louise Poor kid.

Josie We had a ceremony in the garden. We said some prayers and then we erected a tent. She wanted a place of her own where she could always go off and think about her sister.

Louise So I had a good send-off.

Josie I didn't send you off. You left of your own accord. First I thought you'd come back – thought you were just letting off steam. I was the same at your age. And then the fear got me, and I rang all the hospitals – I'd have dredged the canal with my bare hands if I could. I used to see you all the time – your face in a crowd – hear you calling for me. But then as the months went by, I knew I had to let you go. I never stopped hoping though. I always left a light on for you in the porch, just in case.

Louise Red light, was it?

Chinese Elvis Do you want me to pop back in a bit?

Josie Brenda-Marie was on at me every day: 'Where's she gone, where's our Shelly-Louise?' I didn't know what to say to her, Elvis.

Chinese Elvis No.

Louise You could have told her the truth.

Josie I didn't want her to live in hope. We had to mourn you like you were dead. It was easier that way.

Louise Easier without me?

Josie I didn't say that.

Louise But it was.

Josie How did you get to be so hard, Shelly-Louise?

Louise My mother's a prostitute. I learned it from her.

Chinese Elvis Right. I think I'll definitely find Lionel.

Josie No, you're all right, Elvis. I haven't got the strength for this, Shelly-Louise. I'm sorry, but I haven't. (*She gets up to go.*)

Louise Where are you going?

Josie You left us in the lurch, Shelly-Louise. Not a word for four years. How dare you leave us like that? How dare you? And just because you've decided it's time to come back, doesn't mean we can all dance to your tune. I'm sorry. (*She exits.*)

Chinese Elvis I think I'll just go and try another costume. I don't think this one is working out.

Louise I'm sorry, Elvis. This is nothing to do with you.

Chinese Elvis No.

Louise It never comes out right.

Chinese Elvis What?

Louise The things you mean to say.

A knock on the door. It is repeated.

Come in. Come in. Come in. For Christ's sake.

She goes and opens the door. Martha is poised for more knocking.

Martha I've been saying the rosary for you and your mother.

Louise I think we'll need more than that. You can come in. We've finished.

Martha Hello, Elvis.

Chinese Elvis I'm going to try the fat years. See if I have any more luck with them.

They look at him. He exits.

Louise Well.

Martha You have a lot to be grateful for.

Louise Do you think so?

Martha You're not dead for a start.

Louise No. I ought to thank my lucky stars.

Martha And your Mother. You ought to thank your mother.

Louise Mmm. Do you have children?

Martha I haven't been blessed with children myself. But I was a member of the Catholic Mothers' Union.

Louise How did you manange that?

Martha I got in on a technicality. Besides they needed someone who was good at sewing.

Louise Oh.

Martha Gowns for stillborn babies.

Louise What?

Martha We each had a duty. Mine was making gowns for stillborn babies.

Louise How sad.

Martha Yes, but it was a gift too. I made them beautiful, intricate, full of detail. I didn't want to make them any less so, just because the child was – I liked doing it. It helped the parents, I think.

Louise But you don't do it any more?

Martha I got thrown out.

Louise Why?

Martha I had a set-to with a lay member of the Knights of Columbia. Because I wouldn't give up counting for Lent.

Louise You're a funny lot, aren't you?

Martha What?

Louise It must be difficult to be a practising Catholic and still be on the game.

Martha I beg your pardon?

Louise Is Lionel one of yours or one of hers?

Martha One, two, three, four, five. I really don't –

Louise What's your speciality? Do you whip them with your hair?

Martha One, two, three – I clean, four, five – I clean –

Louise The saucy maid thing? No offence, but isn't that a bit seventies?

Martha Five, ten, fifteen, twenty, twenty-five –

Louise Apparently my mother wows them with her honey tongue. I mean I've got to hand it to her for keeping it up for so long. She can't look good in the bondage gear any more.

Martha Thirty, thirty-five, forty –

Lionel enters. During the next, Martha continues to count under her breath and develops an alarming array of nervous tics.

Lionel I think Elvis may have done a bunk. Is everything all right?

Louise We were just discussing the tricks of the trade. What's your thing, Lionel?

Martha (*with difficulty*) Mr Trills is a dry-cleaner.

Louise Oh, I bet my mother gives you gold service.

Martha He cleans and I clean. We both clean.

Louise Mmm. Yes. A very nice line in French-polishing.

Martha Mrs Botting is a counsellor.

Louise That's one word for it. Anyway, if you'll excuse me, there's something I need to do. Have fun. (*to Lionel*) Good luck, Lionel. I bet she goes like the clappers.

She exits.

Lionel Miss Clear, I –

Martha I'm here under false pretences.

Lionel Please let me explain, Miss Clear.

Martha Five, ten, fifteen, twenty, twenty-five, thirty –

Lionel Josie's a good woman. She just felt it was easier not to tell you.

Martha She's a jezebel?

Lionel She's a dominatrix. A madam, yes.

Martha Are you one of her –

Lionel Yes, yes I am. But she's a friend too. I don't do it that often –

Martha I knew there was something funny about you.

Lionel No, you don't understand –

Martha You're a pervert!

Lionel And you're an obsessive-compulsive.

Martha Two wrongs don't make a right, Mr Trills. Excuse me –

Lionel We have to see this through.

Martha See what through?

Lionel There's a rapport between us. Admit it. You feel it too.

Martha I don't like you.

Lionel Why not?

Martha I don't like the cut of your gib, mister. (*She goes to leave.*)

Lionel Where are you going? Martha?

Martha I'm handing my notice in. I will no longer clean a den of sin and iniquity.

Lionel But why? What are you going back to?

Martha The straight and narrow.

Lionel You're lonely. And I'm lonely.

Martha Now that's where you're wrong. I relish my own company. I'm the best company I know.

Lionel I want to confess to you, Martha.

Martha Oh, please don't.

Lionel I visit a madam because I like to dress up in women's clothing.

Martha You what?

Lionel Have done since I was a boy. I just like the feel of a skirt. The swish. The air between my legs.

Martha Hold it right there, Mr Trills.

Lionel Lionel. Please call me Lionel.

Martha Why should I?

Lionel It's my name.

Martha What sort of name is Lionel?

Lionel Jewish. It's a Jewish name.

Martha Holy Mary Mother of God. I'm stuck in a whorehouse with a Jew who likes to wear women's clothing.

Lionel I was brought up Jewish but I don't practise any more.

Martha Oh my God! A lapsed Jew. We're really running the gamut this evening.

Lionel Catholics don't have the monopoly over lapsing, you know.

Martha I really don't have the time for a theological debate, now if you'll excuse me –

Lionel No, I won't.

Martha I beg your pardon.

Lionel I'm not letting you go.

Martha Why not?

Lionel I'll stop you counting. I'll fill your life so full you won't have time to count.

Martha Please don't go all gung-ho on me, Mr Trills.

Lionel I want to dance with you, Martha.

Martha You really fancy your chances, don't you?

Lionel I want to dance the tango with you.

Martha And you'll be wearing a dress, will you?

Lionel I want you to walk barefoot in the snow. I want to hear you laugh in eight different languages.

Martha I'm very sorry, Mr Trills, but I have no intention of venturing out without the benefit of shoes and I'm not a multilingual. Be so good as to tell Mrs Botting that I am never going to darken her door again. Good night.

Martha exits through the French windows.

Lionel Martha! Wait! It's freezing out there. You'll catch your death. (*He looks for Martha's coat*)

The Chinese Elvis enters from another door. He is wearing an Elvis costume and wig from Elvis's last years, with padding.

Chinese Elvis I've been looking for you, Lionel.

Lionel Yeah. Not right now, lad.

Chinese Elvis I'm not having a very good time.

Lionel No, you're not the only one.

Chinese Elvis Nobody's interested in hearing me sing.

Lionel Well, that's showbiz. Do you know what Martha's coat looks like?

Chinese Elvis I think I might call it a night.

Lionel I've paid you till twelve, besides I'm going to need you later on. We're going to have dancing. That's a good costume.

Chinese Elvis I'm representing the late years.

Lionel Are you wearing padding?

Chinese Elvis A bit.

Lionel Nice touch. Now, I'm on a bit of a mission. I've got to deliver a coat to a damsel in distress. You just sit tight and I won't be long.

Chinese Elvis Yeah but –

Lionel I'll make it worth your while. Help yourself to a catastrophe.

Lionel rushes out of the front door after Martha. The Chinese Elvis goes over to the mirror. He starts to sing to himself.

Chinese Elvis
Love letters straight from your heart
Keep us so near while apart
I'm not alone in the night
When I can have all the love you write –

Brenda-Marie appears from outside and watches him. He doesn't see her until right at the end.

Brenda-Marie (*an insult*) You're sad, Chinese Elvis.

Chinese Elvis Yeah, thanks.

Brenda-Marie enters.

Brenda-Marie Nobody's come to find me to see if I'm all right. I've been in my tent for about three hours.

Chinese Elvis Your mum and your sister are upstairs, I think.

Brenda-Marie I'm not going to them.

Chinese Elvis Right.

Brenda-Marie The way I see it, Chinese Elvis, my sister died and my mam told me she was dead and I cried enough tears to fill a thousand ice trays and now she comes back so she either didn't die or she did die and this girl's just a Shelly-Louise impersonator and anyway me mam told me a big bad fib so I'm not going running to them.

Chinese Elvis No.

Brenda-Marie It's definitely going to snow out there.

Chinese Elvis How do you know?

Brenda-Marie I can feel it in my bones.

Chinese Elvis You must have an old soul.

Brenda-Marie You what?

Chinese Elvis Some people are just born full of ancient wisdom. You must be one of them.

Brenda-Marie Do you think so?

Chinese Elvis Yeah.

Brenda-Marie Holy Jo says it's too cold to snow. That's mad, isn't it? I mean, how can it be too cold to snow?

Chinese Elvis Perhaps it's like when people say they're too tired to sleep.

Brenda-Marie I'm never too tired to sleep.

Chinese Elvis Or like when people are really, really upset but they can't cry. They'd like to cry but they can't. They're beyond tears. Maybe it's like that. The sky is just beyond snow.

Brenda-Marie Yes. I suppose so. Do you know, if my mam and my sister come down now and I don't feel like talking to them, I'm going to say I'm very sorry but I'm too cold to snow right now. I'm beyond snow.

Chinese Elvis And if they ask me to sing I'm going to tell them, I'm sorry I'm too cold to snow as well.

Brenda-Marie Good.

Chinese Elvis That's settled then.

Brenda-Marie Is it cold where you come from, Chinese Elvis?

Chinese Elvis I come from Whalley Range.

Brenda-Marie No, your China home.

Chinese Elvis Vietnam. I was born in Vietnam.

Brenda-Marie Was it cold?

Chinese Elvis It can be very cold and it can be very hot. But I don't remember it.

Brenda-Marie Why did you leave?

Chinese Elvis I don't know – I was a little boy. I left with my parents on a boat.

Brenda-Marie You were a boat boy! A Vietnamese boat boy!

Chinese Elvis Yes, I was.

Brenda-Marie But did you always want to be an Elvis when you grew up?

Chinese Elvis No. But I've always liked the way he sang.

Brenda-Marie Do you like being an Elvis?

Chinese Elvis I don't really know yet. Last week I had to do this hen party. And all these women went wild. They threw their knickers at me.

Brenda-Marie Did you like it when they threw their pants?

Chinese Elvis Not particularly. They weren't nice – they'd gone grey in the wash. I think if I'd been the real Elvis, I'd have been a bit insulted. Then I thought it was sad, the way they all came up afterwards and scrabbled around on the floor for them.

Brenda-Marie I would never be a pant-thrower.

Chinese Elvis No, I didn't think you would.

Brenda-Marie Will you be my boyfriend?

Chinese Elvis No.

Brenda-Marie Oh, okay.

Chinese Elvis I'm sorry.

Brenda-Marie No I'm not that bothered. Sometimes I think it would be nice to have a boyfriend because most people do. But most of the time I think I'd rather have Sky television.

Chinese Elvis The thing is, Brenda-Marie, if I was going to have a girlfriend I would almost certainly choose someone like you.

Brenda-Marie That's good to know, Chinese Elvis.

Chinese Elvis But, well, I'm not that fussed about girls.

Brenda-Marie Oh!

Chinese Elvis It gets a bit tricky especially when I'm the Chinese Elvis because I'm supposed to be like this sex symbol to all these women.

Brenda-Marie But what you really want is an Elvis to call your own.

Chinese Elvis I think I'd prefer John Lennon. He's more my type.

Brenda-Marie nods wisely.

Brenda-Marie Chinese Elvis, if the real Elvis walked in right now, how would you feel?

Chinese Elvis Overdressed.

Brenda-Marie No you wouldn't, you'd be cross.

Chinese Elvis Why?

Brenda-Marie You can't just go off and pretend to be dead. It's not fair on the rest of us.

Chinese Elvis Why not?

Brenda-Marie Because when you think that someone is dead, you think about them every day. It's like they're more alive to you because you can't stop thinking about them. You can't just send them down the shops for ten minutes. You have to think about them. And your mam thinks about them and when she looks at you she's thinking about the dead one. And then you find out they're not dead and you think what a waste of time. I could have been thinking about something nice for ten years and going on holiday and eating ice-cream instead of feeling sad sad sad for an alive dead person.

Chinese Elvis But maybe that person had her reasons. Maybe she had to get away for a bit. To find herself.

Brenda-Marie Why couldn't that person find herself in Bolton?

Chinese Elvis People have to go on long journeys sometimes. I had to come from Vietnam to Whalley Range to find myself as Timothy Wong.

246

Brenda-Marie The furthest I've gone is to my tent.

Chinese Elvis Well, you're full of ancient wisdom, you see. You don't have far to travel in this life, because you already know who you are.

Brenda-Marie It's nice talking to you, Timothy Wong.

Chinese Elvis You're the only one that thinks so this evening.

Brenda-Marie I prefer you to Elvis. You should be a Timothy Wong Impersonator.

Louise enters in domination gear, with cuffs, etc., hanging from her belt. She carries a whip.

Louise Brenda-Marie!

Brenda-Marie stares at her sister in disgust.

Brenda-Marie No! I'm too cold to snow. (*She runs out.*)

Louise I'm Miss Popular tonight. Hello again, Elvis.

Chinese Elvis (*uncomfortable*) Oh, hello. All right?

Louise Is Josie around?

Chinese Elvis Not seen her.

Louise Right.

Chinese Elvis Well. I'll just go and see if Brenda-Marie's okay.

Louise Wait a minute. (*changing her demeanour*) Sing to me.

Chinese Elvis What?

Louise You heard me.

Chinese Elvis I already did.

Louise It's not a request. It's an order.

Chinese Elvis I don't really feel up to it.

Louise Get down on your knees.

Chinese Elvis What?

Louise Adopt slave position. Do it now.

Chinese Elvis Is this a joke?

She cracks the whip.

Louise Of course it's not.

Chinese Elvis I can't do it if I'm forced.

Louise Get down on all fours. Sing to me!

She pushes him down. She puts her foot on his back. She forces his head back.
Josie enters.

Josie What do you think you're doing?

Louise Look at me, Mam! Had to try it out for size. What do you think? Am I a chip off the old block?

Josie Take it off right now.

Louise Doesn't it suit me?

Josie If you want to shame me, you'll have to do a lot more than this.

Louise It'll be my pleasure. Come on, Elvis. Let's see what you're made of.

Chinese Elvis This is definitely the worst gig I've ever done.

Louise pushes him down and tries to handcuff him to the table.

Chinese Elvis Mind my costume – you'll fray the cuffs!
Look at that – it's ruined!

Louise fumbles with the handcuffs, gives up.

Louise I'm sorry, Elvis.

Josie takes them off her, ties him expertly to the table.

Josie Give me those. The dominatrix never gives up,
Shelly-Louise. You've got to be in control. That's it!
China boy. Now you sit there nicely for your madam.
You can't show weakness. They smell weakness. And
despair. Oh yes, despair is the biggest turn off. Don't give
them one ounce of yourself. Only problem is you get so
good at it, you lose sight of who you are. You know
you're there. There's a little tight kernel of you hidden
deep, deep down, if you could only find it. Enjoy it in
stolen moments. But you cover your tracks, you see.
Come on, you heard her, China boy. She wants you to
sing, so bloody well sing!

Chinese Elvis (*feebly and quickly*)
When no one else can understand me
When everything I do is wrong
You give me hope and consolation
You give me strength to carry on
And you're always there to lend a hand
In everything I do
That's the wonder – the wonder
Of you –

Josie That's right. I lend a helping hand. That's all I do.
To people in need.

Louise That's not all you do, Mother.

Josie Well, I'm sorry if you saw things you didn't want
to see. It didn't kill you.

Louise You're not sorry.

Josie No – I'm proud of what I am, what I do. I make people happy. I relieve the boredom. The stress of their horrible little lives. I stop them from doing worse elsewhere. It's a scratch and I itch it. I'm not asking for the Nobel bloody peace prize. You don't even have to respect me. Acceptance is all I've ever asked.

Louise Why should I accept it?

Josie Because I'm your mother and I loved you before you loved yourself.

Louise You don't get it, do you?

Josie I tried to protect you. I did my best.

Louise Your best wasn't good enough.

Josie There's nothing I can do now, is there? I can't change the past. I can't bring you up any different now. So you'd better come to terms with it.

Louise I'm going. You know, you were right about one thing. Shelly-Louise did die. I'm Louise, I'm Louise now. (*She goes to exit.*)

Josie You didn't have to go. You didn't have to leave us.

Pause. She turns back.

Louise Do you want to know why, Mother? Why I couldn't live with you any more? I'll tell you exactly. This is a lovely tale for a cold winter's night. Let me paint the picture for you, Elvis. I was home early from school. She'd taken Brenda to the clinic and I was revising for my A Levels, and the front doorbell went. And I wasn't even going to answer it because I thought it won't be for me because none of my friends call round here because I won't let them in, in case they find out. But for some

reason I did answer it. And funny, it turned out it was
for me. Do you know who it was?

Pause. Josie does not say anything.

Chinese Elvis Who was it?

Louise A gentleman caller. Not one of the regulars. A
new client. Recommended by a friend. And there I was
still in my school uniform. Just the thing.

Josie You're lying.

Louise So he asked me how much I was. What do you
want, I said? The full works? Kit and caboodle? I knew
the lingo, you see. Learned it from when I was knee-high.

Josie Please tell me you didn't.

Louise I must have been tight because I never had before.
Wouldn't let any of the fresh-faced boys at school near
me, too busy with my studies. But he didn't seem to
mind. He was a bit rough, wanted to leave his mark on
me. I remember I was revising for my French A level.
And as he was pounding away I was conjugating all the
verbs in my head . . . passive tense . . . Je suis aime. Tu
es aime. Il est aime. I didn't think it would end but it
did. I felt quite proud of myself. I found I had it in me.

Josie Oh my God.

Louise Oh and I liked the twenty quid at the end. I
thought I'll buy myself some clothes, get my hair dyed.
I could do it a few more times, it wouldn't kill me.
Eventually I'll get myself a flat. I won't be dependent
any more. I won't have to be so responsible. For Brenda-
Marie – but for her too. I won't have to carry the weight
of her expectations any more. Be the person she never
was. And that night I slept, but it was a dead sleep, you
know? The sort you wake up and feel like you just need

to sleep all over again. And when I looked in the mirror my lips were bruised and I felt all wonky. Like my smile was going to slide and slide right off my face. But what was more frightening was the feeling that somehow I deserved it. That she'd had to do it, to bring us up. So why should things be any better for me? Why was I pretending that I could be any better, pass exams and go to college? And that scared me, because I thought, that's it, I'll just become her. And I couldn't allow that for myself. So I packed my bags and I wrote her the note saying I'm never coming back. And I went.

Chinese Elvis I'm sorry.

Louise It wasn't all bad. I got a 'B' in French.

Pause

Josie Thank you for telling me. I think you should go now.

Louise What?

Josie (*quietly, with difficulty*) I understand now. And you were right. You should go.

Louise What?

Josie Please. Go now. Do you need money? I'll give you money.

Louise No.

Josie Please.

Louise You really want me to go?

Josie It's the least I can do.

Louise But –

Josie Please – if you ever – I'm asking you – I'm begging you. Forget about us. We'll be fine. Please.

Pause.

Louise All right then. If it's what you want. I'll just go and – get my things together.

She exits upstairs. Silence.

Chinese Elvis Can you undo me please?

Josie Yes, sorry lad.

Josie unlocks Chinese Elvis.

Don't look at me like that. She made the right choice. She had to get out. I'm not going to hold her back. I would never do that.

Chinese Elvis Are you bleedin' mad?

Josie She needed to explain to me. And now I need to let her go.

Chinese Elvis Rubbish.

Josie Who asked you, anyway?

Chinese Elvis Call yourself a dominatrix?

Josie I've lost the will, Elvis.

Chinese Elvis Go after her. For Christ sake.

Josie She doesn't want me to.

Chinese Elvis Yes she does. She came back, didn't she? That must mean something . . . Go on.

Josie (*slowly*) I'd better get my skates on.

She exits. Chinese Elvis sighs, pours himself a soft drink. Martha enters.

Martha Oh, Elvis. Have you seen my coat?

Chinese Elvis I'm not singing for anybody else.

Martha Well, you'll have exhausted your repertoire. Now have you seen my coat? It's freezing out there.

Chinese Elvis No.

Martha Now where is it? One, two, three, four, five. One, two, three, four, five. One, two, three, four, five.

Lionel enters. Martha doesn't notice him at first

Chinese Elvis Why do you count all the time?

Martha Oh Lord, not another one. What is this sudden obsession with my counting?

Lionel We want to know, Martha. Why do you?

Martha (*she jumps*) Oh God. Where did you come from?

Lionel I've been following you. Here's your coat.

Martha Elvis. Ring the police. I knew he was a stalker.

Lionel Yes, go on, Elvis. Ring the police. That's 999. Three numbers which if you invert them become 666.

Martha (*puts her hands over her ears*) No, no, you evil little man. One, two, three, four, five. One, two, three, four, five.

Lionel There's no point putting your hands over your ears, Martha. Me and Elvis are going to sort you out. Tonight we're going to knock you for SIX.

Chinese Elvis You can count me out. I'm not singing any more.

Lionel I'm sure Martha here would be very happy to count you out. I on the other hand may need your assistance. Now, Martha, answer Elvis's question. Why do you count?

Martha Because I have to.

Lionel Not good enough.

Martha Why do you dress in women's clothing?

Chinese Elvis What?

Martha Oh Elvis, did he forget to mention to you that he's a cross-dressing pervert?

Lionel It must have slipped my mind, Elvis. Forgive me.

Chinese Elvis That's okay.

Lionel I dress in women's clothing because I enjoy it.

Martha I count because I enjoy it.

Lionel No you don't.

Martha I've done this ever since I can remember.

Lionel So?

Martha Counting reminds me that I'm alive. Count to ten, my Mother used to say. When they hit you and knock you down. Count to ten. Every time someone ignores me or is rude to me or jostles me in the street. I am so constantly provoked I haven't got time for ten, so I count to five and I know I'm real, I'm still here.

Lionel But what if you didn't count, what would happen?

Martha Something bad. Something bad would happen.

Brenda-Marie enters in a flurry from outside.

Brenda-Marie Chinese Elvis, I require your urgent assistance outside.

Martha You see! What is it, Brenda-Marie? What's happened?

Brenda-Marie It's nothing to do with you, Holy Jo.

Chinese Elvis I'm right behind you.

Lionel But I'm going to need you.

Brenda-Marie I need him most. Come on Timothy Wong.

> *Chinese Elvis goes to go. As he reaches the French windows he turns.*

Chinese Elvis Elvis has left the building.

> *Brenda-Marie and the Chinese Elvis exit. Martha goes to follow them.*

Lionel No you don't.

Martha Brenda-Marie is obviously on the verge of a crisis.

Lionel She'll be all right. She has Elvis with her.

Martha You don't understand, do you? We could all be inches away from disaster.

Lionel You should be thankful to be alive.

Martha I am. I count my blessings.

Lionel You're living your life in fear.

Martha No, I'm living my life in suspicion. It's very different.

Lionel You should throw back your shoulders, open wide your chest –

Martha Are you a lesbian?

Lionel (*suddenly weary*) No, no, Martha, I'm not. Do you want a drink? I need a catastrophe.

Martha It's all a catastrophe. Everything is a catastrophe.

Pause.

Lionel (*he hands her a glass*) It's hard when you go on and on and nobody notices your potential.

Martha Speak for yourself.

Lionel I am, Martha. People don't take a blind bit of notice of you when you're a dry-cleaner. I'm short and I'm bald and I hand them a ticket for clean clothes next Thursday. That's how much I figure. I'm very easy to overlook. But the clothes speak to me. The dirty clothes full of stains. Dirt they want erased. But do you know what? I love the mess because it means people are living their lives. I hate it when you go into a house and you feel like you can't sit on the seats, you can't walk on the carpet, you can't piddle in the toilet. I want to see a house that's lived in, a coat that's worn, a church that's prayed in – all of us have got a use, Martha, all of us.

She sits.

Martha (*a revelation*) I don't want to be like this any more.

Lionel I know you don't.

Martha I wanted to be a nurse. I wanted to have a child. I wanted to go to Graceland. And it's all passed me by.

Lionel No, it hasn't. It needn't.

Martha People look at me like I'm a loonie. I am a loonie. Why are you bothering with me, Lionel?

Lionel Because you've got a lot to offer.

Martha Really I haven't. I'm a deeply unfortunate woman.

Lionel I've got an urge to reclaim unfortunate women.

Martha I'm sorry, Lionel. I just can't.

Lionel Can't what?

Martha This. That. The other. Here. Now. Ever. With you. Sorry.

Lionel You don't find me attractive enough.

Martha It's not that.

Lionel Then what?

Pause. Martha counts softly to herself. She cries silently.

Lionel I'd better go.

Pause. He goes to exit.

Martha No. Please. Lionel. (*quietly*) Have you seen those girls? The girls in town on a Friday night. No more than sixteen some of them. In their best bib and tucker. Well, actually, it's hardly that is it? Wouldn't cover a flea. Half a bib and no tucker to speak of. In their big bovver boots and the sparkle round their eyes. And some of them are in army gear, with their bosoms hanging out and they look at you like they're about to karate chop the living daylights out of you. And I think, they'll catch their death – I would – but they don't. They've got thermostats in their boots. And I look at them, the bobby-dazzler girls, and I think, how did you learn to be like that? Where did you get the courage? I didn't have a minute, a second in my life when I felt a bit like that and I wish I had, Lionel. I wish I'd worn those boots and those clothes and that face for half a minute of my life. I might have stood a chance.

Lionel We can get you combat gear, Martha. That isn't a problem.

She laughs.

Martha I feel like I'm declining slowly into invisibility.

Lionel But I've come along. With X-ray specs.

Martha But I don't want to sleep with you, Lionel. I can't sleep with you.

Lionel That's okay. We'll dance. And you can let down your lovely locks for me, eh?

Martha Like Rapunzel.

Lionel Yes. Like Rapunzel.

Martha It's very fine, my hair. There's a lot of it. But it's very fine.

Lionel I'll be the judge of that. I'll go and find Elvis. Wait there. Don't move.

Martha Yes.

Lionel exits. Martha goes to the mirror, looks at her reflection, tries to pull her dress down to reveal some cleavage, sighs, goes to the hostess trolley, pours herself a very large drink which she drinks in one.
Josie enters.

Josie Martha, have you seen Shelly-Louise? I mean Louise?

Martha No, Mrs Botting. But I'm glad you're here, Mrs Botting because I need to talk to you.

Josie I need to find my daughter.

Martha It really won't take very long. You see, I made a surprising discovery earlier this evening.

Josie Oh?

Martha Concerning the precise nature of the counselling services that you offer here.

Josie Well, bully for you, Holy Jo.

Martha On acquiring this information, I am of course forced to hand in my notice.

Josie Fine. I accept.

Martha What?

Josie You can go right now. Nobody's stopping you. And if you think I'm going to give you a reference, you can think again.

Martha What?

Josie I've enough wackos coming round here as it is without you as well. I'd rather have the place dirty.

Martha You have to give me a reference.

Josie No one tells me what I have to do.

Martha I'll take you to an industrial tribunal! I'll tell them what sort of woman you are.

Josie Go ahead. I'll probably know them anyway. I get a lot of magistrate types round here.

Martha I withdraw my notice. You'll have to sack me.

Josie Avec plaisir!

Martha Don't you talk French to me, lady.

Josie I'll say what I like in my own house.

Martha You'll never find another cleaner like me!

Josie You're right there.

Martha I'm not going! I know my rights! . . . Besides I can't go. Don't make me go, please! Please, I don't want to go!

Josie What?

Martha I can't go because I need to avail myself of your services.

Josie What are you talking about?

Martha The thing is – I need your advice. Some tips. Just the basics.

Josie I'm not with you.

Martha You see I haven't – I've never, I mean even with Gene Pitney, it never got further than my girdle . . . to tell you the truth, I'm scared out of my wits, Mrs Botting.

Josie Holy Jo – are you saying –?

Martha Yes! I'm saying there's a man out there and he's small and he has no hair and he's Jewish and he likes to feel the swirl of air between his legs when he's wearing a dress and I don't know what to do about him. I think I'd like to become a fallen woman. But I need some lessons.

Josie Well I bloody well never!

Martha I'm forty-five and I don't know who else to ask.

Josie We'd better have a master class.

Martha You'll help me?

Josie Come with me.

Josie and Martha exit upstairs. At the same time, Brenda-Marie enters from outside with the Chinese Elvis and Lionel trailing behind her, carrying various bits of her tent.

Brenda-Marie Come on, you two. Lionel, don't lag. I think we'll have it over here in this corner. I can't believe me mam and me sister haven't come looking for me. But if my tent's right under their noses, there'll be no excuses.

Lionel She's gone. Well, I'm not letting this happen. (*He exits upstairs.*)

Brenda-Marie Lionel, where are you going? You've got to help me and Elvis put my tent up.

Chinese Elvis We'll put it up, Brenda-Marie, don't worry. It's easy. We'll have it up in no time.

Brenda-Marie I'll give you directions. You can build it round me.

Chinese Elvis Thanks very much.

He starts to put the tent together. Louise appears. She is back in her ordinary clothes, with her bag, ready to go.

Louise Can I help?

Brenda-Marie It's all right, thank you very much.

Louise Well, you look as though you need some help, Elvis.

Chinese Elvis It depends what you mean by help.

Louise It's all right. I'm not going to tie you up again.

She puts her bag down and they start to build the tent around Brenda-Marie.

Louise Brenda-Marie, I just wanted to –

Brenda-Marie I'm sorry, I'm very busy right now.

Louise Oh. Okay.

Chinese Elvis Just pass me that bit, Louise. Ta.

Pause

Brenda-Marie And here we are in the Heidelburger Stadium. It's minus about a hundred degrees outside. But here's the Botting Sisters from Bolton. Flying split triple-twist. Yes. Perfect. But, oh no! Shelly-Louise has lost her grip. She lets her go. Brenda-Marie's head smashes into the ice. She can't control it. Her skull is sliced in two. The ice is turning red. She's lying on the ice. She's not moving.

Louise Brenda-Marie –

Louise goes to sit in the frame of the tent with Brenda-Marie, while the Chinese Elvis continues to construct the tent.

Brenda-Marie Barry Davies is crying. He says no one will ever take her place.

Louise I'm sorry I went away.

Brenda-Marie Barry Davies is a mess. He's got snot pouring down his face.

Louise I didn't think what it would do to you.

Brenda-Marie Barry Davies is in tatters.

Louise But I didn't stop thinking about you. I don't expect you to understand why I did it. But I want you to know that it was very necessary.

Brenda-Marie You had to find yourself, I know.

Louise (*surprised*) What? Yes, yes I did.

Brenda-Marie Some people can find themselves just sitting in a tent and some people have to go round pretending they're dead. It's very inconvenient but some people just have to do it.

Louise I didn't pretend I was dead. Mam only said that to make it easier.

Brenda-Marie How could it make it easier?

Louise I'm sorry, Brenda-Marie.

Brenda-Marie Some people think that just by changing their name that people will start treating them different. But that's a load of cobblers.

Louise Yes, you're probably right.

Brenda-Marie I think you'll find I am right. I was born with ancient wisdom, you see.

Louise Who told you that?

Brenda-Marie A Chinese acquaintance of mine.

Chinese Elvis That's the frame up.

Louise It's so good to see you, Brenda-Marie.

Chinese Elvis Shall I cover you up now?

Brenda-Marie No, we'll do that, Timothy Wong. You have a rest in my tent now, you've worked very hard.

The Chinese Elvis sits in the tent while they put the canvas over it.

Louise Do you remember what Mam said about the night we were born?

Brenda-Marie It was cold, cold, icicles everywhere.

Louise And she thought there was only one of us.

Brenda-Marie And Shelly-Louise popped out quick as you like.

Louise Like shelling peas.

Brenda-Marie She had no hair. She were a baldy.

Louise And then they said –

Brenda-Marie 'Hang on a minute, there's another one in here!'

Louise But Brenda-Marie wasn't coming out.

Brenda-Marie No, she was staying put. Heave ho!

Louise And they dragged her out, bawling and shouting.

Brenda-Marie (*giggles*) She had loads of hair. Like fur. All over 'er. To keep her warm.

Louise She was the big surprise.

Brenda-Marie (*delighted*) A bonus baby. Two for the price of one!

Louise But she wasn't a big surprise to me. Because I always knew she was there. Before Mam knew, even. That's why I was never lonely. Even when I came out and she stayed put we were never apart. So that means – even when there's hundreds of miles between us, we'll always be together.

Brenda-Marie You're going away again, aren't you?

Louise I'm sorry, Brenda-Marie.

Brenda-Marie Don't go.

Louise Some things don't work out the way we want them to.

Brenda-Marie You're a bitch.

Louise Brenda-Marie.

Brenda-Marie Get away from me.

Louise I'm sorry.

Brenda-Marie I hate Advent. Because you wait and you wait for the really important person to come and then they come and then they just go away and you have to start waiting all over again, don't you Elvis?

Chinese Elvis Leave me out of this.

Louise Brenda-Marie, maybe I could write to you –

Brenda-Marie Shove over, Elvis. I need to get in. (*She gets into the tent and zips it up.*)

Louise Brenda-Marie?

Pause

Shit.

She picks up her bag. Josie enters.

Josie Before you go, I need to ask you something.

Louise What?

Josie Why did you come back? You told me why you went. But why did you come back?

Louise It doesn't really matter now, does it?

Josie Please.

Louise (*casual*) I dunno. It was your birthday. I thought I'd surprise you.

Josie You did. You did surprise me. Thank you. It was very brave of you.

Louise Well, I should –

Josie takes the snow globe out of her pocket and hands it to Louise.

Josie Here. Something to remember us by.

Louise I don't need anything –

Josie Bren gave it me – go on. Give it a shake. Watch the snow fall.

Louise does so. She looks at the globe.

Good girl. I'm glad you came back, you know. I didn't realise it till just now – but for the last four years – it's

like I've been frozen – suspended in animation. You left
and I stepped into a casket of dry ice. But then you came
back and that's when it happened – this miraculous
thing! Soon as you appeared I could feel this tingling
feeling up my spine. And then down me arms – at first
I didn't know what was happening to me. Go on, keep on
shaking. And then I realise. I'm getting the feeling back.
I'm thawing out. And that's a medical impossibility.
I was frozen and you've brought me back to life. I am
alive again because of this prodigal return. This brave
and prodigious return. So full of good things that I can't
begin to count them. So whatever your reason I thank
you – because this is the best birthday present that I have
ever ever had.

Pause

Louise There's a man. He wants to marry me.

Josie Yes?

Louise A good man – not a – you know –

Josie No. Shake it again. Go on.

Louise And I don't know what to do about him. I can't
even you know – sleep with him – properly –

Josie Keep on shaking –

Louise I thought none of this mattered – where I came
from – I thought it was all in the past – that I could just
wipe you all out as if you never existed – but it's not that
easy.

Josie No.

Louise I've been feeling terrible – I can't sleep – I can't
do anything –

Josie That's love for you.

Louise I wanted to tell you. That's all. I just wanted to pop by and tell you.

Josie Shake it again, Louise. And you listen to me. I need to say this to you before you go. All I want is for you to be happy. You and Brenda-Marie. Swap hands if it's hurting. Because my love for you and her knows no bounds. When it comes to love, I'm a Goliath. I've been practising all my life. And I don't care if you're Shelly-Louise or Louise or Louis the bloody Fourteenth, you'll never stop me. So if you want to be a bride, I'll run up the aisle with you and if you want to be a lap-dancer I'll fix you a table and if you want to take another break from me I'll just keep on snowing till you come back. So that's it. The most I've ever said without the aid of a whip . . . You can stop now. Let the snow settle. Let it settle.

Pause. They watch as the snow falls.

Josie Does your wrist hurt?

Louise Yes.

Josie I'm getting you in training for married life.

Louise Mam –

Josie I know.

Louise I've never –

Josie I know.

Louise I really –

Josie I know.

Louise It won't be all plain sailing.

Josie I know. I know that. Come here.

Josie and Louise embrace. Brenda-Marie appears out of the tent.

Brenda-Marie (*sulky*) You've found her space in your heart again then, Mam. I'll have to shove over.

Josie No you won't. I've improved my capacity. We're gonna have to go and see about this sky television, aren't we?

Brenda-Marie (*smiles*) Yeah.

Josie Why don't you show your sister what I made you for Christmas?

Brenda-Marie Okay.

Josie Go and put it on, then.

Louise Shall I come and help you?

Brenda-Marie No, wait here. I want it to be a surprise.

She exits.

Josie (*indicating the tent*) What the hell's she brought this indoors for?

Louise (*whispers*) Elvis is in there.

Josie goes to the tent.

Josie Elvis, are you in there, love?

Chinese Elvis Yes.

Josie Are you all right?

Chinese Elvis I'd like to keep myself to myself, if it's all the same to you.

Lionel enters looking very glum.

Josie And look at the face on him!

Lionel She's barricaded herself in the bathroom. She won't talk to me.

Josie Martha?

Lionel I thought I'd won her.

Josie But you hardly know her, Lionel.

Lionel I've made a fool of myself.

Josie I'll go and see to her. Wrestle the Jay-cloth from her bare hands if I have to.

She goes to see Martha, just off.

Louise I might be getting married.

Lionel Good for you.

Louise It's not definite.

Lionel No. It never is.

Pause.

Josie re-enters, looking shocked.

Josie Lionel.

Lionel What?

Josie It's your birthday. And Christmas. Come at once.

Lionel What?

Martha enters. She is wearing a low-cut sexy Spanish flamenco dress. Her hair is tied at the nape of her neck, but with most of it flowing. She has a flower in her hair. Chinese Elvis pops his head out of the tent.

Josie Go on. Tell him.

Martha Lionel. I have a real urge to lick your bald head.

Louise Do it, Martha.

Josie Yes, but do it front to back, Martha, it's more hygienic.

Martha Stand back, please.

Martha licks Lionel's head from front to back.

Martha I could stimulate your follicles, Lionel Trills.

Chinese Elvis Bloody hell.

Louise (*at window*) Oh Mam, look, it's started to snow.

Josie So it has. Let's go outside.

Louise Yes.

Lionel (*to Martha*) Come on, bobby-dazzler.

They exit. Brenda-Marie enters. She is wearing a replica of Jane Torvill's dress from the Ravel 'Bolero' routine. She rushes in, then seems deflated that no one is here.

Brenda-Marie Mam? Shelly-Louise?

Chinese Elvis You look nice.

Brenda-Marie This is me 'Revel's Bolero' dress.

Chinese Elvis You look like – (*He can't quite put a name to it.*)

Brenda-Marie No I don't. Because I can't really dance, you see. On the ice. I made that up.

Chinese Elvis Well, nobody wants to hear my Elvis impersonations.

Brenda-Marie No. The thing is, Elvis, we all know you can do Elvis, now we want to hear you sing like Timothy Wong.

Chinese Elvis Timothy Wong can't sing.

Brenda-Marie Come on, sing for me now.

271

Chinese Elvis I can't.

Brenda-Marie Nobody's listening. I'll tell you if you're shit. I'll throw my pants at you.

Chinese Elvis I'm sorry, Brenda-Marie. I've had enough tonight. I'm not a performing seal.

Brenda-Marie Prima donna.

He zips up the tent. She thinks for a minute. Then she stands up. She addresses the tent.

Brenda-Marie Ladies and gentlemen, I'd like to introduce to you, Mr Timothy Wong. He used to be a Vietnamese boat boy, but now he's a poofter living in Whalley Range.

The Chinese Elvis unzips the tent.

Chinese Elvis What?

Brenda-Marie His name is Timothy Wong. He hasn't sold any records. His name is Timothy Wong. He hasn't made any films. His name is Timothy Wong and he's my friend and he's appearing for one night only in my tent in my front room.

Pause

Brenda-Marie His name is Timothy Wong –

Chinese Elvis All right. All right. We know what his name is.

Brenda-Marie Go on, then.

He begins to sing in his own voice. He starts off tentatively and gains in confidence as he sings. Brenda-Marie gives him a hand to get out of the tent. At the same time he sheds his Elvis layers down to just a T-shirt and shorts.

Chinese Elvis
Oh I wish I was in the land of cotton
Old time's there are not forgotten –

Brenda-Marie And he's brilliant. You're brilliant,
Timothy Wong! You're better than Elvis.

Chinese Elvis
Look away, look away, look away Dixieland –

Brenda-Marie Sing it, Timothy Wong!

*She begins to dance. She kicks her feet awkwardly.
She's quite clumsy.*

Chinese Elvis
Oh I wish I was in Dixie
Hooray, hooray!
In Dixieland I'll take my stand
To live and die in Dixie!

*Slowly, slowly her arms lift with an awkward grace
and this becomes an 'ice-dance'.*

Brenda-Marie Oh bloody hell. It's comin, Mam, it's
coming. The ice-dance is welling up inside me.

The front of the stage becomes an ice rink.

Chinese Elvis
In Dixieland's where I was born –

Brenda-Marie Mam! I'm ice-dancing!

During this, the others walk back in and watch her.

Chinese Elvis
Early on one frosty mornin' –

Brenda-Marie One minute I'm the Torvill. Next I'm the
Dean. And where's Barry Davies when you need him?

Chinese Elvis
  Look away, look away, look away Dixieland –

Brenda-Marie Mam, I'm wearing the see-through tights and the big pants and I'm queen of the ice!

Josie You are.

Chinese Elvis And Timothy Wong can sing!

Lionel He can. He bloody can.

Brenda-Marie And my sister's a bride!

Lionel And so are you, Brenda-Marie.

  At the word bride, Josie, Martha and Lionel start to throw handfuls of confetti in the air. Timothy Wong continues to sing 'Glory, Glory, Hallelujah'. The confetti starts to fall from the ceiling, too. Brenda-Marie continues to dance. The lights on the Christmas decorations start to twinkle.

Brenda-Marie And it's snowing, Mam! That's amazing. It's snowing in the house.

Martha Look at the mess!

Lionel Leave it, Martha. We love the mess.

  When Martha begins to count it is as if she is trying to count the falling pieces of confetti.

Martha One, two, three, four, five –

Lionel No, Martha, no. Let it fall.

Martha One, two, three, four, five –

Louise Let the snow fall.

Martha One, two, three, four, five –

Josie Let it settle.

Brenda-Marie No, she's trying to say something. I know what she's trying to say.

Martha One, two, three, four, five –

Brenda-Marie Say it, Holy Jo! Say it!

Martha One, two, three, four, five –

Brenda-Marie She's judging me. She's giving me my marks!

Martha Six!

Chinese Elvis Technical merit?

Martha Six!

Louise Artistic presentation?

Martha Six!

Lionel Hallelujah!

Martha Six! Yes!

Brenda-Marie I did it, Mam! I did it! I got the perfect number!

She spins and spins in her final move. The others watch rapt. The 'snow' continues to fall. The fairy lights twinkle. The final 'Glory, Glory, Hallelujahs' from An American Trilogy *play.*

Blackout.

HUMBLE BOY

For my parents

Humble Boy, presented in association with Matthew Byam Shaw and Anna Mackmin, was first performed on the Cottesloe stage of the Royal National Theatre on 9 August 2001, with the following cast:

Felix Humble Simon Russell Beale
Mercy Lott Marcia Warren
Flora Humble Diana Rigg
Jim William Gaunt
George Pye Denis Quilley
Rosie Pye Cathryn Bradshaw

Music played live by Charlotte Bradburn (*saxophone*), Adam Caird (*piano*), Zoe Martlew (*cello*)

Director John Caird
Designer Tim Hatley
Associate Costume Designer Lucy Roberts
Lighting Designer Paul Pyant
Music Joe Cutler
Sound Designer Christopher Shutt
Company Voice Work Patsy Rodenburg

Characters

in order of appearance

Felix Humble

Mercy Lott

Flora Humble

Jim
the gardener

George Pye

Rosie Pye

Act One

SCENE ONE

*Set: a pretty country garden. Perhaps the suggestions of
a house or a glass conservatory from which the characters
enter into the garden. A patio area, perhaps with a
path through the garden. At the back there is an area
for gardening tools; a gardening chair or stool. There
is a garden hosepipe wound up there. Something of a
lawn with borders. A rose bush. At the end of the garden
there is a large beehive. The suggestion of an apple
tree – perhaps just some overhanging branches with a
few apples.*

*The stage is in darkness. There is music. Perhaps
resonant of 'The Flight of the Bumblebee'. The beehive
lights up to suggest the bees leaving the hive. The lights
fade up on the rest of the garden. The music is still
playing and the hive continues to throb with light.*

*Felix Humble walks in a stumbling, uncertain way
into the garden. He is transfixed by the hive. He is an
overweight but not unattractive man of about thirty-five.
He wears old and slightly greying cricket whites, despite
the fact that he is not a sportsman by any stretch of the
imagination. He climbs up the steps and takes off the
lid of the hive and looks in. The music ends.*

*Mercy Lott enters the garden. She is wearing black
clothes with brown shoes. She is in her late fifties, a
petite and timid, mousy woman. She watches Felix with
concern. She approaches him but doesn't get too close.
Felix glances at her, then returns his attention to the hive.*

Felix (*he stumbles on the letter 'b'*) The b–b–b–bees have
gone.

Mercy Yes, dear. Will you come in now?

Felix They took the b–bees away. I saw them.

Mercy Your mother isn't cross. She just wants you to come in.

Felix There were four of them. The bee-keepers. All in white.

Mercy I'm sure if you just say a little sorry to her –

Felix They looked like astronauts.

Mercy Did they?

Felix Or cosmonauts. Depending.

Mercy On what, dear?

Felix If we were in Russia.

Mercy Is it still called Russia? Russia?

Felix What?

Mercy Russia? Is it still called Russia? I can't keep track. Anyway, your mother's waiting inside for you.

> *Felix puts the lid back on and climbs slowly and awkwardly down.*

Felix What do you call a group of b–bee-keepers, Mercy?

Mercy Is this a joke? I'm not very good with jokes, dear.

Felix No, I mean what's the word? Like a flock of sheep, a herd of cows, a pack of dogs, a – an exaltation of larks.

Mercy Is it really? An exaltation. How lovely.

Felix What is it for b–bee-keepers?

Mercy Do you know? I've no idea.

Felix What is it for astronauts? A group of astronauts?

Mercy Shall we discuss it inside, dear?

Felix Something to do with them being white. And weightless. And silent.

Mercy We shouldn't leave your mother on her own with all the others.

Felix I just have to find the right word.

Mercy We really should support your mother.

Felix (*a flash*) I can't go in until I've found the right words. Come on. A swarm of b—bees. A what of b—bee-keepers? A what of astronauts? A what? There must be a word for it. The word must exist. I just need to get this — just . . . think logically. There were four of them. They were dressed in white — they took the bees away.

Mercy A heavenly host?

Felix What?

Mercy A heavenly host! A heavenly host of bee-keepers, stroke astronauts. I like it. (*Mercy glances anxiously towards the house. She sees Flora approaching.*) Please let's go in now.

Felix Or an apocalypse. An apocalypse of bee-keepers.

Mercy Lovely. Even better. That's settled. In we go then.

> *Flora enters. She is a very attractive woman in her late fifties. She looks young for her age. She wears a stylish navy blue dress and Jackie Onassis glasses.*

Mercy Flora! We were just coming in. Weren't we, Felix? We were just sorting out what you call a group of bee-keepers and then we were right with you. Do you need me to do more sandwiches? She's not angry. You're not angry, are you, Flora?

Flora No.

Mercy There. I told you she wasn't angry. We can all go in now. Your mother isn't angry with you.

Felix Yes she is.

Flora (*calmly*) I am not angry, Felix. I am incandescent with rage.

Mercy Oh dear.

Felix (*stammering badly*) An apocalpse of b–b–b–b–bee-keepers. What do you think of that for a collective noun, Mother? It's not b–b–bad, is it?

Flora Stop that, Felix. You haven't done that since you were at prep school.

Mercy He's just a little jittery.

Flora He's doing it to annoy me.

Mercy I'm sure he's not – you're not, are you, Felix?

Flora He can speak perfectly well, if he wants to. He's doing it on purpose.

Felix (*extreme frustration*) I'm trying to b–b–b–b–b–

Mercy (*supplying the word for him*) Behave? He's trying to behave, Flora.

Flora (*coolly*) I'm afraid, Felix, you will not get the sympathy vote. Today your father has a prior claim.

Felix I saw them, Mother. The apocalypse of b–b–b– (*He gives up.*) They were here. While my father was being consigned to dust. You got rid of them immediately. His be– his be– be–

Flora I got rid of the bees on professional advice. They were swarming. Since your father's death they have developed very alarming tendencies.

Felix P–perhaps they were angry.

Mercy Felix.

Felix I came home and I went through the house and I find all my father's be–be–be– all his things gone. All his clothes.

Mercy Flora very kindly gave them to me. For the Romanian orphans.

Flora His bee-keeping suit is still there. In the garage. It is a constant reminder.

Mercy I could have taken it but Jean who runs the shop was worried there wouldn't be much call.

Felix I come home – and there is just an absence.

Flora Don't question what I do, Felix. You weren't here.

Felix I'm trying to find the right words.

Flora Oh yes, Felix, you carry on. That is what this day has been lacking. Yes. There we all were, waiting in the church for you to find just the right words. Waiting for my clever son, my golden boy, the Cambridge don, to deliver his father's oration.

Felix I'm not a don.

Flora There we all were, thinking he will make this bloody bloody awful thing . . . better – oh, we will cry but we will be uplifted. But instead you, let me find the exact word now, you absconded.

Felix I'm not well.

Flora Buggered off.

Felix I have p–pills.

Flora And so it falls to an amateur entomologist, an insect man, not even a close friend, a passing acquaintance of your father's, to find the right words. The *bon mot*.

Mercy He did very well, considering.

Flora He did not do well, Mercy. He compared my husband's career to the life cycle of an aphid.

Mercy I liked the bit about you spinning a web around him.

Flora Oh yes, there was no end to his metaphorical prowess. Men who spend their waking hours studying the mating rituals of arachnids should not be allowed out.

Felix They're his friends.

Flora They *were* his friends. Friends of the *late* James Humble. A group of tedious entomologists. No, no, let me adhere to the linguistic rules that have been imposed on us today. A boredom of entomologists. A woeful irritation of insect men. Open up their collective thorax and you will not find a beating heart among them.

Mercy Shall I go and make some more sandwiches? I thought the beef paste was going down rather well.

Felix I haven't b–b–been well.

Flora Your father is dead, Felix. Your being unwell barely registers on the Richter scale.

Felix I tried to sp–speak – to sum his life up –

Flora We are every one of us unwell. Do not deceive yourself that you hold the monopoly. Mercy's not well. She hasn't been right in years.

Mercy Well, a little arthritis in my back –

Flora And I am recovering from major surgery.

Mercy Oh, she is.

Felix (*quietly*) P–plastic.

Flora What did you say?

Felix A nose job is not major surgery.

Mercy Oh, but her face was black and blue. You should have seen it. Even now if you look under those glasses – ah, the bruising, she looks terrible –

Flora Shut up, Mercy.

Mercy I only meant –

Flora Did you not have a more suitable pair of shoes?

Mercy What?

Flora I've told you about wearing brown and black together.

Felix You're not wearing b–black.

Flora Black is too draining. Anyway this is Jean Muir. And I have to say I find it rich, yes, ripe that I am being criticised on my choice of – look at you! Did you seriously think that this was appropriate attire for your father's funeral? You don't even play – you were a horror when it came to ball games. In fact I don't recognise you. Look at yourself. You've grown fat and unkempt. How could you do this?

Mercy Should I pop home and change them?

Flora Oh please go in, Mercy. See to the insect men. Wreak havoc with some potted shrimp, for Christ's sake.

Mercy Right. Yes. Good idea. You'll be all right?

Flora Oh yes, yes. My husband is dead and my only son, who has grown fat and strange, has just run away from his own father's funeral. I'll be fine. Fine. At least those bastard bees are gone.

A moment, then Mercy leaves apologetically.

Mercy Yes. Yes. Sorry, Flora.

Felix and Flora stand there.

Felix B–b–blessed are the p–p–peacemakers.

Flora For they shall irritate the hell out of you . . . I saved up a long time for that operation.

Felix I know.

Flora Your father wanted me to – (*carefully*) he didn't not want me to – he knew what it meant to me.

Felix Yes.

Flora I didn't even know he was in the garden. I was upstairs, resting, when he collapsed. I couldn't hear – the bandages covered my ears, muffled the sound. But I knew. I was reading *Vogue* and suddenly it dropped from my hands. Just fell to the floor. But there was nothing – he was dead in an instant, you know, his heart –

Felix Yes.

Flora I couldn't bear to have his things. I couldn't bear –

Felix It doesn't matter.

Flora Perhaps I should have kept – for you – but really, you haven't been here in such a long time –

Felix Just because you can't see something doesn't mean that it isn't there.

Flora (*sharply*) What?

Felix B–black holes. They're not observable. Well, without very sophisticated microlensing techniques they're not.

Pause. Flora is wrong-footed.

Flora Don't try and blind me with science, Felix.

Felix I'm not.

Flora You made me look like a fool in that church. This is not something that I will be able to forgive, Felix.

Felix No.

Flora This is not something that I will be able to forget.

Felix No.

She turns to go, turns back.

Flora What pills are you taking?

Felix It's nothing. Nothing. For nerves. Just to help me sleep.

Flora I always know when you are ill.

Felix Yes.

Flora Well, you're too old now for me to . . . Are you going back today?

Felix I don't know yet.

She looks at Felix intently. The gardener Jim walks into the garden. He is in his sixties, thoughtful and quiet, even absent-minded, with a gentle sense of humour. Felix stares at him, Flora does not look at him. He carries a hoe and a bucket of ashes and tea leaves. He scatters the ashes under the rose bush, spreads them. Flora looks away, around the garden.

Flora It's such a beautiful day. Shame.

She walks back into the house, giving the hive a wide berth. Jim glances at her as she leaves. Felix continues to look at Jim. Jim notices him watching.

Jim I know, I know. I thought twice about coming today. But what with this hot weather, it all needs doing and your mother can't bear it getting out of hand, can she?

Felix No, she can't.

Jim (*looking at the roses*) This has definitely come out of itself today . . . (*He dead-heads the bush.*) I like the floribundas but Mrs Humble is fond of the hybrids. They smell sweeter of course. That always swings it for her. I'd go for more variety but she only wants the scented flowers. And I do as I'm told.

Felix Yes.

Jim This one's a hybrid tea, *Rosa 'Josephine Bruce'*. Don't know who she was, Josephine, but she's got quite a jolly flower named after her. Beautiful dark crimson, lovely scent – and so easy. Positively rampant. Makes me think Miss Bruce must have been a bit of a goer in her day.

Felix She might not be dead. Josephine B–b–b–

Jim No, you're right, she could still be at it. But often they are, aren't they? Dead, I mean. And this is a nice way of carrying them on. For their family.

Felix Yes.

Jim You'd be surprised how many are named after the strangest people. There's a pink climber called Bobby Charlton. Not that he's dead. Or is he? Anyway, it's a real blowsy thing, I always wondered if he had a hand in choosing it for himself. I rather hope he did . . . Sorry, listen to me, I'm not thinking. Are you all right, lad?

Felix The b–b–bees are gone.

Jim I know, it's a sad day. Very sad. A hive without its bees. It says it all, doesn't it?

Felix I saw it. There were four of them. An apocalpse. In all their regalia. White with their veils on, carrying their boxes and the – you know – (*He searches for the word.*)

Jim Smokers?

Felix Yes.

Jim To pacify the bees, I know.

Felix It was strange. No, it was beautiful.

Jim (*smiles*) Was it? (*Jim enjoys the story of the bee-keepers.*)

Felix I was watching from upstairs and the sky was black with bees. But the bee-keepers didn't panic.

Jim No. They wouldn't.

Felix They placed a white sheet on the ground and reached up towards the bees. And what was odd – from where I was upstairs, from that angle, with the blackness of the sky and the whiteness of their suits, it seemed like they lifted right off the ground. It made me – I can't describe it exactly – but it, it made me want to cry.

Pause.

Jim Don't tell Mrs Humble, but there's still some left.

Felix What?

Jim Bees. The ones that got away. They've outwitted her. God love 'em.

Felix But the hive is empty.

Jim No, not in the hive. *Bombus hortorum*. The garden bumblebee. There's a nest underneath the shed. I found it just the other day. At least they look like *hortorums*.

Felix You didn't tell her?

Jim If she wants her flowers, she should be thankful for some friendly neighbourhood bees. Anyway, they'll die off soon. They'll only last the summer, not like the honey-bees. I think we should leave them in peace, don't you?

Felix Yes. Till the end of summer. Yes.

Jim Good lad. It can be our little secret.

Felix I'd better get in now.

Jim Yes. There's quite a gathering in there.

Felix They'll want to see me.

Felix stumbles away, perhaps steadying himself on the hive as he goes. He looks back at Jim.

Jim Nice talking to you, Felix.

Felix nods and exits. Jim starts to hoe around the rose plant.

SCENE TWO

A beautiful sunny day in midsummer. The summer solstice. About two weeks after the funeral.
Jim picks up his gardening implements and exits. As he does so, George Pye enters. Jim looks at him but George does not return the glance. George is a beefy, well-built man of about sixty. He has a large portable CD Walkman on and he carries a jug of Pimms or the equivalent. The headphones are very large. Music –

Glen Miller's 'In the Mood' – plays quietly. He puts the jug down.

George (*he shouts towards the house, rather too loud*) Out here, bunny!

He turns his Walkman up. We hear 'In the Mood' more clearly. He stretches luxuriantly. He pours himself a Pimms, he is already jiggling along to the music. He dances absently around the garden, banging out percussion on the hive. He comes to the rose bush. He tries to pick a rose off the bush. A thorn pricks him.

Bugger. Bloody bugger it. (*He sucks his finger, then rips the flower from the bush.*) Got you, you swine.

He places the rose on the hammock. He checks in his pocket, takes out a ring box. He puts it back in his pocket. This gives him a burst of energy. His moves become more exuberant. He is definitely 'in the mood', dancing as if no one were observing him. He starts conducting the plants of the garden, as if he were Glen Miller. He brings some garden furniture out and sets it up, dancing all the while. Flora enters. She looks radiant in cream. She watches George, amused in spite of herself. He spots her.

Flora George. What are you doing?

George Bunny!

He grabs her and swings her into a jive. For a moment they dance well together. But she is reluctant and tries to stop him after a few extravagant moves.

Flora (*laughing*) Stop it, George.

George Can't hear you, bun.

Flora You great fool! I can't even hear the music.

George Don't need to. Just follow me, bunny.

Flora What if someone saw us – stop it – what if Felix . . .? Turn, it off.

He turns it off. Takes it from his waistband. The music stops.

George He's still here, is he?

Flora Apparently he intends to stay till the end of summer.

George After what he did to you at the funeral. The little shit.

Flora He is my – I can't – anyway, he doesn't seem . . . himself.

George snorts in response. He pours her a glass of Pimms. Flora sits, rearranges herself, undoes a button to catch more sun. She looks at the CD player.

Flora Is that your new toy?

George It's bloody excellent, isn't it? I even wear it when I'm driving.

Flora Isn't that illegal?

George Bollocks! I'm going hi-tec, bun. Stereo, On-Digital, widescreen, DVD, that's me.

Flora No holding you back.

George Rosie bought it for me. I tell you, it comes to something when it's your child telling you to turn your music down.

Flora I take it she's not a fan of the big band.

George Christ no! I love her to bits but she's like her mother. Born without an ounce of swing.

Flora laughs. Pause.

George This is good, Flora. Being out here with you.

Flora Yes.

George I could get used to this. Flora –

Flora (*interrupting*) You haven't said anything, George.

George Eh?

Flora The bruising's completely gone down now.

George What?

Flora My nose.

George (*mock surprise*) Bloody hell!

Flora What?

George It's magnificent!

Flora You hadn't even noticed.

George I had. I was just savouring it. It's bloody tremendous. It's positively Roman.

Flora It's not Roman. I didn't ask for Roman.

George When I say Roman, I mean . . . Neopolitan.

Flora Neopolitan?

George Yes! The Neopolitan nose is soft, with delicately flared nostrils and a certain very appealing button-mushroom quality. As far as noses go, it's a bloody classic. It's the Lamborghini of noses.

Flora Yes, but is it me?

George Let me see . . . And the other side. Yes. It's definitely you.

Flora I mean, does it suit me?

George You're a vision of loveliness.

Flora I don't think I like it.

George Oh bun! After all that.

Flora Oh, I mean the nose is fine. The nose is quite pleasing, but I'm not sure if my face lives up to it. Somehow it makes the rest of me look – tired. I might need a little lift.

She pulls her skin back and up. George takes her hand away.

George You look fine to me.

Flora Well, you're biased. Hand me my cream before my wrinkles reach the point of no return.

George Let me. (*He puts sun-cream on her face.*)

Flora Ah yes, anoint me. That's nice.

George Oh Flora.

Flora Please don't get ardent, George. It's only half past twelve.

George You know what I want, damn it. I know it's too soon, but, I mean bloody hell. I've been waiting in the wings for a long time now.

Flora I know.

George And it doesn't come naturally to me. I'm not a back-seat driver, Flora. It's a terrible shame, a shock about James and everything but you've been worrying about telling him for so long, I think we should just do it. Grab it by the balls. We can wait a few months, but let's not piss about, the sooner the better, bun. Anyway I've already got you the ring.

Flora Really?

298

George I'll make you bloody happy. The words 'pig' and 'shit' spring to mind. In a more classy sort of way.

Flora You're such a romantic, George.

George How do you want me to do it? On bended knee?

Flora Please don't, George, you might never get up again.

George I'll swing from the ruddy trees if you want. Shout it from the rooftops, thatched or otherwise.

Flora This is a small place, George.

George I don't give a bishop's bollock what anyone thinks.

Flora George!

George I mean bloody hell, Flora. It's not as if you were happy with him.

Flora Please don't talk about that.

George He was dull. You told me he was dull.

Flora That was the wrong word to use.

George Look, lover, we've both paid our dues and neither of us is getting any younger.

Flora I don't need reminding of that.

George (*pleadingly*) Bunny, please . . .

Flora Show me the ring.

He takes the box out. She looks at it.

George It's a black opal. Bloody unusual, apparently. I can change it if you don't like it.

Flora Is it old?

George Antique.

Flora Mm. What sort of ring did Mary have?

George I don't remember, it was years ago, some cheap thing, we were completely brassic at the time –

Flora I'm not ready for another ring.

George It's not Mary's ring. Rosie has that.

Flora I don't like the idea of someone having worn it before.

George I can change it, get a new one. I knew I should have let you choose. I've got bugger-all taste.

Flora A diamond might have been nicer. (*She closes the ring box and hands it back to him.*)

George Is this a no?

Flora No. I'll have to think.

George Is this a provisional yes?

Flora We'd have to wait a bit. Till after – till the end of summer.

George You're a star.

Flora You'd have to make an effort. With Felix. I know he's – but I don't want any more upset. I can't take it.

George I like Felix. We just got off on the wrong foot.

Flora What about Rosie?

George She wants what I want.

Flora But after what happened between her and Felix?

George Water under the proverbial.

Flora I haven't ever spoken to Rosie. Properly, I mean.

George Rosie's not a problem. She wants her old ⌐
be happy. They're both old enough and wise enough

Flora Yes, I suppose so.

George We'll have a little party, invite them all.

Flora Nothing showy.

George No, no, discreet. My middle name.

Flora Yes. It's about time we all got civilised.

George Absolutely.

Flora This is not a yes.

George gets the rose he picked earlier and gives it to her.

George It's enough.

She takes the rose, smiles and smells it. Felix enters the garden. He watches his mother. He is wearing his cricket whites but with an old-fashioned coloured tank top over them.

Flora That's funny.

George What?

Flora Doesn't smell of anything.

He takes the flower and smells it.

George 'Course it does.

Flora No. It doesn't. (*She goes to the bush, smells the rest of the flowers.*)

Felix Mother?

Flora Felix! Darling. You made me jump. Come and join us. Felix, you remember George Pye, Rosie's father?

Felix Yes. I do.

George Felix. I was just offering my condolences. I'm very sorry about your father's –

Felix Yes.

Flora Thank you, George. (*to Felix*) You're back very early.

Felix Half-day closing.

Flora On a Monday?

Felix Jean is a very whimsical woman.

She looks at him oddly.

Flora What is that top you're wearing?

Felix Perk of the job.

Flora It doesn't suit you, darling. Felix has been helping Mercy out at the charity shop. I'm not sure why.

Felix Apparently I'm a natural. Jean says I've got a job for life, if I want. I shifted more in two hours than Mercy does in a week.

George Oh yes?

Felix But then it's for a good cause. The Romanian orphans. And I have a particular affinity with them, being half way to orphan status myself. I like the second-hand nature of it all. Used goods do have a special appeal all of their own, don't they? (*He spots the jug of drink.*) Ah, nectar! It's a scorcher today, isn't it? Of course it's the summer solstice. The longest day. It's all downhill from now on. (*He helps himself to a drink.*)

Flora (*a slight edge*) You're very honey-tongued today, Felix . . . But I think you should calm yourself, don't you?

Felix Oh I am calm. I am wonderful. And you are looking ravishing, Mother, if I may say so.

Flora Thank you.

Felix Not even a hint of widow's weeds.

Flora laughs.

Flora (*a little forced*) He's only joking.

Felix Oh yes, it's all in jest. Now how are you? How is your fleet, George Pye?

George What?

Felix Pye's Coaches.

George Well, I'm semi-retired now. Some other bugger does the dog work for me. I still do the odd Oxford run though, if we're short. I'm not proud. Can't quite hang up the old driving gloves, you see.

Felix No, I bet you can't. What was the legend now? 'Travel Pye –' don't tell me – 'travel Pye –'

George (*pleased*) '– if you want to fly.' 'Travel Pye if you want to fly.'

Felix Ah yes. A fleet of Flying Pyes. Did you come up with that?

George I did, as a matter of fact.

Felix Genius. Absolutely inspired.

George Thank you very much.

Felix Only thing is, I remember being rather disappointed the first time I travelled on one of your coaches. It was all curiously earthbound, you see. Not at all P–pye-in-the-sky-ish. But then you weren't driving. Perhaps they needed George himself at the helm to really make them lift off.

Flora It's just as well, Felix. You don't really have a head for heights.

George When are you going back to your – erm, studies?

Flora He hasn't completely decided, have you? A little break will do him good.

George Astrology, isn't it?

Felix What?

George Your bag. Astrology.

Felix No.

Flora It's like astrology, darling. It's not a million miles away.

Felix Theoretical astrophysics. I think the differences between the two could be measured in light years.

George It's all the same to me.

Flora And me. But he's a clever boy.

George Don't believe in it myself, anyway.

Felix What?

George Horoscopes. A load of balls.

Felix Really? I bet you're a Taurean then, aren't you?

George (*as if he is getting the joke*) Ah! Yes! Good one.

Felix Yes, definitely Taurus, the b–bull. Born in the month of May. When's your birthday, George Pye? When's his b–birthday, Mother?

Flora Well, you know, it is May. It is May, isn't it, George? But you could be on the cusp.

Felix Bullseye. Perhaps you're right, George Pye. Perhaps astrology is, after all, my b–bag. Here I was thinking that all the other sciences were woolly and descriptive, that there was something p–pure and exact and fundamental about theoretical physics, that it would unveil for me the secrets of the universe but now I see I was mistaken. I should have got myself a sparkly waistcoat and a pair of coloured contact lenses and started b–bandying a few predictions about. At the summer solstice, with the happy conjunction of Venus and Saturn, all Taureans born on the cusp will find themselves going out on a romantic limb.

Flora Stop it, Felix.

George Look, son –

Felix I am not your son. Did you know my father well?

George In passing . . . Your father was a very decent man.

Felix Decent. Decent? Yes. I'm compiling a list of adjectives, you see. My father's true nature is proving very difficult to pin down. Decent. Upright. Upstanding. Clean-living. Respectable. But not b–brave, no, we wouldn't go as far as b–brave. No, brave doesn't come into it. Just outside the spectrum. Although there is passion there, yes, give him his dues, he was passionate about his bees.

Flora Felix. I want you to stop this now. I am asking you nicely.

George Don't worry, Flora. I must be on the road.

Felix The Egyptians believed the first bee was created from a teardrop of the sun god, Ra. Did you know that, George Pye?

George No, I didn't. Thank you for the drink, Flora.

Felix The sun cried bees. I like that. One minute it's raining cats and dogs. The next it's shining bees. You could say it about today, couldn't you? It's shining bees. Except technically the bees have gone, banished by my mother. The bee-loud glade is suddenly beeless. Apparently sans bee.

Flora I don't know why he's suddenly so attached to the idea of the bees. You used to be more against them than me.

Felix No I didn't.

Flora You hated the noise, the droning, while you were studying. And you point-blank refused to eat any more honey.

George I ought to be going. Just a 'flying visit'.

Flora Yes. Yes. I'll see you out, George. I'm sorry about this.

Felix Don't forget your flower, Mother. It's already beginning to wilt.

Flora Don't push your luck, Felix Humble.

Felix I wasn't aware I was lucky, Mother.

Flora takes the rose and exits. George follows her.

Fly, Mr Pye, fly.

George turns round sharply. Flora has gone.

George I don't give a shit if you piss your life away but you keep away from my daughter. You've fucked her life up once already and you're not doing it again.

Felix (*quietly*) No.

*George exits. Felix walks upstage. There is a very
quiet humming sound. He reacts to it, as if it were
tinnitus in his ears.*

Oh no. Please.

Flora comes back on.

Ma.

*She sees that George has left his CD player behind.
She tuts and picks it up, then sits and puts the
headphones on and turns the CD player on. We hear
music quietly: Glen Miller's 'Don't Sit under the Apple
Tree'. Perhaps she mouths the words to the song.
There is a lighting change. It is as though time slows
down for a moment. She cannot hear Felix.*

Ma, I keep dreaming that I am at home and I am a baby
and you place me on the lawn. Ever so gently you place
me down on my tummy. On the lush, green grass. And
you are smiling and I am complete. And then suddenly
it shifts and I am like I am now. And I lie myself down
on the grass on my stomach and it is green and cool and
it takes my weight. And I p–place a gun in my mouth.
It stops the kickb–back this way. I know this. And I
want to b–blow my b–brains into a thousand p–particles.
I want to see the green lawn turn red. And I look at you
standing there above me. And you are smiling.

*Suddenly Flora senses him still near her. She switches
off the music. The humming continues quietly.*

Flora Felix, don't lurk.

Felix The grass is so green this year, isn't it, Ma?

Flora I'm not speaking to you!

*Flora takes the CD player off and exits with it. Felix
is left on his own. Slowly the humming sound builds.
Now it is as though time is speeding up.*

Felix No, please. I can't b–bear it. I can't –

He goes upstage to where the hosepipe is snaked.
He picks it up and slowly he places it round his neck.
The humming increases to a terrible pitch. He pulls the
hose tight. He feels what this feels like. Time passes.

SCENE THREE

Mid-July.
Jim comes on. He is carrying a tray of seedlings and
some compost, and a trowel. He proceeds during the
scene to plant the seedlings in pots. He is whistling
'Don't Sit under the Apple Tree'. He looks at Felix. Felix
sees him. He is embarrassed. The humming stops. Felix
looses the hose from around his neck.

Felix I'm sorry . . . I was just – I was experimenting . . .

Pause.

I often use a garden hose. As an analogy, I mean.

Jim Oh yes?

Felix Yes. Yes. With superstring theory there need to be
six or seven extra dimensions. We can't see them but it's
like with a garden hose. If you stretch it out between two
posts in a field and then you walk half a mile away and
look back, it just looks like a one-dimensional line.

Jim I'll take that off you, shall I? (*Jim takes the hose off*
him and starts to wind it up again.)

Felix Yes. Yes. But if you look at the hose through
binoculars, if you magnify it, a second dimension – one
that is in the shape of a circle curled round the hose –
becomes visible. So in the same way there could be extra
dimensions in space but you can't see them because

they're small and curled up, furled around one another.
You see?

Jim Mmm . . . Well. Knowing my luck, they'll ban them
soon anyway.

Felix What?

Jim Hosepipes. Last time we had a summer like this, by
this time in July there was all sorts of rules.

Felix Yes.

Jim I know lots of people ignore a ban, but I'm not like
that. I watched all the plants flounder. And then I go
next door but one and they've got a symphony of
sprinklers going off. Drowning the plants, they were.
I wanted to report them.

Felix Garden rage.

Jim But then their plants got blight and died anyway.
What goes around comes around.

Pause.

Felix I haven't seen any of the bees yet.

Jim The drones will be out and about soon. Buzzing
round the queen. Seven or eight of them joining the mile-
high club. Then after they've done their bit she flies away
with their torn-off genitals still attached to her. That's
women's lib for you.

Felix smiles.

Felix I'd like to see them. Before I go. I'd feel better,
I think.

Jim You will.

Felix I just can't seem to – I can't seem to ask the right
questions . . . I need to make a decision about what
I should do next.

Jim You want to stop asking all the questions.

Felix But it's so hard – with my work, I must question everything. I must –

Jim stops what he's doing. He looks at Felix.

Jim Felix, you know, bumblebees shouldn't be able to fly. Aerodynamically they're too big, their wings are set up all wrong. They don't obey the laws of physics. But they fly anyway.

Mercy comes out into the garden. She looks around, although she does not address Jim directly.

Mercy Doesn't the garden look lovely?

Jim looks at Mercy. She smiles but does not look at him.

Jim Thank you.

Then he works on in the garden unheeded. Felix glances at him from time to time but he is absorbed in his work.

Mercy Such a beautiful day. I can't remember a summer like it. Mind you, I wish it would rain . . . Now I just popped round with those clothes for you. Jean says she doesn't want any money for them. I've put the bag in your room. But you know I don't think the jacket will fit you, dear. Unless you like a very snug fit.

Felix It'll be fine, Mercy, thank you.

Mercy Because we've just had another suit in. It's a bit worn round the seat region and the lapels are on the wide side, but apart from that –

Felix (*a little too sharply*) I don't want another suit. I want the suit you brought me.

Mercy Well, you know your own mind. (*absently looking at the garden*) Isn't that African lily marvellous?

Jim *Agapanthus umbellatus.*

Mercy But then I love all the lilies. White lilies.

Jim *Lilium candidum.*

Mercy Tiger lilies.

Jim *Lilium tigrinum.*

Mercy And the sweet peas. I do love sweet peas.

Jim *Lathyrus odoratus.*

Felix You know all the names.

Mercy Yes.

Jim I only know the right names for my little world.

Mercy Even from here, they smell heavenly, don't they? (*She stands awkwardly for a few moments.*)

Mercy So. What are your plans?

Felix What do you mean?

Mercy Your mother tells me you're not going back till the end of summer?

Felix Does she?

Mercy Have you fixed on an exact date?

Felix No.

Mercy Your mother says you're taking pills.

Felix Oh.

Mercy What are they for?

Felix doesn't reply.

Mercy Have you stopped taking them?

Felix Are you on a retainer?

Mercy What?

Felix Or do you just enjoy it, doing duties for her, carrying out her little schemes –

Mercy Felix –

Felix Of course she won't do anything that might chip her nail polish.

Mercy Your mother didn't ask me to do anything for her.

Felix Mercy. You are not a convincing liar.

Mercy It's only because she cares –

Felix How exactly do you fit into the equation, Mercy?

Mercy I've known you since you were born. Your mother and I would play with you here in this garden. I'm a very close, personal friend of your mother's.

Felix Ah yes. I see. You like to orbit round her?

Mercy Yes, no, I don't know.

Felix You should be careful. That's the problem with black holes. The gravitational attraction is so strong you can't resist. But they warp you, they pull you out of shape.

Mercy Please don't be sharp with me, Felix. I am of a very nervous disposition.

Felix I'm sorry.

Mercy It's beyond the pale, really it is.

Felix I'm sorry, Mercy.

Mercy Is it your work? Is everything all right with your studies?

Felix Fine.

Mercy Are you a professor yet, dear?

Felix No. Research fellow.

Mercy Really? Isn't that wonderful? And I remember when you failed your eleven-plus. What is it that you're looking for again?

Felix What?

Mercy In your studies?

Felix It's complicated.

Mercy Oh! I like hearing all those funny words.

Felix I'm working on M-theory – trying to unify the various strands of superstring theory.

Jim Go on.

Mercy Mmm.

Felix At the root of everything we believe, I believe – a billionth of a billionth of a billionth of the size of an atom, so many noughts it would dazzle you, the perfect Planck length – there is a loop or a filament of energy – what we call a string – which is the fundamental building block of the universe. And these strings are stretched like the strings on a violin and they're vibrating to and fro.

Mercy Really?

Felix I know they're there – the strings – the superstrings – and they will bring everything together into a perfect elegant supersymmetry – the jittery, frenzied world of quantum mechanics and the gentle curving geometry of gravity. You see we know the rules for the big things like the cosmos and we know the rules for the small things like the atom, but the rules don't agree – it's the superstrings that will bring the forces together. The superstrings will give us a quantum theory of gravity – that's what I want, what we all want . . . You know, I'm so close, I can hear them! I can hear the little vibrating strings inside my head. Even though I can't prove absolutely that they're there, I can hear the patterns they're making, like they're ringing in my ears.

Jim The music of the spheres.

Felix Mmm. I've just run out of the maths. The equations don't exist for what I can already sense. The excitation modes – the ringing has too many layers I can't – hold all the notes, all the variables, all the harmonies in my head. But one day soon, I hope, I'll have it, M-theory, the mother of all theories, a unified field theory. The theory of everything. And once I've done that – I'll be able to rest.

Jim Yes.

Mercy Well, isn't that something, Felix? I mean, if you had to research anything, everything would be the thing to research, wouldn't it? If my brain wasn't so puddled, I'd probably be after it too.

Felix I'm just waiting for my moment of intuition. My Eureka moment.

Mercy I'm sure it will come.

Jim It will.

Felix Einstein called his moment the happiest thought of his life.

Jim You'd better try and have some more happy thoughts then, hadn't you?

Jim moves further away. Felix smiles as he exits.

Mercy Divine inspiration, that's what you need. Even when I'm arranging the flowers in church I pray for a bit of that.

Felix I can already sense what it would feel like.

Mercy Can you?

Felix I don't mind if it's a quiet moment.

Mercy No. Quiet moments can be very agreeable.

Felix Stephen Hawking had his breakthrough when he was getting into bed. But because of his motor neurone disease it took him an age. Throwing back the sheets, plugging in the electric blanket, hauling himself up, tucking himself in, required a gargantuan effort. The nerve cells in his spinal cord were disintegrating, his muscles were playing tricks on him, but all the while his brain was buzzing with complex equations. They went showering through him, like Shakespearean sonnets. By the time he set his alarm clock he'd cracked it.

Mercy He should have had a duvet. I resisted for a long time, but they're so easy. You just throw them on.

Felix Mercy, you are an original.

Mercy What a lovely thing to say!

Felix It's true.

Mercy You'll have your moment, Felix. Probably when you least expect it. Bingo! There it'll be: 'Humble's unified theory of everything.'

Felix I have a terrible fear that I will go through life just missing it. Walking past the love of my life.

Mercy Well, we've all done that.

Felix Have you ever seen an apple fall? Actually fall?

Mercy I don't know. I must have done, mustn't I?

Felix goes over to the apple tree.
  During this Flora comes out and listens. She carries a gift. Felix and Mercy do not see her.

Felix I've never seen it. I once sat out here, I was ten, I must have just learned about Newton and the force of gravity and I thought I'd watch an apple fall from a tree – I wanted to see that moment – well, what would it be, say, the half second that it takes an apple to drop four metres. I sat out here for eight hours. Nothing. In the end my mother made me go in for my tea. I wasn't even hungry – I nearly choked the food down. I came back out after half an hour and there were three of them on the floor.

Mercy Well, Newton just got lucky.

Felix And he didn't have my mother.

Mercy I'm sure she didn't mean it.

Flora On no, it was clearly my fault.

Mercy (*jumping*) Flora!

Flora You don't know this, Mercy, because you have never been blessed with children, but ultimately everything that goes wrong in your child's life can be laid squarely at your feet. It's what they call chaos theory, isn't it, Felix? I sneezed in public in 1968 and as a result my son found it difficult to connect in social situations for the rest of his life.

Mercy He's just shy.

Flora I picked up a sweet wrapper that he dropped when he was three and consequently he's a total failure with women.

Mercy He went out with Rosie Pye.

Felix This is not chaos theory, Mother.

Flora Oh well, pardon me for failing in my use of scientific terminology. I didn't have the benefit of your very expensive private education. Mercy, do you mind leaving us for a minute? I want to talk to my son alone.

Mercy Of course. (*Mercy exits.*)

Felix (*to the exiting Mercy*) End of your commission. Report back for duty later on.

Flora Felix –

Felix You've got her well-trained, Mother. She's like a very earnest springer spaniel. She flushes the wild fowl off the water so you can come and take a pop at them.

Flora She has precious little else to keep her occupied.

Felix I hope she gets rewarded.

Flora Of course. She gets to bask in my reflected glory . . . You know, paranoia is very unattractive in a man, Felix.

Felix What do you expect with my education? I have been taught to apply the uncertainty principle to every p–problem.

Flora Do you know how utterly bored I am by all this science? I have been doubly unlucky in my life. To marry a biologist and give birth to a physicist. Who on earth said God didn't play dice?

Felix Do you want me to go?

Flora If I had been Marie Curie I would have used my bunsen burner to make *crème brûlée*.

Felix Just tell me to go.

Flora I found three more grey hairs this morning. They were not there a week ago.

Felix What do you want me to do about that?

Flora I want you to – you are always welcome, this is your home but I can't bear to see you lolling about out here –

Felix Lolling? Is that what I am doing?

Flora I don't know. I have no idea what you are doing. You never speak to me properly.

Felix You never listen.

Flora Stop it! Stop this! I can't bear it! Your father would have hated this. (*Pause. She touches him lightly.*) Do you remember the first time we took you to prep school? I didn't want to leave you there, you seemed so small, but your father said I had to be strong. And I stood and waved to you while you walked up the long driveway and James was telling me that we ought to go but I didn't stop waving. I wanted you to know that I wouldn't go away that easily. And you got smaller and smaller and further away until you were nothing but a black dot, but I kept on waving. Even when you'd stopped being a black dot, I kept on waving.

Pause.

Flora (*handing him the gift*) This is for you.

Felix It's not my b–birthday.

Flora No, well. It's not a birthday present.

Felix I don't need presents.

Flora No, well you don't need to need it. That is the appeal of gifts.

Felix What is it?

Flora Why are you always so analytical? Really, you were like this when you were a child. Why don't you open it?

> *He opens it. Flora smiles a little. He takes out a smallish earthenware pot with a lid on it. He is obviously a little baffled by the gift.*

Felix What –?

Flora It's a copy of an ancient honey-pot. Etruscan or Egyptian or something. It's not really to my taste. But your father bought it for me. I thought you would like it.

Felix Thank you. (*Felix smiles a little, he takes off the lid.*)

Flora Careful!

> *He inadvertently spills a little of the contents – a fine powdery ash.*

It's filled quite full.

Felix Oh, Jesus.

Flora What?

Felix Is this what I think it is?

Flora I didn't like the other receptacle they sent them in.

Felix You mean *the urn*?

Flora It was a very ugly, horrible vulgar tinny thing. I thought a honey-pot would be much more appropriate.

Felix This is him?

Flora The ashes, yes.

Felix Oh, Jesus.

Flora You criticised me for throwing his belongings out.

Felix I just spilled some! I just lost a bit of his nose or something.

Flora I lost more transferring it to the new pot. I had to use a funnel.

Felix Jesus Christ.

Flora They got stuck to the sides and I had to rinse them out.

Felix I don't believe this.

Flora I've thrown the funnel away.

Felix I think you're psychotic.

Flora Oh well, I can't do anything right.

Felix This is my father. You have just handed me my father in a pot.

Flora Don't be so melodramatic.

Felix You wrapped him up, for God's sake.

Flora I . . . I . . . thought it would make it more formal – more precious.

Felix You wrapped him up in 'Happy Birthday' paper.

Flora Well, it was all I had to hand . . . I thought this would help. I thought you could say the words that you were going to say. I thought that was what was making you so miserable. I thought that we could have a little ceremony. And that then you could scatter him.

Felix What's left of him. You tipped half of him down the sink.

Flora Of course there's no guarantee that this is your father. These crematorium places are often very slipshod in their arrangements. And let's face it, one man's ashes is . . . another man's ashes.

Felix What are you saying?

Flora I am saying that your father is gone. I am trying to help you come to terms with this fact.

Felix Well, I'm sorry, Mother. I am very sorry that I do not have the same facility as you for letting go –

Flora I said my goodbyes at his funeral like any sane person would.

Felix You spent nearly forty years of your life with him –

Flora You are a selfish, selfish boy. I know what this is about. I know why you couldn't speak about your father. Because you think that you are better than him. What on earth could you have said? He was only a teacher, after all. Head of Biology. And at a girl's school, of all places! Oh, and he dabbled in bees. Some might call it a pathetically small life. What did he ever achieve, compared to you?

Felix Mother –

Flora So you look down on him and me and this place. It's all too middling for you with your grand ideas and your big life.

Felix That's not true.

Flora Well, you don't have to say anything. I know what you think. Just scatter the ashes and be on your way. That can be an end to it. Your father's car is out there, I'll give you the keys.

Felix I'm not ready to scatter them.

Flora Well, give them to me then, and I'll scatter them.

She tries to grab the ashes off him. There is a small kerfuffle.

Felix Mother, please. Stop it. I'm not ready yet. Just give him b–b–back. Let him b–b–b–be.

Flora All right. All right. This is so undignified. And mind my nose. I've just paid hundreds of pounds for it.

There is the noise of a car horn off. Flora breaks off. She takes a small compact out and checks her appearance.

Felix What are you doing?

Flora I'm going out now. I'm leaving you to your own devices.

Felix Is it George P–pye?

Flora He has been a very good friend to me since James died but he is afraid to even come near the house for fear of encountering you.

Felix Don't go.

She puts lipstick on.

Flora He's taking me out of myself.

Felix Stay here with me.

Flora Don't begrudge me my little bit of pleasure. At least I'm making an effort.

Felix P–please, Ma. Don't.

Flora Felix? What is it? Why ever not?

Felix I don't like him.

Flora No, well, I'm sure the feeling is mutual. After what you did to his daughter.

The car horn goes off again.

Felix I didn't do anything – it was –

Flora Felix. Must you always have the last word? Do you not realise that the last word is my prerogative?

Felix goes to speak and thinks better of it. Flora smoothes down her dress.

I'm going to have a lunch party later on in the summer. Just a small group of people. I hope you will be able to come. But if you are going to be in one of your moods then I would rather you didn't. (*She goes to exit. As she does:*) And you should be wearing a hat in this sun.

She exits. Felix stands. The humming begins again. He looks at the honey-pot. He takes off the lid and stares inside. He looks as though he might be about to scatter it but he thinks better of it. He puts the lid back on and cradles the pot to him. He walks slowly off. The humming ceases.

SCENE FOUR

The stage is empty. An apple falls from the tree just after Felix has exited.

Just afterwards a young woman comes into the garden. She is in her early thirties, healthy-looking but quite plain. It is Rosie Pye. She does not pay much attention to her appearance. She looks around the garden. She sees the apple on the floor. She goes and picks it up. She polishes it on her clothes. Then she sits and takes a huge bite out of it. She swings herself on the hammock and continues to eat the apple in a hearty fashion.

Felix enters the garden again. He is wearing a sun-hat and still carrying the ashes. He talks to himself and occasionally addresses the pot. Rosie stops swinging and eating and watches him with increasing horror.

323

During this scene the sun starts to set.

Felix (*intoning*) James Humb–ble was a b–b–biologist and a b–b–bee-keeper. And a husb–band, and a father. A b–b–beloved –

Rosie It's only a suggestion, but perhaps you should go for fewer 'b's.

Felix nearly jumps out of his skin, almost drops the pot.

Felix Oh, Jesus God!

Rosie (*proffering him the apple*) Do you want a b–b–bite?

Felix Rosie. Rosie. Rosie.

Rosie Well, that's a start.

Felix Yes, I . . . I was hoping, I should have, I meant to, I really wanted – I thought ab–bout coming to see you, I started to write, I wanted to phone . . .

Rosie What about e-mail? Did you consider that?

Felix I'm sorry.

Rosie Can you put the pot down, please? Just for a minute.

He does so, reluctantly. Rosie goes up to him and slaps him hard across the face.

There. I've been saving that up for a long time. Yes. We can be friends again now. Here. (*She hands him back the pot.*) Now tell me what's wrong.

Felix Rosie –

Rosie Oh no. Not that tone of voice, please.

Felix But I want to explain.

Rosie It's all right, Felix. I fell in love with you, you weren't as in love with me, you tried to be, you failed, you ran away because you weren't emotionally evolved enough to talk to me about it, you threw yourself into work, I didn't wash my hair for five months, blah, blah, blah, you failed to write, I got angry, I got over it. In a nutshell.

Felix Right.

Rosie I tried therapy but it was shit. Tae kwon do was much better. A short course in the ancient Korean art of hand-and-foot fighting. Worked wonders. I wasn't very precise in my movements but apparently my battle cries were very convincing. Now take that hat off and let me look at you.

Felix does so.

That's good.

Felix What?

Rosie I'm not in love with you any more. I thought I wasn't but I couldn't be sure until I saw you again.

Felix It's b–been a long time.

Rosie Seven years, five months, fourteen days.

Felix Oh God.

Rosie I'm joking. I've no idea exactly how long it's been. It's about seven years. My dad told me you were around again. And against all the odds, I got a slight itch.

Felix I've got fat.

Rosie Mm.

Felix I don't look good.

Rosie Mmm.

Felix I haven't b–b–been on top of things.

Rosie Since your dad died?

Felix B–b–before, b–b–but worse since.

Rosie What's with the stutter?

Felix It's funny, sometimes I don't have it. Some days it's fine. I used to do it when I was little but then recently it came b–back. I had to p–present a p–paper, ab–bout b–b–b–black holes. I was supposed to do a follow-up about the B–b–b–big B–b–b–b –

Rosie Bang?

Felix Thank you. I never got that far. My father died so I left. I've b–been at home ever since.

    Pause.

I don't think I can go b–back.

Rosie You've given up?

Felix Every time I try to – I hear this ringing –

Rosie (*interrupting*) That's great, that is!

Felix What?

Rosie You left me to become the great white hope of theoretical physics and now you're jacking it in. It was really much better for my self-esteem when I knew I'd been chucked in the pursuit of a Nobel Prize.

Felix It's p–percolating my b–brain, Rosie.

Rosie You're just upset about your dad.

Felix I wasn't close to him.

Rosie Of course you were.

Felix For me, it was always my mother. It was always about her. She b–burnt more br–brightly. Eclipsed him.

Rosie Mothers have a tendency to do that, Felix.

Felix It's like my mother was the big force – gently warping everything around her. And my father was the little force, fizzing away quietly on a microscopic level. But I can't bring them together. I'm trying to understand the extreme conditions that would have brought them together. I mean, I know the geography of it. It was outside the exam halls of the School of B–biology. London University. My father had just finished his Finals and he walked out and my mother was just p–passing. She'd p–paused to light a cigarette. She was on her way to sign up to a modelling agency. He went up to her and asked her if she'd dropped from the sky. She never got to the agency.

Rosie That doesn't sound so extreme.

Felix But that's not the physics! The physics of what attracted them and what kept them together.

Rosie Maybe you are what kept them together.

Felix looks at her a moment.

Felix (*shaking his head*) There are too many questions. And now all I have is this b–b–bloody p–pot.

Rosie What?

Felix He's in here.

Rosie looks confused, then slightly disgusted.

Rosie Oh.

Felix Do you want to look?

Rosie Does it smell?

Felix No, of course not.

Rosie Just quickly then.

He lifts off the lid for her. She sniffs slightly.

Felix Don't sniff at him.

Rosie We buried Mum. I prefer that.

Felix I feel strangely attached.

Rosie It's got bits in it.

Felix shuts it rapidly.

Felix No it hasn't.

Rosie I don't think this is healthy, Felix.

Felix I didn't say it was healthy. Did I say it was healthy?

Rosie When my mum died, I could have fallen apart, I really could. But I didn't allow myself to dwell on – the fact of her death. I know it sounds simplistic – but I made myself think about all the happy times we had together – (*She stops herself. Pause.*) It does get easier, Felix. Time doesn't heal, but it accommodates.

Felix I look forward to that, then.

Rosie I'm trying to help you –

Felix It's all right, I'll get myself a book. 'Happy bereavements. How to grieve in twelve easy steps.' I'll be over it in no time.

Rosie Fine, you do that. Good luck. (*She goes to go.*)

Felix No, please, Rosie. You're right. I'm sorry.

Pause.

It's just I – can't remember – a time of being close, you know. I mean feeling close, feeling – like he was my father . . . The only good memory I can think of is watching the Apollo moon-landings with him.

He stops. She coaxes him further.

Rosie Yes?

Felix I was in my astronaut phase.

Rosie laughs.

Felix I know, I know, but I was only seven . . . It's still so clear – it's four in the morning, the latest I've ever stayed up in my whole life. I can barely keep my eyes open but then it's the countdown and he reaches out and he takes hold of my hand. And it's like a charge passes from him to me, like he super-adrenalates me. I know this is something huge. I'm suddenly wide awake. We don't speak. But I look at him and he's crying. I am seven years old and I can't b–believe it. I can't b–believe my father is crying . . .

Rosie looks at him and then leans in to him and kisses him on the lips.

Felix What are you doing?

Rosie Put him down. (*She takes the pot out of his hand.*)

Felix I don't understand.

Rosie You need to get out of your head, Felix. (*She kisses him again.*)

Felix I really don't think you should be doing this.

Rosie It's all right, I'm a nurse.

Felix No you're not.

Rosie Yes I am. I trained. After you left.

Felix Did you?

Rosie The world didn't stop turning, Felix.

Felix No, of course not.

Rosie I'm training to be a midwife now. You get more glory. When's the last time you had sex, Felix?

Felix Are you asking that in your professional capacity?

Rosie It's been a long time, hasn't it?

Felix (*a lie*) No.

Rosie I'm not in love with you, you know.

Felix Then why are you doing this?

Rosie Because I'm not in love with you.

Felix That doesn't make sense.

Rosie You can't apply logic to everything. Even in your vacuum-packed little world.

Felix No.

Rosie Take off your tank top.

Felix I'm not doing this.

She takes his top off.

Get off!

Rosie Yes you are.

Felix You can't force me.

Rosie You'll really enjoy it.

Felix I really really won't.

Rosie Just lie back and think of the Big Bang.

Felix Please. Please. Stop. You're scaring me.

Rosie stops what she is doing.

Rosie I just wanted, I thought it would take you out of yourself.

Felix I know. And you're – beautiful, brilliant, better than me –

Rosie At least it's shocked you out of your stutter.

Felix I'm sorry.

Rosie You were going to name a star after me. You were going to find a new star and call it Rosie's Star.

Felix I only work on stars after they've collapsed.

Rosie Well, then you could have named a black hole after me. I'm not fussy.

Felix 'Rosie's hole.'

Rosie Some people would find that curiously appropriate.

Felix You have always been absolutely yourself. That is why I loved you.

Rosie I should bloody well hope so.

Felix Look at me, Rosie. I'm fat, I'm – look at me.

Rosie I don't care. Sometimes time stands still. Just for a moment.

Felix goes up to her and kisses her tentatively.

Felix I loved the way you used to sleep with both your arms flung above your head. I think about that a lot.

Rosie Felix. You liked me when I was asleep because I was quiet.

He kisses her again. It gets awkwardly passionate. Rosie breaks off. She picks up the pot and moves it to a place of safety.

Sorry, Daddy Humble. If you could look away. (*She walks back in a mock-sexy way towards him.*) Ten. Nine. Eight. Seven. Six. Five. Four. Three. Two. One. (*She straddles him.*) Houston, we have lift off.

There is the noise of a car pulling up outside.

Oh, Felix. Take me to the long grass. Please.

Felix The long grass?

Rosie The long grass.

He lifts her up suddenly and carries her to the hammock. It is all a bit clumsy and improvised.

Rosie My big brave astronaut.

Felix I think I'm out of my depth.

Rosie I'll super-adrenalate you.

Felix I don't want to take any more clothes off.

Rosie I'd forgotten what you tasted like.

Felix I don't even know if it's fully operational down there any more.

Rosie You taste like fruit.

Felix You might not be able to find it. You might need the Hubble Telescope.

Rosie Apricots. Yes. Ripe apricots.

Rosie laughs throatily. Felix stops suddenly.

Felix What's that? What's that?

Rosie What?

The sound of laughter off. Flora and George are arriving back in high spirits.

George (*off; singing*)
A–B–C–D–E–F–G–H
I got a gal in Kalamazoo
Don't wanna boast
But I know she's the toast of Kalamazoo
Years have gone by, my my how she flew
I liked her looks when I carried her books
In Kalamazoozoozoo.

Flora (*off, laughing*) George.

Felix Oh God!

Rosie Don't panic.

They lie quietly in the hammock or run to a place where they cannot be immediately observed. It is quite dark by now. A moment then George lurches into the garden. He is fairly drunk. He does not see them.

George Bun, bun! Bunny girl. (*He almost stumbles into the hive. He knocks on it.*) Anyone in there? Or have you all buzzed off? (*He is very amused by his joke.*) We got the better of you, you little bastards. Buzz. Buzz. (*He starts to buzz disdainfully, then laughs so asthmatically he has to lie down on the grass.*) Just need a little rest. (*He looks at the sky.*) Bugger me. Look at the size of it. The moon is out for us tonight, bunny girl. Bunny! Come and look at this.

He starts to sing or whistle the tune to Glen Miller's 'Moonlight Serenade' loudly, while kicking his legs in the air occasionally. Flora enters from upstage. She does not come right into the garden. She is a little tipsy. George lies on the grass and sticks his arms in the air.

George Do you wanna dance?

Flora George! Be quiet, you'll wake up my thirty-five-year-old. (*She laughs.*)

George Bunny, the sky is falling on me. I require your urgent assistance.

She giggles, then hushes herself.

Flora No, no, shushy. I'm making some coffee.

George No coffee. I'm allergic. I need your urgent-lying-down-here assistance.

Flora giggles.

Flora I'm not lying down anywhere.

George Why in God's name not?

Flora I'll get wet. I never get wet.

George Oh no, bun. Look it's bone dry, dry as toast here.

Flora Keep the noise down, Georgy.

George Shushy! Georgy is very shushy now.

Flora Come and get your coffee.

She exits. During the next he staggers to his feet.

George Don't go, bun . . . Look at that wonderful arse!

She waggles it for him and then exits.

Bunny! It's very, very dry. It's a ruddy heatwave. We're in a drought, bunny. I'm dying of thirst. (*He is on his feet, but still a bit wobbly.*) It's a bloody desert out here. Needs irrigating. (*He undoes his trousers and urinates in a zigzag fashion across the lawn.*) This is a very dry bit. You want to talk to the sod who looks after your garden for you, bun. 'S very, very patchy. It's a good job I'm so full of piss. (*He laughs and then he comes across the pot of ashes.*) Who left a bloody pot in the middle of here? Bloody pisspot. (*He urinates a bit on it and then laughs*

334

and steps daintily around it. To the pot:) Excuse me.
Much obliged. (*He does his trousers up.*) Bun! I've done
this garden a big favour, I can tell you. It's positively lush
now.

> *He exits unsteadily. After a pause, Rosie sits up. She
> does her top up, straightens herself out.*

Rosie I hope he's not going to drive.

Felix We've got to stop this.

Rosie Well, he says he drives better when he's rat-arsed.
He says it doesn't matter if you live in the country.

Felix No. My mother. And him.

Rosie What?

Felix She's making a fool of herself. She doesn't know
what she's doing. She's b–bereaved.

Rosie Are you serious?

Felix I know he's your father, but he's taking advantage
of her.

Rosie You really don't know?

Felix What?

Rosie This has been going on for years. Everyone knows
about it.

Felix What?

Rosie They've been having an affair for years. Five or
six at least. Look, I thought you knew. I'm sorry.

Felix But this is terrible.

Rosie Felix, if you're like me, you'll keep out of it.
They're old enough to know their own minds.

Felix This is – this is –

Rosie This is not about you. Or me. I'm sorry, I've really got to go.

Felix No, please, Rosie, stay and talk to me. I have to talk to you ab–bout this.

Rosie My mum died a long time ago. My dad injected her with a sixth of a grain of morphine every four hours. She begged him to kill her, but he wouldn't. I don't like your mother, but I want him to be happy. He deserves to be happy.

Felix No, don't leave me, Rosie.

Rosie I have to. I've got to get back for the babysitter.

Felix What? Oh yes. I'm sorry. Your baby! You haven't said anything about your baby.

Rosie I don't remember the conversation ever being steered in the direction of my life.

Felix I'm sorry – I wasn't thinking. Tell me about your . . . baby.

Rosie (*curt*) Well, she's not a baby any more, thank you for asking.

Felix Oh. Right. I'm sorry – I'd forgotten – not forgotten – it had slipped my – I can't imagine you – with a child –

Rosie Thank you.

Felix No, I mean – I don't know what I mean. I'm sorry.

Rosie So you did know about her?

Felix Yes. Yes. My mother told me you'd had a child, not long after –

Rosie (*quickly, quietly*) No, not long after.

Felix But I was in the middle of, you know – and I should have written to congratulate you – but I didn't know if it was appropriate.

Rosie No.

Felix How old is she now?

Rosie (*slowly, looking at Felix*) She's nearly seven. Her name is Felicity. And yes, she's just like her father.

Felix What? What? Rosie? Are you saying . . .?

Rosie For someone who is supposed to have a brilliant mind, you really are slow on the uptake, aren't you?

Felix But my mother said – she said you'd – she said you were with –

He trails off. Rosie smiles wryly.

Rosie And Felix always believes everything his mother tells him. (*She goes to go.*) I'll see you around.

Felix Wait, Rosie. I need to talk about this. You can't just –

Rosie Felix, do your trousers up, eh?

Rosie exits. Felix stands there. He does his trousers up slowly. The humming starts again but it is more dissonant now. The humming increases in volume.

Felix I can't be her – I'm not a – I don't even have a –

He lies himself face down on the lawn on his stomach by his father's ashes. He stretches himself out.
    Suddenly a light is shone in his face. He looks up blinkingly. Jim, the gardener walks on. He is holding a torch and a packet of salt. He walks up to Felix lying in the middle of the lawn. The humming starts to recede or become more harmonious.

337

Jim Hello. (*He shows him the salt.*) I was just looking for slugs.

Felix (*indicating himself*) Bingo.

He holds out a hand and helps him up. Jim shines his torchlight once more round the garden. It is almost black except for the torchlight. He shines the torch on the hive. He lingers for a moment. Then the light snaps off. The humming stops.

End of Act One.

Act Two

Late summer.

As for the first act, except now the garden is set for a party. There is a large table which has been laid for five people. Flora has gone to quite a lot of effort. During this act the light fades very slowly.

Jim is there. He is tidying up round the garden. He sees the pot of ashes on the floor. He absently picks it up and places it on the table. He exits at the same time as Mercy enters. Perhaps he makes way for her.

Mercy comes out, carrying a very large bowl of soup, with a ladle. Her shoes are a little too high and she proceeds with extreme caution. She is dressed rather eccentrically for the party and in a state of excitement.

Mercy (*shouts back towards the house*) I can manage! (*She places the soup and ladle on the table. Shouts back:*) Oh it looks heavenly out here, Flora. (*She puts out her hand to check for rain. Shouts back:*) I think it'll hold out, you know. (*She adjusts several settings on the table. Shouts back:*) We're a chair short, Flora. (*She waits for a response. There is no response. She sighs, looks around and sees the gardening chair that Jim sat on earlier. She brings it over to the table. It is considerably shorter than the other chairs.*) That'll do for me.

Then she tastes the soup. She wrinkles her face, indicating that the soup needs something. She spots the ashes, which are now next to the salt cellar on the table. First of all she adds a little salt. Then she takes the lid off the honey-pot and sees what she thinks is pepper. She takes a sprinkle and adds it to the soup.

339

She tastes again. She is still not sure. She adds a bigger handful. She tastes. She is more pleased.

George enters. He looks dapper. He carries flowers and a bottle of champagne. He comes up behind Mercy and pinches her bum. Mercy is absolutely delighted. She is obviously infatuated with George.

George There she is, the little corker!

Mercy George!

George Looks delicious.

Mercy Gazpacho. Although I held back on the pimentos. I'm worried it hasn't got enough zing.

George Gazpacho! Where did you learn to make that?

Mercy Oh, I just followed a –

George Don't tell me, Spanish Civil War?

Mercy What?

George Don't try and fool me. I can see through the innocent act, Mercy Lott. You were out there with Franco, giving it some.

Mercy giggles, hits him playfully. She revels in this attention.

Mercy (*laughing*) You know I've hardly even been outside the Cotswolds.

George Balls! We've got a little red under the bed, haven't we? She's only small but she's at the nub of things. Cuban Missile Crisis. Fall of the Berlin Wall. There she is in the background, waving. Cooee!

Mercy You do tickle me, really you do.

George Where's the main girl?

Mercy Inside making the salad. I did the starter and the pudding. To help Flora out, you know. I've done my fig tart.

George Well, bugger me.

Mercy giggles.

I hope you're not intent on giving us all the trots.

Mercy laughs.

Mercy No. Although I say it myself I think it's quite a good one. I added a little twist, marinated the figs in honey and thyme.

George I'd better go in to her.

Mercy Oh yes, listen to me wittering on.

He claps his hands together and rubs them gleefully.

George I'm looking forward to this. (*He goes to go.*)

Mercy George – don't you think it will rain? I said to Flora that it wouldn't because she's cross, you know, at it not being sunny, but I think it might.

George Nothing is going to spoil this day. Where's Little Lord Fauntleroy?

Mercy He's getting changed.

George So he's going to make an effort, then?

Mercy Oh, I think so.

George He'd better keep his arse in check, or there'll be hell to pay.

Flora enters behind them. She looks immaculate.

George My *chérie*, look at you, I could eat you up.

Mercy (*a little forced*) Leave some room for my fig tart.

George Bunny girl.

*He ignores Mercy, embraces Flora, kisses her hand.
Mercy looks away, embarrassed.*

Mercy Those black clouds are blowing over now.

Flora We're not going to have any upset today. We're
going to be civilised. Felix has told me he's going to
behave and so will you.

George I'm always civilised. (*He hands her the flowers.*)

Flora Thank you. (*She smells them. She looks momentarily troubled.*)

George What is it?

Mercy Shall I put them in a vase for you?

Flora Yes. And give Felix a shout, will you?

Mercy exits.

I don't know why she thought she was invited.

George (*intense, sexual*) Hello, bunny.

*George immediately tries to steal a moment with
Flora. She is evasive.*

Flora And George, you can go and get the wine out of
the fridge. Then once Rosie arrives we'll be more or less
there.

George What is it?

Flora It looks like we've seen the last of summer.

George What's wrong, bunny?

Flora I just want it all to go well.

George It will. This is the beginning of everything for us.

Flora Yes. Yes.

They kiss.

You will see to the wine though?

George Don't worry. (*He exits singing.*)
Love is in the air, everywhere you look around
Love is in the air, every sight and every sound –

*Flora smiles. She is left on her own. She looks around
the garden, shivers slightly. She checks the table,
moves a few things that Mercy had rearranged. Then
she sees the pot of ashes.*

Flora Oh Felix.

*She is about to move it when Rosie enters and
interrupts her. She puts the pot back down.*

Rosie Hello, Mrs Humble.

Flora Rosie. I'm glad you could come. It's a crime we
see so little of each other.

*They think about it and then embrace awkwardly.
Rosie hands her a bottle of wine.*

Rosie I'm not sure if it's a very nice one.

Flora looks at the label dubiously.

Flora Actually I never drink Italian white. It doesn't
agree with me. But I'm sure we can find a use for it.

Rosie smiles knowingly, nods. Their chat is stilted.

Take a seat. The others will be out in a minute.

Rosie doesn't sit.

Rosie The garden looks lovely.

Flora I'm worried it's going to rack and ruin.

343

Rosie The flowers smell wonderful.

Flora Do they? This summer I don't seem to be able to –
How is the nursing?

Rosie I'm training to be a midwife now.

Flora Your father said. How lovely.

Rosie Yes. Although I get sick of the dads. The weeping
and overwhelmed fathers. I could do without them.

Flora Mmm.

Rosie Probably because I had to go through it all on my
own.

Flora Yes. (*She knows her name very well.*) How is . . .?

Rosie Felicity.

Flora Oh, yes. I should remember that.

Rosie She's tremendous, in a little alien kind of way.
At the moment her mission in life is to part her hair in
the middle, in a perfect, undeviating straight line.

Flora You should have brought her.

Rosie I don't think so. I'm still at the protective stage.

   Pause.

Flora I would have liked to have a daughter. I was
convinced mine was going to be a little Jennifer. I knitted
ferociously in pink. But it turned out to be a Felix.

Rosie Felicity is desperate for a little brother.

Flora I only had one viable fallopian tube and that had
to be blown through. After Felix was born, I decided to
rest on my laurels. It's a funny thing, realising that you
are no longer the heroine of your own life.

Rosie Mmm.

Flora (*awkward*) You must bring her round another day.
Let her play in the garden.

  Rosie looks at her a moment.

Rosie You didn't tell him that Felicity was his daughter.
He didn't know.

Flora (*carefully*) I told him the facts as I knew them.
I thought if there was something important to say, that
you would say it.

Rosie In your infinite wisdom.

Flora As far as I remember, just after Felix left you
seemed to have rather a lot of male friends. In any case
we didn't really talk about you.

Rosie No, of course not. It must have been a relief.
I didn't cut the mustard, did I? Oh, it doesn't matter.
I'm very much of the 'fuck you, Mrs Humble' line of
thinking. It just makes all this today a little bit ironic,
doesn't it?

  George re-enters with the chilled wine, followed by
  Mercy, who has put the flowers in a vase. She places
  them on the table. George makes a huge fuss of Rosie.

Rosie Here he is. Romeo himself. Hello, Mercy.

Mercy Hello, dear. Don't you look pretty?

George She's not a looker but she's got character and
I love her.

Rosie Thanks for that, Dad.

Mercy How's little Felicity?

Rosie She's a ball of energy.

345

George (*discreetly to Rosie*) You're feeling okay? About –

Rosie I'm fine.

George That's my girl.

Rosie Let's have some wine.

George Yes, let's get this party on the road. (*George starts to pour the wine.*)

Mercy Not too much for me.

Flora Where's Felix?

Mercy Oh, I gave him a shout and he says he's coming. He was just sorting out the post.

Flora (*bewildered*) The post?

George ushers Flora to sit.

George Come on. Let's not worry. He'll be down in a minute, I'm sure.

Flora and Rosie sit.

Rosie Sit next to me, Mercy.

Mercy Oh, thank you, dear.

George seats himself at the head of the table opposite Flora. The only seat left is the small gardening stool.

George First of all I'd like to propose a toast. Raise your glasses. To Flora and her future happiness.

As they raise and drink their glasses, Felix enters. He is wearing the suit that Mercy got him from the charity shop. It is far too small for him. His ankles and wrists are very much on display. It is, in fact, one of his father's old suits. When Flora sees him she nearly chokes on her wine. The others react strongly.

Felix Oh, wait for me. I don't want to miss anything. (*He snatches up a glass and raises it. It is empty.*)

George (*sotto voce*) Jesus Christ.

Rosie (*amused*) I think you ought to review your capsule wardrobe, Felix.

Mercy I told you it would be an odd fit.

Flora Where did you get that?

Felix From the charity shop.

Mercy I could take the hems up.

Flora (*to Felix*) How could you?

Mercy It won't take five minutes.

George What is it? Bunny, what's wrong?

   Felix helps himself to a glass of wine.

Flora It's James's suit. He's wearing his dead father's suit.

Mercy Oh. Oh, dear.

Felix I wanted to be smart for you, Mother.

Rosie Come on then, give us a twirl.

Felix You can never be overdressed, according to my mother.

George Take it off.

Felix And also there is a deplorable lack of good, affordable millinery around these days. Isn't that right?

Flora Just ignore it, George. It's fine. Fine. We're going to have a pleasant day. I'm not going to get upset. It suits you, Felix. Very grunge, darling. (*She takes a sip of wine.*)

Felix What's on the menu?

Mercy Gazpacho soup.

Felix Yummy.

Mercy I've never made it before. I hope it's all right.

Felix goes and sits on the stool. He barely reaches the table.

Flora Please find yourself a more suitable chair.

George He's fine.

Felix Oh yes, I'm fine. Suitably low status.

George Come on then.

Mercy Let me serve it up.

Felix (*to Rosie, a little awkward*) How is Felicity?

Rosie Fine. She's at a friend's birthday party.

George Causing havoc, no doubt.

Mercy gets up and starts to ladle the soup out. She goes round the table.

George All right, bunny?

Felix Sorry. Point of order. Sorry. Can I just inquire about that? Call me old-fashioned but I'm afraid it troubles me. My mother being referred to, even affectionately, as a rabbit.

George She likes it.

Flora And it's very accurate, Felix.

Felix What?

Flora For a brief and rather enjoyable period in the early sixties, I was a bunny girl.

George Complete with fluffy tail.

Rosie (*under her breath*) That makes sense.

Felix What happened? Did you contract myxomatosis?

Flora No, I married your father and he brought me here to Moreton-in-the-Mud to rot my life away. The world did not begin at your conception, Felix, as troubling as that may seem . . . Did you say something, Rosie?

Rosie This looks lovely, Mrs Humble.

Flora Mercy made it.

Rosie Mmm. I must get the recipe.

Flora Of course I was thrillingly thin in those days. Before my son robbed me of my figure.

Mercy goes to serve Flora.

Not for me. I won't have any, thank you.

Mercy Oh Flora. Please.

Flora I'm not really hungry. I don't seem to have much of an appetite these days.

Felix You're anosmic.

Flora What?

Mercy Anaemic?

Felix Anosmic.

Rosie You mean anorexic.

Felix No. Anosmia. No sense of smell. It affects the appetite.

Flora What?

George She's not fucking anosmic.

Rosie Dad.

Mercy Perhaps it's because of the nose job.

Felix It's not because of the nose job.

Rosie You've had a nose job?

Flora I haven't had a nose job. I have had my nose slightly rephrased. That is all.

George And she's not fucking anosmic. If she was fucking anosmic, I'd be the first to know about it.

Felix Thing about George, he can always be called upon for an elegant turn of phrase.

George Piss off.

Mercy Does anyone want bread with it?

Felix You have been anosmic, Mother, since the day my father died.

Rosie No thank you, Mercy.

George Why don't you take a running jump? Preferably in close proximity to a cliff.

Flora George.

Felix Do you think that's the best way?

George What?

Felix No, really, I'm interested. What is the best way to do yourself in, so to speak? More wine, Mother?

Flora proffers her glass. Felix goes round refilling for everyone.

Rosie Pills. But not paracetomol. They're too slow and they do funny things to your liver.

Felix So speaks the nurse.

Rosie The worst is drinking sulphuric acid. You burn yourself inside out.

Mercy I really don't think we should be talking about this at the table.

Flora I'd put my head in a gas oven.

Felix Ah. The housewife's choice.

Flora Anything is preferable to cleaning it.

Mercy I've got an Aga.

Rosie It doesn't work any more.

Mercy Well. It's a bit temperamental to light.

Rosie No, I mean, you can't do it with a gas oven. They changed it so you can't.

Flora Killjoys.

Mercy I don't think you could do it with an Aga either. No.

George (*slowly, considered*) A length of hose. Easy.

Felix (*sharp*) What?

George Only way to do it. In the car. A length of hose from the exhaust pipe. Wind the window up. A glass of whisky in my hand and Glen Miller on the stereo. I'd have an upbeat number first. 'Chattanooga Choo-Choo' or 'Pennsylvania 6–5000'. Followed by 'Moonlight Serenade'. I'd just drift off. Easy.

Rosie Dad!

George Christ. I never would, Rosie love. It's a mug's game.

Felix A length of hose. Yes.

Flora What about you, Felix? What is your preferred method?

Felix Well, in an ideal world, I'd like to jump through a black hole.

George I'm sure it could be arranged.

Flora Why, Felix?

Felix Just a whim of mine.

Flora Tell me why.

Felix Well, I'd find out what it was like inside.

George How thrilling.

Felix It would be for a theoretical physicist.

Rosie Who doesn't get out much.

Felix Theoretical physicists don't get out much.

Rosie Well, come on then, enlighten us.

Felix You get to pass through the event horizon and down into the state of singularity. The point where all mathematical equations break down and you break up into a thousand million particles. I think that would be quite satisfying.

Rosie Doesn't sound much fun to me.

Felix The beauty of it is you get to carry on. Well, maybe you do.

Rosie But it wouldn't be you. It would just be bits of you.

Felix It'd be the essence of me. I'd be recycled. The particles of my body would go off and form another universe. It's a kind of immortality.

Rosie If it's immortality you want, I think it's easier just to have a baby.

Flora Is that what you want, Felix? How very mundane. If you can't make your mark while you're here, what's the point?

Mercy Nobody's eating my soup.

Felix Do you think my father made his mark?

Flora No. Sadly. I think he would probably feel that he hadn't.

Felix You know, Mother, one day scientists at NASA pointed the Hubble Telescope at what they thought was an empty speck of the sky and they saw a void teeming with galaxies. They saw clusters of stars billions of years old that they never knew about.

Flora (*sharply*) What are you trying to say, Felix?

George Yes. If you've got something to say, I think you ought to say it.

Mercy Couldn't we save it till after the first course?

Felix I rather thought that it was you and my mother who had something to say.

Mercy I'll get some bread.

Flora Sit down, Mercy. You invited yourself, so you can sit through this.

Mercy sits down.

Rosie Felix, why are you being so difficult? You know what they want.

Mercy He can't think on an empty stomach.

Rosie They want to get married. Big deal. You take everything too much to heart.

Mercy You're getting married?

George Yes, we are.

Mercy (*a little crestfallen*) Oh. How lovely.

Felix (*raising his glass*) Yes! Isn't it! Come on, Mercy. Raise your glass for the Humble Pyes! A match made in Moreton!

George I don't give a fart for your opinion, sonny.

Felix And I'm not talking to you, Pops. Just answer me this, Mother. What do you see in him?

Mercy Oh. There's a lot to see in George. He's a very nice man underneath.

George Thank you, Mercy.

Mercy You're welcome.

Flora I do not need your blessing, Felix. But it would be nice.

Felix It's a bit late for my blessing, isn't it? My father died two months ago but –

Flora At last Felix is up to speed.

Felix – but this has been going on for years. The world and his wife are privy to this information.

Rosie Leave it, Felix.

Mercy I didn't know for ages.

Felix How could you do this? How could you do this to my father?

Rosie There's no need for all this.

Flora James knew about it.

George What?

Flora I told him about George. I told your father that I loved him but that he wasn't enough. He accepted that fact.

George You told James? About me. You've never told me that –

Flora It didn't concern you.

George I can't believe you didn't tell me.

Felix starts to laugh.

Felix Bravo, Mother. What a tactician!

Flora Your father was generous to a fault.

George (*working it out*) But if he knew – and I didn't know that he knew – and he knew that I didn't know that he knew – that . . . that gave him more power than me.

Flora It wasn't a question of power. It was a question of balance.

George Well. This doesn't change anything now. It doesn't make any difference to how things are now.

Felix Are you sure of that, George?

Flora You are desperate to turn this into a tragedy, Felix, but you will not be able to.

Felix My father fell down dead in this garden. And you were upstairs waiting for your new nose to recapture your lost youth so that you could go off and shag Biggles here –

George Watch it –

Felix – and all the while my father was dying. His heart was giving up on him. His heart was bursting.

355

Flora No. That is incorrect. His heart was not bursting. He did not die of a heart attack.

George Oh yes, boyo, you just wait for this.

Felix (*wrong-footed*) What do you mean?

Mercy (*a warning*) Flora.

Flora Give me a cigarette, George.

George You don't smoke.

Flora No, well, I am branching out.

George gives her a cigarette and lights it for her.

Felix What is she saying?

Mercy Don't, Flora.

Felix Jesus! What?

Flora No, he's asked for this.

Felix What did you do to him? Dear God, did the pair of you – what did you do to him?

Flora Not me, darling. Not me and George, although that would have made sense, I grant you. No, it was his bees. James Humble was killed by his beloved bees.

Mercy It was a tragedy.

Flora No. It was not a tragedy. Sad and pathetic and shockingly stupid, ironic, funny even, yes comical, hilarious, but not a tragedy.

Felix I don't –

Flora Anaphylactic shock. He was allergic to the bee-sting.

Felix Don't be ridiculous. He kept b–bees for years.

Rosie You can develop it over time, without knowing.

Flora Thank you, Rosie, if we want a little Nurse Pye nugget, we'll ask for it.

Felix What are you saying?

Flora He knew, but he couldn't give it up. May that be a lesson to you about the dangers of obsessive behaviour.

Felix What? I don't b–b–b–believe my –

Flora If it's any consolation, the bee died as well. I found your father on the lawn, with the bee close beside him. Neither of them was moving but I squashed the bee underfoot anyway. There is something deeply satisfying about the crunch of a dead bee.

Felix I don't want to hear this –

Flora Your father always said to me that, when it was time to go, that there was no debate to be had. He said that bees have a finite number of wingbeats and once they are used up, the bees just fall from the sky. In the same way we have a finite number of heartbeats. I doubt whether he would have been satisfied with his quota. But no doubt the bee had a case for grievance as well . . . So there. (*She stubs out the cigarette.*)

Felix Why didn't you tell me?

Flora I would rather that he died of a heart attack. I am more comfortable with that version of events.

Felix More comfortable?!

Flora For his sake. It makes him look less of a fool.

George This doesn't change anything.

Flora You have said that once already, George.

George Your mother and I are still going to be married. Whatever you think.

Rosie If it's any consolation, after the wedding, I will be your sister and your daughter will also be your niece. If you weren't fucked up before, this will really send you reeling.

Flora Ah, Rosie. Just when the conversation was flagging.

George Rosie. Fliss isn't his – you promised me she wasn't –

Flora She's not his daughter.

Mercy I don't think I can cope. (*Mercy starts to cry silently.*)

George Rosie – you said it was that long-haired lad from The Bell. You promised me.

Rosie She's Felix's daughter.

Flora Not without DNA evidence she's not.

George You don't know that for sure, do you? Rosie?

Rosie I'm her mother and I know.

Flora I'm not a grandmother. She's lying –

Rosie I'm not.

George But there's no proof, is there, love?

Flora Of course there isn't.

Felix (*desperate*) Rosie. I have been walking around with this for four weeks. I have b–been trying to rise to this. I have been trying to feel what this feels like. Please don't lie to me.

Rosie I'm not lying. After you left, I . . . I did sleep with a few men –

Flora I'm sorry. Forgive me for being pedantic but 'a few' is not the correct collective noun in this case.

Rosie Dad, tell her.

George You did put yourself about, Rosie love.

Rosie I was heartbroken at the time.

Felix stands up.

Felix I'm sorry. This is too much.

Flora Sit down. You will not walk out on me again. I deserve more respect from you.

Felix Why?

Flora Because I am your mother.

Felix You have to do a bit of mothering in order to earn that title. And sadly that has never been your strong suit, has it?

Flora What?

Felix You don't love me, Mother.

George Oh, Christ on a bike.

George takes out his headphones and puts them on during the next.

Flora Of course I do. You are my son.

Felix That doesn't follow. You know that.

Flora You're talking nonsense.

Felix I am sure you tried. But you couldn't do it.

Rosie Love embarrasses you, Felix. You can't turn it into an equation. There is no constant as far as you are concerned. Dad. Take them off.

George I'm not listening to his crap.

He turns the music up. He taps away to it.

Mercy There is no point in being constant in love. It's seen as a sign of weakness.

Flora (*to Mercy*) Oh God! I don't know why you're crying.

Mercy I may as well throw the soup away.

Flora None of this has anything to do with you.

Rosie Oh Mercy, don't cry. It's all right.

Flora Take those bloody headphones off right now, George, before I rip them off.

George (*he can't hear*) What? (*He takes them off.*)

Rosie (*to George*) Mercy's upset.

Mercy (*crying*) I'm sorry, sorry, sorry. I get these brief bursts of unutterable sadness. I'm taking a herbal remedy.

Rosie Are you?

Mercy Yes. It's for people who soldier on in the face of complete hopelessness, but it hasn't made any difference –

George You've got nothing to cry about, little Mercy.

Flora Of course she has. She has never been married, she has no dress sense to speak of and she has always been in love with you, George.

Rosie You're a bitch.

Mercy (*to Flora*) What?

Flora It's true, Mercy.

Mercy (*terribly embarrassed*) No! No! No. I have not – I like George, but I have never really – you are very rude to me, Flora.

360

Rosie She thinks she's too good for all of us.

Mercy And if you four are anything to go by I'm very glad I've kept myself to myself, thank you very much.

George Absolutely.

Mercy It's people like you that give people who live in the countryside a bad name.

George Hear, hear.

Mercy I know that I am a negligible sort of person. But I won't stand for it. I've always looked up to you. Always.

Flora You have no life of your own so you constantly leech off mine.

George Flora, stop it.

Flora I did not choose you to be my friend. It was an accident of geography. Because I am stuck in this bloody awful middle-England middle-class bloody rural bloody idyll.

Felix (*with sudden authority*) Stop it, Mother. ENOUGH! That is enough now. You have said enough. We have all said enough. It's a beautiful day and . . . and I think we should eat now. Whatever our differences – I think we should eat.

    Pause.

Perhaps you'd like to say grace for us, Mercy. Then we can eat your delicious soup.

Mercy I don't know.

Felix Please. We are all going to be calm now. We have exhausted ourselves. See.

    Everyone is quiet round the table.

Mercy Very well. (*Mercy goes to stand up. She cannot quite look George in the eye.*) I don't have those sort of feelings for you, George.

George No, of course not.

Mercy So long as you know that.

George I know that.

She stands up a little shakily. They all bow their heads, except perhaps Flora.

Mercy For what we are about to receive, which none of you really want to eat but which I stayed up till two in the morning to make and I didn't even have any pimentos and had to improvise round them, may the Lord, whether you believe in Him or not, I know you don't, Felix, because you're a scientist so you're not allowed to and anyway I don't know if I do, because of things like James dying in the way that he did and little Felicity not having an identifiable father and the terrible things that Flora has said to me and the little fat bumblebees just dropping down dead from the sky. And I know that what James said about the finite number of heartbeats should be a comfort, but it is not. And maybe I don't have much of a life but up to now God has filled all the gaps but now there do seem to be holes that He can't fill so perhaps you are right, Flora, because even though I still do the flowers in church and my various parish duties really I would say that I was unofficially on a sabbatical from God at the moment because everything is really so unsettling and I'm sick to my heart of trying all the time, trying, trying, trying, and I don't like it, I don't like it at all so may the Lord, even though we're not on speaking terms, make us all, and I mean all of us, truly grateful. Amen.

George Amen.

Felix Very well put, Mercy.

George Let's eat. I'm starving. (*He takes a mouthful.*) It's bloody delicious.

Rosie It's got a real zing to it.

Mercy There isn't too much seasoning?

Felix No. It's just right.

They all eat, making some noises of satisfaction and reassurance for Mercy. Suddenly Flora stops, puts her spoon down.

Flora One minute.

Felix (*a warning*) Mother?

Flora I would really rather prefer it if Felix took his father off the table.

Felix takes the urn off the table. He holds it to him. Mercy watches him.

Mercy That's –

Flora The remains, yes. He insists that he is not ready to scatter them but I think we can do without them at meal-times. Thank you, Felix.

Mercy No! No! No! Don't eat it! Stop! Don't eat it. I'm sorry.

George What's the matter, Merc?

Mercy No, please. I forgot a vital ingredient. I did something inadvertent. (*She's grabbing the plates off everyone and pouring the soup back into the tureen.*) It's contaminated. It's dangerous. I'm sorry. Give it back to me at once.

Flora I thought you were dying for us to eat it.

Mercy No, no, no, I'm not. I'm leaving now. This is a very bad day.

Rosie It's lovely, Mercy.

Mercy Oh no. No. No. No. Please excuse me. Ignore me. Chat among yourselves. I have to – urgently attend to the fig tart. (*Mercy grabs the tureen and exits.*)

George I think she's flipped her lid.

Flora You took her part against me.

George No I didn't. I feel a bit sorry for her, that's all.

Flora Well, some people are just unfortunate, it's not my fault.

Felix Mother, go and apologise to her.

Flora What?

Felix Say sorry to her.

Flora I will not.

Felix She is lonely and she thinks the world of you. Tell her that you didn't mean it. You'll feel terrible tomorrow if you don't.

Pause. Flora gets up.

George Do you want me to come?

Flora No, I do not. In any case it won't take long.

Flora exits. The other three are left. George is quite drunk by now. Rosie sits quietly and Felix holds his dead father's ashes.

Rosie Well, it's all going very well so far.

George stares at Felix.

George What does he look like?

Rosie Dad.

George Winnie the bloody Pooh! Here, Winnie, I'm going to marry your mother, whatever you –

Rosie Dad. Let's change the subject. Talk about something different. There must be something that we can talk about calmly.

Pause that stretches towards a silence.

I know the range of possible topics is fairly limited. But come on. Let's have someone's starter for ten.

Felix Glen Miller took a long time to find his sound, didn't he?

George Yes.

Pause.

Rosie Okay. Another go.

Pause.

George Do you know why I called my coach firm the Flying Pyes?

Rosie What you going on about, Dad?

George No, no, Rosie. It's kosher. He wanted to know this. He asked me.

Felix I did, after a fashion.

George See, Rosie, love, just a friendly little chit-chat. Go on then, ask me.

Felix Why did you call your coach firm the Flying Pyes?

George For my dad. (*casually*) He was RAF, flew in the war. Lancasters, Halifaxes, Stirlings. He said the noise of the engines was unbearable – a droning so terrible and the planes were unpressurised and cold, twenty degrees below zero, Fahrenheit that is, so cold you couldn't think. He had to piss into a funnel, the desert lily they called it. They gave them all a survival kit with Horlicks tablets and a Mae West flotation jacket.

Felix Really?

George Yes, really. See, Rosie, it's all going nicely. We're getting on like a house on fire. May I continue?

Rosie Go ahead.

George He went on thirty sorties, he flew with two engines gone, he flew with dead and wounded aboard. He baled himself out of fatal spins, where the G-force could suck your insides out. Then one day he was chatting to one of the other pilots, a mate of his, lad from Northampton, queer as a coot apparently, and as he was talking to him he saw his face turn into a skull.

Rosie You're making this up!

George And this lad, the gayboy, went out on a raid on the Ruhr that night and got himself shot down and killed. And then my dad started seeing it all the time. The skull lurking beneath the face. And every time he saw it in a lad's face he knew the boy wouldn't make it. He could tell from just looking at their faces. In the end they kicked him out, said he couldn't fly any more, he was gutted . . . LMF. Lack of Moral Fibre. Bastards.

George goes up to Felix. He grabs hold of his face and pulls it closer to him, looks at him.

Rosie Dad, stop it right now. You're drunk. Go on. Go away.

George No. Just what I thought. (*George lets go of his face dismissively and walks out. Pause.*)

Rosie He's harmless really.

Felix Mmm.

Pause.

Felix Rosie –

Rosie No, that subject is vetoed.

Pause.

Felix My father once said that a beehive was the blueprint for a Utopia in which the sexual impulse would cease to exist. He must have been going through a difficult time when he said it . . . But I don't think he was right. I think a hive is a blueprint for a world in which the men are totally useless. The women do all the work and the men, once they've fertilised the women, the men, well . . . die.

Rosie Seems like a good system to me.

Felix Clearly.

Rosie Felix. What did you expect me to do after you left me? Hie myself to a nunnery?

Felix I think you should have told me.

Rosie You didn't deserve to know.

Felix You used to be straight with me.

Rosie Well, things aren't black and white for me any more. That's what it's like to be a parent. Anyway, I don't care what you think of me. I brought up my daughter on my own. She is a credit to me. I am a good person.

Felix I know that.

Rosie Good.

Felix Why did you want to have sex with me again?

Rosie I don't know. It wasn't just a casual fuck, if that's what you mean. Nothing with you is ever casual, Felix.

Felix I tried to imagine what it would be like if we were together again –

Rosie Don't waste your time. I wouldn't have you.

Felix No. Good call.

After a pause they both smile. Rosie looks at her watch.

Rosie I've got to go and collect her. She gets anxious if I'm late.

Felix Did you really name her after me?

Pause. Rosie shrugs.

I tried to picture it, you know, the last four weeks, introducing myself to her. I don't even know what a seven-year-old looks like.

Rosie She doesn't have your eyes, if that's what you're asking. She's her own little person.

Felix That wasn't what I meant.

Rosie She's about this high. Her face is full of freckles from the sun. She's just lost her front tooth. And her knees are covered in scabs. She's the most gorgeous child you'll ever see.

Felix I bet she is. (*Felix smiles. Pause.*)

Rosie She wants to know who her father is. She wants to know his story. This is for her, you know, not for me.

Felix goes to speak.

She is the best thing, Felix. I started writing a diary the day she was born – to record all the important moments, you know. The first time she spoke, caught a ball properly, tied her own shoelaces, rode a bicycle without stabilisers. I know it might sound dull from where you are standing –

Felix No, no, it doesn't. Eureka moments.

Rosie Yes, that's nice. My life is full of Eureka moments now I have her.

Felix Yes.

Rosie I would like you to meet each other.

Felix What?

Rosie She would like you –

Felix No –

Rosie She wouldn't show it for a bit, you'd have to put a bit of work in, but she's so thirsty for knowledge, for answers, for how the world works –

Felix (*quietly*) I don't know how the world works.

Rosie I mean things like all the names of the stars, the constellations –

Felix You can get a b–book for that.

Rosie A book isn't the same.

Felix Rosie. I would be next to useless.

Rosie Well, that's not as bad as completely useless.

Felix It's worse than useless. At least with useless you know where you are.

Rosie No you wouldn't be.

Felix Rosie. I can't do this . . . I'm sorry. I'd like to give you some money, though –

Rosie Oh, shut up, Felix. You have spent too much of your life theorising. Don't you realise how brilliant this offer is, how generous I am being? I am offering you a chance to be. Just to be.

Felix It's too late.

Rosie Of course it's not. She is a child! If she is up for having a dad after seven years of being without one, then you bloody well should be. (*Rosie goes up to him. She embraces him, kisses his head.*) It's probably the best offer that you will ever ever get.

He nods. She goes. Felix stays where he is.

Felix (*quietly, rehearsing it, clumsily, unconvinced by his performance*) Felicity. Felicity. This is Cassiopeia and Andromeda and that is Pegasus and Ursa Major of course, and . . . erm . . . Ursa Minor –

Flora enters.

Flora Talking to yourself? Where's George?

Felix I don't know.

Flora Has Rosie gone?

Felix Yes.

Flora Oh. Right. Mercy's calmed down, thankfully.

Felix I'm going today, Mother.

Flora I see.

Felix I'll have to get my things in order. (*Felix puts the ashes down. He takes a letter out of his pocket. He hands it to his mother.*)

Flora What's this?

Felix It came today. I wanted to give it to you earlier b–but there wasn't a right moment.

Flora It's addressed to your father.

Felix Yes. I opened it, I hope you don't mind.

Flora What is it?

Felix It's from the Royal Entomological Society.

Flora Oh. I'll look at it later.

Felix No, look at it now.

Flora opens the letter. She reads it. He watches her. She folds it up and puts it away.

You were wrong about him. He did make his mark. In his own small way. (*He goes to go.*) Oh, and Mother, you know you told me about the day you took me to prep school and how you waved and waved to me until I was a b–black dot. Until after I was a black dot . . . The thing that you've forgotten, Ma, is that I didn't look b–back. I never looked back.

Perhaps he goes to get the ashes and then changes his mind. He exits, leaving the ashes behind him. Flora watches him.

Flora Felix?

He does not turn round. She is left on her own. She picks up the ashes gingerly and holds them to her for a moment. George enters.

George There you are, bun. I've been looking for you.

She puts the ashes down carefully on the steps to the hive. He watches her.
    She is distracted.

George What is it, bun? What's happened?

Flora James discovered a new species of bumblebee before he died.

371

George What?

Flora An official letter came.

George That's good.

Flora It's such a shame that it arrived late. That he never read it. The recognition.

George Yes.

Flora It's something he always wanted to do – to find and name a new species. He said it was the best way to make your name as a bee-keeper. The only way to have your name live on after death.

George Good for James.

Flora It's a variety of the small garden bumblebee, *Bombus hortorum*, only the queen is smaller and more delicately built.

George (*humouring her*) Is she?

Flora But the point is, he didn't name it after himself, you see. He named it after me. *Bombus floratum*. Flora's Bumblebee.

George Well, that's nice of him. I bet she's a looker.

Flora I can't marry you.

George Bun –

Flora I'm very, very sorry.

George What are you saying?

Flora It's not right.

George Bollocks.

Flora Our families hate each other.

George Our families can go to hell.

Flora And I am already married.

George No, well, we'll live in sin. Bugger it.

Flora No, George.

George You said James wasn't enough for you. You said –

Flora He wasn't. But neither are you. I'm sorry. I am a deeply ungrateful woman, I always want more and it is my undoing, you see.

George I'll be more. I'm only just getting into my stride.

Flora It doesn't feel right. Being here in this garden. With you. Since James died nothing has felt right.

George We'll move. We'll get somewhere else.

Flora Don't you see that it only worked when there were three of us? Everything had a place. And now there is no equilibrium.

George You're just disorientated. You're feeling guilty.

Flora Yes.

George I understand.

Flora No, you don't. I feel like I've lived my whole life in miniature. And I am not a miniaturist. I have tried my hardest to break out but I cannot.

George We can, we will . . . When Mary died I couldn't function –

Flora Yes. Poor Mary. Poor Mary, George.

George Yes, God love her, she went through it, she didn't deserve it but my life with her was humdrum, Flora. Charming but humdrum. But when I think about you . . . I fee . . . like –

373

Flora (*interrupting*) Oh spare me the metaphor. At our age it's all such a cliché.

George Why? Why should it be? What do you want?

Flora I don't want. To want things has always been my gravest error. I am going to stifle it.

George Rubbish –

Flora George. I am so old. Not even the royal jelly will save me.

George You are beautiful –

Flora Beauty is not enough. It is never enough. Nature's cruel trick. When I was little I always thought that I was marked out, special, that I was on the verge of something momentous happening. I used to tingle with anticipation, I had legions of butterflies in my stomach. No that's not right. A flutter of butterflies, is it?

George What?

Flora James was very good with words. Knowing the right words.

George Please don't compare us. You said you never would.

Flora No, and I don't because it is impossible. You pale in each other's comparison. (*laughing*) Oh you, you George, you are a monumental man. When all this nonsense began I would be at the sink and the thought of you would catch me in my throat, wrap around me, flay me . . . You lack – precision that is all. But it doesn't matter.

George It does matter. I will change. I will be what you want me to be.

Flora It's too late. It has gone sour.

George No, it hasn't. You're just upset. Today has been –

Flora I am not upset. I am in a state of terminal disappointment.

George Please, Flora. Don't do this. I beg you. I can't cope with this. Everything will come right, I promise you. (*George is practically on his knees.*)

Flora (*hard*) We've been fooling ourselves, George.

George I haven't.

Flora We're just going through the motions.

George I'm not.

Flora It's all so vulgar. The whole bloody lot of it.

George No. I love you, please, bunny. Bunny girl.

*Felix enters. He is wearing the cricket whites that
he was wearing in the first scene. He interrupts them.
He is embarrassed.*

Felix I'm sorry. I didn't mean to – I was just getting my things together. I needed to – I forgot the –

Flora They're over there.

Flora points at the ashes. Felix goes to get them.

Will you be able to get a train at this time?

Felix I thought I might take the car, if that's all right?

Flora Fine.

George starts to laugh uncontrollably.

George Owzat!

Felix What?

George There he is. He's done it. He's won the bloody ashes.

375

Felix I'm going now.

George (*sourly*) Yes! You go. You've done your worst, now you bugger off.

Flora George.

George I'll tell you something for nothing. I'm glad you're not my son.

Felix puts the ashes back down on the steps to the hive.

Flora This is not Felix's fault.

George You bastard. You big fat lazy bumbling bastard.

Flora (*to Felix*) George and I have separated.

George Do you feel happy now? Now you've fucked everyone's life up?

Felix No.

George Perhaps Rosie was right. We're not good enough for the Humbles. We don't live up to their elevated standards.

Flora That is not true.

George And here he is, the highest flier of them all. Felix Humble. You want to be careful, you could be heading for a fall. You know what happened to Icarus, don't you? Oh sorry, did I shock you all there with a literary allusion? I do beg your pardon, getting above my station.

Flora George –

George Well, Icarus and his dad, I can't remember his name but he was a boring old fart whoever he was, he probably kept bees in his spare time, well they decided they'd go for a little fly, like you do, so they made their wings of wax – ah! wax, see, from the buggering bees he kept on the side –

Flora I think we're familiar with the story.

George Don't interrupt me, Flora, not when I'm at full throttle. So they made their wings of wax and feathers and shit and then Icarus, Icky to his mates, not that he had many, Icky flew slap bang into the sun, like the stupid twat that he was.

Flora George –

George So my advice to you, Humble boy, is head for the skies. Yes, do us all a favour and keep following that star.

Flora I think you should go.

George You're a beautiful woman, Flora, but your problem is you disappeared up your own arse some time ago. You want to wake up and smell the roses. Oh dear, sorry, *faux pas.*

Felix goes up to him, takes him by the arm.

Felix You've said your b–b–bit.

George Good, wasn't it? I thought I put it quite well. (*George shakes Felix off roughly.*) I'm going, I'm going.

George starts to walk away. He is calm but just before he exits he picks up a hoe from the back wall where all the garden equipment is kept. He swings round and charges at Felix. Felix at first defends himself with the gardening stool. The fight continues around the garden, over the table, round the hammock. Various garden implements get used: the trowel, the garden fork, a pair of secateurs. Perhaps at one point Flora picks up the small water sprayer and sprays George with it. The dialogue continues through the fight.

Right. Let's be having you, you bastard.

Flora George, stop it, stop it right now.

George Let's see how light he is on his feet.

Felix Please stop. I don't want this –

George Not bad for a lardy. Come on, run, come on Icky, let's see you fly.

Flora George, this is ridiculous.

> *Suddenly Felix turns round and attacks him back.*
> *George starts to overpower him.*
>   *Felix suddenly stops. He is breathless.*

Felix Don't hurt me.

George I knew you didn't have it in you.

Felix No, you're right. I don't.

> *George approaches him.*

Flora Oh no, please don't hurt him.

> *But suddenly George stops as well.*

George What the –?

> *He is swatting his hands around him in a demented fashion. At the same time as he does this Jim the gardener comes on. Felix sees him, but Flora and George do not look at him. George is swatting away a bee that is attacking him.*

George Get off me, you little bastard. I thought you got rid of them. Get off. (*He continues to swat the bee away and move from spot to spot to try and get rid of the bee.*)

Felix (*looking at Jim*) They're back.

George Do something, Flora.

Felix The bees are back.

George Get a spray, for Christ's sake.

Felix Let there be b–bees!

Flora You mustn't fight it.

George It's bloody mental.

Flora Don't threaten it.

George It's trying to bloody kill me.

Flora Well then, go! I've told you a hundred times to go.

George Jesus Christ!

> *George makes a very inelegant exit. He is still pursued by the bee. Flora still has her back to Jim.*

Jim Exit pursued by a bee.

> *Flora reacts strangely to Jim's voice. She doesn't turn round.*

Flora What?

Jim That was the queen. Lovely little thing, but don't rile her!

Flora Oh my God.

Felix You can hear him? Mother! Please tell me you can hear him.

> *Flora nods.*

Jim She's probably the only one left now. The others will have dropped out of the sky.

Flora A finite number of wingbeats.

Jim That's right.

Felix Turn around, Mother. Look at him.

Flora He's here?

Felix All summer he has been here with me. In the garden.

Flora Oh my God.

Felix Like pointing a telescope at a blank bit of the sky and seeing a star that I have never seen before.

She turns around slowly. She looks at him. Slowly there is music.

Flora James.

Felix You can see him?

Jim *Bombus floratum.*

Flora Yes!

Jim Flora's Bumblebee. Do you like her?

Flora I do.

Felix All summer he has been with me. But I didn't know what to say.

Jim Flora.

Flora (*to James*) The first time I saw you, I knew.

Jim Yes.

Flora I knew that no one would ever look at me like this again.

Their speech overlaps slightly as they feed each other with the lines.

Jim Outside the exam halls –

Flora – of the School of Biology –

Jim – I had been writing about flowers –

Flora – the pollination of flowers –

Jim – and I saw you. The sun is shining around your head –

Flora – and you come towards me – your gown flapping in the wind –

Jim – like I'm flying towards you –

Flora – and you look at me –

Jim – I look at you –

Flora – and you say –

Jim Did you drop from the sky?

Pause.

Felix (*quietly*) Eureka.

Felix looks at both of them. They are transfixed with each other. They come together.

Jim My Flora.

Flora James Humble. Bachelor of Science.

Felix is apart from them.
He stumbles off.

Flora James, I'm sorry – I'm so sorry –

Jim (*to Flora*) Hush. I have to tell you about the flowers – all the flowers I have planned for you . . .

Flora Yes. Tell me the names. The names of all the flowers.

As Jim lists the flowers, Flora slowly starts to cry.

Jim *Papaver dubium.*

Flora A poppy?

Jim Doubtful poppy. To help you sleep. *Dianthus barbatus*. Sweet William. For peace.

Flora Yes.

Jim *Mimosa sensitiva*. For scent. *Zinnia elegans*. Elegant like my Flora.

Flora A sunflower, I'd like a sunflower.

Jim *Helianthus multiflorus*.

Flora And some love-in-a-mist.

Jim Whatever you want.

Flora Some love-lies-a-bleeding.

Jim *Amaranthus procumbens*.

Flora Some St John's wort –

Jim *Hypericum perforatum* – for sadness. *Lythrum salicaria* – purple loosestrife, for contentment. *Oenothera biennis* – evening primrose, for ease of heart.

Flora Some bluebells.

Jim *Campanula rotundifolia*. For the spring.

Flora And more scented flowers. I need more scent. I need to be able to smell them again.

Jim *Lavandula spica*. Blue and white varieties. *Passiflora caerulea*. Passion flowers. *Dianthus deltoides*. *Syringa vulgaris*. Some sweet-scented heliotrope. Clematis and honeysuckle. My bees love that. Buddleia for the butterflies. Scented hyacinths. French marigolds. *Tagetes Patula*. *Aster multiflorus*. *Amaryllis aurea*. Can you smell them all?

Flora Yes. Yes, I can. I think I can.

Jim Good. (*He goes to go.*)

Flora No, please, James. Please don't go.

Jim All the bees have gone now. It's only the queen left. *Bombus floratum*. She'll have to do the winter on her own, but she'll manage that. She's strong.

Flora No. No, I can't.

He leads her to the rose bush. He bends down and smells it. He gestures that she should do the same. She does so. She breathes deeply, takes in the scent.

Jim There.

Flora Yes.

He exits. As he does, the hive lights up, and then fades. She looks up.
    The music changes suddenly to a humming, resonant of bees and a revving car engine. Flora reacts as if she had tinnitus in her ear.

Flora I can't do the winter on my own. Felix. Felix? Oh my God. Please God – Felix!

She runs towards the exit. Felix appears.

Flora I thought you'd gone – I thought you'd –

Felix I was just starting up the car.

Flora Suddenly I had this terrible feeling you'd . . . I don't know what I thought. It was stupid of me.

Felix No, no, it wasn't stupid. At the beginning of the summer I thought I was going to – But I'm not brave enough to let go.

Flora Thank God!.

Felix B–b–but I just want . . . the p–possibility . . . of another life, Ma.

Pause. Felix picks up the ashes.

Flora Say the words. You know them. You've always known them.

Felix (*with difficulty*) The night we watched the moon-landings together, Dad cried. And in that moment, he made me want to fly. He held my hand and he gave me the courage to defy physics and fly anyway. The day that a man landed on the moon Dad cried. And the day he died the sun cried bees. The sun cried bees. (*He takes the lid off the pot.*) I release my father to space. To the limitless quiet of space. To fly in unending silence. Through a black hole. Past the event horizon. To the state of singularity. Dust to immortal dust. And out and on and beyond. To a new universe. A parallel world.

Flora A better place.

Felix The land of milk and honey.

Felix scatters the ashes. They watch them settle in silence.

There.

Flora Yes.

An awkward moment between them.

Will you still be going back –?

Felix In a little while.

Flora It's getting dark, maybe you should set off in the morning, when it's light. And you've eaten next to nothing –

Felix (*a hint of irritation*) Mother.

Flora looks at Felix, perhaps she touches him lightly but unsentimentally.

Flora Well. (*She goes to go in.*) Don't expect me to wave you off.

He smiles. The sound of a bee humming somewhere in the distance.

Felix Let b–b–b–be.

Flora smiles and exits. He is left alone in the garden in the failing light. Felix pauses, swallows and smiles.

Let be.

Lights fade.